Birth, Death, and Femininity

Birth, Death, and Femininity

Birth, Death, and Femininity

Philosophies of Embodiment

EDITED BY ROBIN MAY SCHOTT

*With contributions by Sara Heinämaa,
Robin May Schott, Vigdis Songe-Møller,
and Sigridur Thorgeirsdottir*

Indiana University Press
Bloomington and Indianapolis

This book is a publication of

Indiana University Press
601 North Morton Street
Bloomington, Indiana 47404-3797 USA

www.iupress.indiana.edu

Telephone orders	800-842-6796
Fax orders	812-855-7931
Orders by e-mail	iuporder@indiana.edu

⊗ The paper used in this publication meets the minimum requirements of the American National Standard for Information Sciences—Permanence of Paper for Printed Library Materials, ANSI Z39.48-1992.

Sara Heinämaa's work has been funded by the Academy of Finland.

Manufactured in the United States of America

Library of Congress Cataloging-in-Publication Data

Birth, death, and femininity : philosophies of embodiment / edited by Robin May Schott ; with contributions by Sara Heinämaa . . . [et al.].
     p.   cm.
Includes bibliographical references and index.
ISBN 978-0-253-35535-5 (cloth : alk. paper) — ISBN 978-0-253-22237-4 (pbk. : alk. paper) 1. Death 2. Birth (Philosophy) I. Schott, Robin May. II. Heinämaa, Sara, [date]
   BD444.B54   2010
   128—dc22

                                                            2010016977

          1 2 3 4 5   15 14 13 12 11 10

We dedicate this book to the memory of
Eva Gothlin (1957–2006).

CONTENTS

ACKNOWLEDGMENTS

This book is a result of cooperation and dialogue. Over several years we have been studying original sources and contemporary research contributions together, discussing arguments, concepts, and methods for studying birth, death, and femininity. Over this period, we have become indebted to many institutions and individuals, whom we would like to acknowledge here.

The authors of this book originally met in November 1999 at a conference entitled "Rereading the Canon: Feminist Interpretations of the History of Philosophy," organized by Lilli Alanen at the University of Uppsala. Without Lilli Alanen's initiative, which was groundbreaking in the Nordic countries, we would have had neither the idea nor the opportunity to initiate this collaborative relationship. We would like to thank NOS-H for supporting our research, first through a project-planning grant and subsequently through a research grant. Without this support, this project would not have been possible.

We have held research meetings and symposia at, or received support from, the University of Bergen, the University of Copenhagen, Helsinki University, and the University of Iceland (in particular the EDDA Center of Excellence). We held additional meetings at the Finnish Institute in Rome (with special thanks to Simo Orma and Mika Kajava at Villa Lante for providing us this opportunity on several occasions), the Norwegian Institute in Rome (with special thanks to Turid Karlsen-Seim for hosting a meeting), and the Fondation Maison des Sciences de l'Homme in Paris. The Academy of Finland and Helsinki Collegium for Advanced Studies funded the "International Symposium on Femininity and Embodiment" held in Helsinki in 2007, where we presented some of our work. We also had the opportunity to present work at the meeting of the International Association of Women Philosophers at the University of Gothenborg in 2004.

Sara Heinämaa would like to give special thanks to the following people: Penelope Deutscher, Robert Hanna, Juha Himanka, Dan Lloyd, Turo-Kimmo Lehtonen, Timo Miettinen, Anthony Steinbock, Joona Taipale, and Dan Zahavi. She would also like to thank Dan Zahavi for hosting her research period at the Center for Subjectivity Research at the University of Copenhagen in 2006, and the Academy of Finland and Helsingin Sanomat Foundation for supporting this work financially.

Sigridur Thorgeirsdottir would also like to thank the Center for Subjectivity Research at the University of Copenhagen for providing working accommodations during a sabbatical in 2007, and the Deutscher Akademischer Austauschdienst for a grant for a research visit to Germany in 2008. She is very grateful for comments on her chapters from Penelope Deutscher, Daphne Hampson, and Werner Stegmaier and his Nietzsche Colloquium at the University of Greifswald.

We would also like to thank Claudia Card who provided very useful suggestions for the manuscript.

Finally, we are grateful not only to those who enabled our collaboration, but for the fact of this collaboration itself. Our meetings have provided us with intellectual inspiration, direction, humor, and solace that have made this collaboration one of the outstanding events in our academic careers.

Birth, Death, and Femininity

Birth, Death, and Femininity

ONE

Introduction: Birth, Death, and Femininity

ROBIN MAY SCHOTT

The concept of death has excited interest from the earliest sources of Western philosophy. In the pre-Socratic tradition, Heraclitus discussed death and birth as two equal principles of life. Death was viewed not as liberation of the soul into an otherworldly realm, but as the becoming of life of another worldly being. Thus, death and birth both belonged to an unending cycle of becoming. This approach to death as part of a vital life-cycle has been celebrated by later philosophers, in particular Friedrich Nietzsche and his followers. In the Platonic tradition, by contrast, death appears as liberation from the cycle of life. In the *Phaedo,* Socrates argues that in death, the philosopher's true self or soul is liberated from the body and can rediscover its original contact with eternal ideas. Plato presented Socrates as an example of the philosophical attitude that does not grieve when confronted with the ultimate prospect of dying.

But fewer philosophers have looked to the concept of birth in order to find a horizon of meaning or an inspiration for philosophical reflection, as Heidegger and innumerable other philosophers have done with the topic of death. Birth indeed figures in Plato's *Symposium,* which is an inquiry into the nature of love. In the dialogue, Socrates tells about the wisdom of his teacher Diotima, who claims that philosophers are the most perfect lovers because knowledge of the good is the highest form of love. She distinguishes between those whose "procreancy is of the body, who turn to woman as the object of their love" and "those whose procreancy is of the spirit rather than the flesh" (*Symposium* 208e–209a). Socrates' account of Diotima's speech echoes the view expressed earlier in the dialogue that vulgar love of the body is oriented toward women and human propagation, whereas the love of a man leads to a more lasting form of fatherhood (Schott 1993: 13). Thus, the concept of birth that is central for Platonic philosophy is not human birth, but the birth of knowledge. As Vigdis Songe-Møller has argued, Plato uses metaphoric images related to sexuality and birth in order to "facilitate a particular understanding of philosophy: philosophy as the highest form of reproduction—the reproduction of the One and of Likeness—with immortality as its objective and a radical homo-eroticism as its precondition" (Songe-Møller 2002: 112). Certain aspects of the feminine become absorbed into philosophy through the use of metaphors, but in a desexualized manner. Hence, Socrates describes himself as a midwife in the *Theaetetus*, in the following terms: "My art of midwifery is in general like theirs; the only difference is that my patients are men, not women, and my concern is not with the body but with the soul that is in travail of birth" (*Theaetetus* 150b). In this context, birth indeed becomes a concept for philosophical reflection, but only in the sense that philosophical birth frees one of human origins.

Nietzsche is another philosopher who turns to birth for philosophical inspiration. Sigridur Thorgeirsdottir argues that the metaphor of birth is at the center of Nietzsche's philosophy of embodied life. Yet he is highly selective about which aspects of the body and birth he incorporates into his conception, and he excludes significant dimensions of inter-relationality from his reflections on birth. Hannah Arendt brought the concept of birth into philosophical discourse through her reflections on human action and speech, and thereby poses the question: how does the concept of natality contribute to philosophy more generally?

Given the expansive philosophical literature on death and the more limited philosophical interest in birth, one might expect that a specifically *feminist* philosophical analysis would rethink philosophical concepts through the primacy of birth, rather than the primacy of death. This is what Grace Jantzen sought to do when she placed "natality—the fact that we were born, we are all 'natals'—against the fact that we shall all die, that we are all 'mortals'" (Jantzen 2004: 6). Our project is different. We too approach these topics as feminist philosophers; we too interrogate the role of sexual difference in life and thought. But we do not focus on natality alone as the clue to human existence. Instead, we seek to refocus attention on both the concept of natality and the concept of mortality within a shared frame of reference. By doing so, we do not primarily develop a "philosophy of death" in the fashion that many sociologists have contributed to a "sociology of death, dying and bereavement" (Bauman 1992: 10). Nor do we primarily seek to contribute to a "philosophy of birth," as Iris Marion Young did in her phenomenological study of the pregnant body, or as Julia Kristeva did in her study of the split nature of maternal subjectivity during pregnancy (Young 1990, Kristeva 1980). Rather, our project shows how both the concept of natality and the concept of mortality contribute to reflections on fundamental questions in philosophy, including questions about identity, temporality, and community.

All Men Are Mortal

Simone de Beauvoir began her book *The Ethics of Ambiguity* with a quotation from Montaigne, "The continuous work of our life is to build death" (Beauvoir 1962: 7). Humans can be said to be born dying, and the threat of death is already present in the first hour of life. The emphasis on death as the defining characteristic of human existence is already found in earlier existentialist philosophers. In *The Second Sex* Beauvoir cited the importance for Sartre of Heidegger's dictum that the real nature of man is bound up with death. She wrote, "if death were not resident in human life, the relation of man to the world and to himself would be profoundly disarranged—so much so that the statement, 'Man is mortal' would be seen to have significance quite other than that of a mere fact of observation. Were he immortal, an existent would no longer be what we call a man" (Beauvoir 1974: 7–8).[1] Beauvoir later conducted a thought experiment in her novel, *All Men Are Mortals:* what would a human being become, if he were immortal? Could he love, could he grieve, could he commit himself with conviction to his projects, if time stretched endlessly before him while his beloved were fated to die? The character Fosca who in the year 1311 drinks a potion that gives the gift and curse of immortality finds out that one can have a political future for a time, but not forever; one can love and lose and love and lose again for a time, but not forever; one can use sleep to refurnish one's vital powers for a time, but not forever. His immortality becomes a curse that cuts him off from not only passionate, but also bearable, relations to other people and himself; and his immortality becomes a contamination that robs all those whom he touches of the meaning in their lives. Mortality provides the internal limits on human existence, which enables humans to exist in the dialectical relation between finitude and infinity, and between temporality and eternity, which is quintessentially human. In *Sickness unto Death*, Søren Kierkegaard articulated this dialectical relation, without which a human being would be only a thing or would be God, but not a man or woman. Nietzsche also focused attention on the existential presence of death in life, through the partings that make up the continuous process of living.

Not all thinkers have agreed that death is meaningful for understanding what it is to be human. The Nobel Prize winner Elias Canetti argued vehemently against death. He wrote, "My character, my pride consist in my never having *flattered* death. . . . [N]o one can say that I have bowed to it, that I have acknowledged or whitewashed death. I find it as useless and as evil as ever, the basic ill of all existence, the unresolved and the incomprehensible" (Steiner 1998: 16–17). Not only did Canetti hold death in contempt, he argued that it cannot and must not be meaningful. But the history of philosophy provides many examples of philosophers who did struggle to capture meaning by thinking through the significance of death, or to provide a conceptual framework for its significance.[2]

For instance, death has been viewed as part of the cycle of genesis, and Heraclitus was the first of the pre-Socratics to mention the word "death" (*thanatos*). Death has been viewed as the liberation of the soul from the body into an eternal essence or idea, as in Pythagoras and Plato. Death has been viewed as caused by human sin, as in Christianity; but Christianity also accords believers in Christ a form of eternal life. Death has been explained in mechanistic terms, as in Descartes's view that death is an effect of the breakdown of the bodily machinery, whereby the soul is set free. Death has been viewed as ultimately nonexistent by philosophers of nature such as Leibniz, who argue that one can change one's perspective and view every death as a birth. Death has been viewed as part of the unity of life, as in German idealism, where death is viewed as a passage from a limited form of existence into an all-embracing form of existence, and hence as a reconciliation with the absolute. In the late nineteenth and the twentieth centuries, whereas positivists declared that "Death as a motive is moribund" (Jacobs 1899), existentialists and philosophers of life focused on the possibility of death as having fundamental significance in the consciousness of the living. Death has been viewed as a merely technical limitation of freedom, as Herbert Marcuse argued, which could be overcome by individual and social efforts. Death has been viewed as immanent in life, and Derrida's view that death is the principle that makes apparent the impossibility of identity calls to mind German idealism. Death has been viewed as carrying moral weight, as in Levinas's view that I am responsible for the other right up to dying for the other, and my responsibility is responding to the other's death.

In fact, death has had such a prominent position in the history of philosophy that Grace Jantzen argued that it is an obsession that displays the necrophilia of Western culture. In her view, the preoccupation with death is one of the constitutive features of the Western symbolic. She writes, "From militarization, death camps and genocide to exploitation, commodification and the accumulation of wealth, from the construction of pleasure and desire to the development of terminator genes, from the violence on the streets to the heaven-obsessed hymnody of evangelical churches, preoccupation with death and the means of death and the combat with death is ubiquitous"

(Jantzen 2004: 5). She invoked the term "necrophilia," meaning the love of death or of dead bodies, to signify the cultural fascination and obsession with death and violence. And she viewed necrophobia—the dread of death that typifies so many of our efforts to medicalize death, to keep it out at a distance or out of sight—as rooted in this more fundamental fascination with death and dying. Jantzen argued that the language of death is rooted in philosophy, not only through the philosophical reflections on death, but also through the metaphorical use of "death" in modernity, as in twentieth-century preoccupations with the death of God, the death of man, the death of the subject, and the death of the author. She suggested that this fixation on death in philosophy is connected to a conceptual and methodological interest in opposition and conflict. She pointed out, for example, that since Hegelian dialectics is built on the procedure of thesis, antithesis, and synthesis, then conflict is presupposed as the necessary condition for progress; and that in Anglo-American philosophy, an aggressive, adversarial method has dominated philosophical debates for decades (Jantzen 2004: 14–15).

Jantzen proposed that this obsession with and dread of death is gender-coded in Western culture, and argued that women are typically linked with death in this symbolic system, often as the cause of death. Her analysis is based on a feminist interpretation of a Freudian psychoanalytic paradigm that she applies to the realm of culture. In her view, the obsession with death in the Western symbolic is a displacement of something more basic that is silenced and rendered invisible by the mechanism of displacement. For her, the association of women and death ultimately signifies the problem of the maternal body, which becomes an obsessive locus of interest and a source of phobia. The identification of women with death, and the obsessive interest in death, is a displacement of "the real locus of the problem" (Jantzen 2004: 17). By this mechanism, one has achieved a silencing of the maternal body.

The association of women and death is well established in cross-cultural studies and interdisciplinary studies, including studies in anthropology, art, and religion. Many other feminist theorists have also reflected on the connection between women and death. The history of this association can be traced back at least to the eighth century BCE with Hesiod's description of Pandora, where woman was identified with death and misery. When Pandora opened the jar given to her by Hermes or Zeus, misery spread over mankind:

> For ere this the tribes of men lived on earth remote and free from
> ills and hard toil and heavy sickness which bring the Fates upon
> men; for in misery men grow old quickly. But the woman took off

the great lid of the jar with her hands and scattered all these and her thought caused sorrow and mischief to men. Only Hope remained there in an unbreakable home within under the rim of the great jar. . . . But the rest, countless plagues, wander amongst men; for earth is full of evils and the sea is full. Of themselves diseases come upon men continually by day and by night, bringing mischief to mortals silently. (Hesiod n.d.: lines 90–105)

Pandora's jar represents the grave jar in which the spirits of the dead were stored. According to this myth, without women there would be no mortality.

In the Judeo-Christian tradition, it also has been argued that the first woman brought death to human beings. When Eve was persuaded by the serpent to eat of the tree of knowledge of good and evil, she gave the fruit to Adam as well. Thus, they knew their nakedness and felt shame. God punished woman by intensifying the pangs of childbirth and making her husband master over her, while man's punishment was to toil for survival: "Until you return to the ground from which you were taken; For you are dirt, and to dirt you shall return" (Gen. 3:1–19). Hence, in traditional interpretations it was through Eve's sin that death enters human life, though the meaning of death first becomes apparent when Cain kills his brother Abel.

Simone de Beauvoir used a major part of the first book of *The Second Sex* to demonstrate the powerful association between women and death. She wrote, "In most popular representations Death is a woman, and it is for women to bewail the dead because death is their work." And "From the day of his birth man begins to die: this is the truth incarnated in the Mother." Women become the material representation of alterity or otherness. And that which is a hostile other—the flesh, and death as the radical other of life—becomes attributed to woman (Beauvoir 1974: 166, 187, 189, 202). As Sara Heinämaa argues in her chapter "The Sexed Self and the Mortal Body," Beauvoir analyzes on a pre-conceptual and pre-symbolic level how men have projected through myth the qualities of finitude and mortality onto women, and how women often have accepted this projection. In Beauvoir's view, the association between women and death has been a primary strategy for men to handle the ambiguity and anxiety of existence.

Thus, we find different answers to the questions: What is the primary emotion that motivates the association of women and death? And what does this link signify? For Jantzen, the primary motivating emotion is the fear of sexual difference in the shape of the maternal body. For her, the association of woman and death signifies something fundamentally wrong in the Western symbolic, something that in different ways is involved in all the misfortunes of human life—from wartime atrocities, to violence on the streets and in the homes, to representations of violence in the media, to the exploitation that underlies the pleasures of consumer culture. In this approach, all that is negative in human existence becomes located symbolically with death. By implication, Jantzen locates symbolically all that is positive in another pole—natality.

For Beauvoir, the primary motivating emotion is the fear of alterity and finitude, which become projected onto the feminine. But she does not assume that alterity, finitude, death, and woman represent all that is negative in human existence. Rather than making such equations, she explores how the association of women and death marks the *ambiguity* of human existence. This idea is worth explicating. The term "ambiguity" is derived from the Latin *ambiguitas,* meaning doubt, uncertainty, or paradox (Langer 2003: 89–91). Ambiguity is usually associated with lack, failure, and hence it often has a negative connotation. But this association presumes that it is possible to achieve doubtless certainty in our efforts to know the world and to act ethically in it. Beauvoir's understanding of the concept of ambiguity is based on a different approach. She rejected the Cartesian criteria of clearness and distinctness both in epistemology and in ethics. She followed Merleau-Ponty, who formulated the implications of human ambiguity in the following way: "By definition, it seems that there cannot be any consciousness of ambiguity without ambiguity of consciousness" (quoted in Langer 2003: 90). The concept of ambiguity has been defined in several different ways, but all definitions point to the indeterminacy and duality of existence. For Beauvoir, ambiguity referred to the paradoxical condition of human life, which is stretched between two oppositional poles: infinity and finiteness, separation and bonding. The most fundamental paradox of human existence is the contradiction that "the continuous work of our life is to build death." Thus, human existence is marked by what existentialist philosophers referred to as lack, failure, or negativity. For Beauvoir the most honest response to the paradox of human existence is not to deny it or seek to flee it through projecting one half of this paradox onto another, but to "assume our fundamental ambiguity" (Beauvoir 1962: 9). Should one fail to recognize the ambiguity in the constitution of the self, then one projects one's unacknowledged negative qualities onto the other. The concept of ambivalence refers to this denial and projection, which stems from the unresolved tensions within human subjectivity.

Death exemplifies the paradoxical character of human life. On the one hand, death is a form of existential evil that constantly haunts life (Schott 2003: 229–32). On the other hand, mortality is that which makes human life human, and distinguishes it from the repetitive life of animals and from the eternal or atemporal life of gods. Hence, to view the symbolism associated with death as solely negative is to deny the duality of death. In reading Western philosophy and culture as necrophilic, as Jantzen does, she misses this dual character of death. Her alternative is to locate all the positive dimensions of life within the concept of natality. She thereby also overlooks the duality that is located in the concept of natality.

All People Are Natals

There is a long history of philosophers' reflecting on the problem of mortality, but most philosophers have ignored the problem of natality. And yet, all human beings are born, and indeed are still of woman born, as Adrienne Rich noted (Rich 1976). Birth is the condition not only of one's own individual life, but of the life of the species. And without the continuous renewal of human birth, the human species would die out, as other species have done before it.

P. D. James's book *Children of Men* is a thought-experiment about what would happen if there were no more births. The dystopia is set in the year 2021, and twenty-five years since the last human birth anywhere on earth. England is ruled by the dictator Xan, who maintains order by harsh regulations, including mass "voluntary" suicide for the elderly, strict control of foreign workers, and endorsement of unbridled brutality on the Isle of Man for all those deemed to be criminals or misfits. Since crumbling buildings and wild gardens will outlast the aging and dying human race, there can be no interest in sustaining a shared future for newcomers to the world. Nor can there be any but the most marginal academic interest in the past, since knowledge gained about the past will also be without a future. Since the present has lost its future, and lost a meaningful relation to the past, society becomes imbued with lethargy and acquiescence. Miraculously, the quarter century of infertility is ended by the birth of an infant. The Oxford professor Theo Fanon, who has risked his life to protect the pregnant woman he loves, kills the dictator, his cousin, who has hunted down the fugitives in order to control this new life and era. Yet this new beginning is also darkened by shadows, as Theo puts on the ring of power, which "wasn't made" for his finger. And one recalls the portion of the funeral service recited earlier in the book, "Thou turnest man to destruction: again thou sayest, Come again, ye children of men" (James 1992: 278, 224).

When Jantzen introduces her concept of natality, she treats it as the source of creativity rather than violence, of hope rather than despair. She characterizes the concept of natality by the following features (Jantzen 1992: 36–38): First, natality implies the birth of an embodied individual. As such, an understanding of natality undermines the mind-body dualism, and the concomitant valorization of the mind or soul and the devaluation of the body, that has underlined so much of Western philosophy and religion. Hence, natality shows the importance of a this-worldly approach to justice and freedom that can enable the flourishing of human bodily needs. Second, natality reflects the primacy of gender in human existence. In reference to a new life (at birth, or already during the early scanning of a fetus), one asks: is it a girl or a boy? And it is disturbing if the answer is "neither" or "both."[3] Third, natality reveals the role of particular relations in human existence. To be born means to be dependent on a web of relationships, without which one could neither thrive nor survive. And fourth, as illustrated by James's dystopia, natality is necessary for hope to exist. Each new life brings new possibilities for human existence.

Jantzen catches sight of many important features of natality. But she misses others, and these gaps contribute to her view that if the symbolic of death is wholly negative, then the symbolic of natality must be wholly positive. One of the thinkers who has contributed most to the development of the philosophical concept of natality is Hannah Arendt, who in *The Human Condition* wrote that "natality, and not mortality, may be the central category of political, as distinguished from metaphysical, thought." (Arendt 1958: 9) For Arendt, one of the key features of natality is spontaneity. Natality represents the principle of beginning, which is the source of hope for human life. It brings forth the idea of an unexpected event, that something radically new is possible in human endeavors and experiences. Secondly, dependency is a central feature of natality. But dependency does not merely mean the dependency of one individual on another, as in a child's need for its caregiver to survive and flourish. It also implies the dependency of an individual on the plurality of individuals in a human community. Arendt finds in St. Augustine an important emphasis on the relation between part and whole, a theme that also is important in the work of Husserl and Heidegger. An individual human life can have meaning, in Arendt's view, only if it is part of a whole, part of the public space of community that consists in a plurality of individuals. Thirdly, for Arendt, temporality is a crucial feature of natality. As a created being, one is always in the processing of becoming and changing. In this sense, one always exists in relation to one's origin, which as past is also the source of one's becoming, and in relation to the future. In the case of human beings, life is futural also in the sense noted above, that human beings can through speech and action begin something new and unforeseen. Fourthly, the concept of natality shows the centrality of memory for human existence. It is through memory that a human being connects to his or her origins, hence memory becomes the path for achieving self-consciousness.

Arendt is interested in natality as a political concept, on how new life presupposes the ongoing life of a community into which one is born, and from which one learns language, history, values, and in which one can act. She focused not just on qualities of natality, but on capacities inhering in it. For Arendt, these capacities include the faculty of memory, by which we relate to that which is past and that which is future. The past gives shape to our future actions, since it is reminds us of what we seek to rediscover or disavow. Natality reveals both the conditions of human life which are given and on which one is dependent, as well as the capacity for acting and shaping one's relation to the world in a spontaneous and creative manner; hence, natality is also a source of resistance to that which is given. In this sense, there is an implicit tension in natality—between what is given and what is constituted—that is insurmountable; this tension also constitutes the concept of natality as complex. The tension between what is given and what is constituted, what is past and what is future, implies that natality cannot be viewed in simply positive terms. As Arendt notes in *Origins of Totalitarianism,* the crisis of our time has brought forth "an entirely new form of government which as a potentiality and an ever-present danger is only too likely to stay with us from now on . . ." (Arendt 1973: 478). If what is past includes totalitarianism and atrocities, then new spontaneous action relates itself to this particular past. One either contests these previous conditions, or perpetuates them in new forms, or both. All of these possibilities and risks are imminent in the notion of natality, as P.D. James also hints.

One might object that this double-face of natality, which shows both the positive and negative risks inherent in human action, applies only to the notion of natality as a political concept, which was the context of Arendt's analysis. Why isn't human birth as such—in a nonpolitical meaning—always intrinsically positive, and even redemptive? For Arendt, such an idea would be absurd because the biological process of birth as such can have no meaning, either positive or negative. It is only through human action and speech that one is able to create new meanings or to activate old ones.

Moreover, a one-sided focus on the positive dimensions of natality looks away from the problematic or miserable conditions in which human birth can take place. Human birth can be subject to racist, totalitarian government policies, as with the Lebensborn program of the Nazi government.[4] And poverty can so undermine a mother's ability to provide housing and economic support for another child that she chooses abortion, as Carmen Climaco did. At the age of twenty-two years, and as the mother of three children, she began serving a thirty-year prison sentence for having an abortion in El Salvador. In El Salvador, abortion is criminalized in all cases, including in cases of rape, incest, fetal malformation, and a threat to the life of the mother (Hitt 2006). Pregnancy is a threat that affects all women who are raped, whether in Bosnia, where forced impregnation was an explicit strategy of war; in Iraq, where both women civilians and detainees in prisons run by Americans have been raped (Rosen 2006); in the Congo, where thousands of women and girls have been raped by soldiers in the nation's army (Leopold 2006);[5] in Haiti and Liberia, where UN peacekeeping troops have subjected teenage girls to rape and prostitution;[6] in South Africa, where in the twelve-month period ending in March 2005, police reported more than 22,000 cases of child rape; in the U.S., where there were 188,960 reported rapes in 2005.[7] And poverty and poor health conditions can make birth a fundamentally dangerous event, as the anthropologist Nancy Scheper-Hughes showed in her study of poor rural women, mostly black or brown, in northeast Brazil, where the infant mortality rate is so high that mothers often do not register the death of their children nor attend their funerals (Scheper-Hughes 1992). In reference to human birth, the political dimension of the concept is inescapable.

Does this mean that the concept of natality is solely a political concept? Would the features of dependency, temporality, and the capacity to reflect on what is past in order to act on what is future not also be central categories for metaphysical thinking? One can easily understand why Arendt argues that it is natality, and *not mortality,* that is central for the political. After all, although death is the inevitable fate for every individual, it is not necessary for the political community. Instead, as Arendt notes in *The Human Condition,* "the common world is what we enter when we are born and what we leave behind when we die. It transcends our life-span into past and future alike; it was there before we can and will outlast our brief sojourn in it" (Arendt 1958: 55–56). But when Arendt argues that it is natality that is the central concept *for the political* she is also abdicating on the metaphysical project of philosophy. Her distinction between political and metaphysical concepts must be understood in relation to her overall views about the constitutive primacy of appearance. In *The Life of the Mind,* she writes, "In this world which we enter, appearing from a nowhere, and from which we disappear into a nowhere, *Being and Appearing coincide*" (Arendt 1978: 19). For Arendt, like for Heidegger, metaphysics referred to the attempt to find absolute grounds for human knowledge and actions—for example, in Ideas, in Nature, in the rational will, or in God (Villa 1996: 166)—and as such is a project that has reached its closure. When Arendt focuses on natality as a preeminently political concept, she also implies that there is nothing behind this political concept, no Being behind the appearing. Her conceptual revolution consists not only in focusing on the process of appearing and becoming (as many other philosophers before her also had done), but in establishing natality as the primary concept for appearing. It is through natality that human beings navigate the groundlessness of their thinking, find the source of spontaneous action, and affirm themselves as unique individuals living amongst a plurality of human beings.

Natality and Mortality

I have chosen to sketch some of the features of the concepts of mortality and natality through the thinking of Simone de Beauvoir and Hannah Arendt, two of the most prominent women philosophers in twentieth-century Western thought. For Beauvoir and Arendt, these respective concepts bring focus on the temporality of human existence; on the groundlessness of human projects and the need for human beings to provide their own, always contestable, justifications for their actions; and on the urgency of human freedom and dependency. But there are significant differences between these philosophers' accounts as well. For Beauvoir, mortality points to the tension within subjectivity between finitude and infinity, as well as between different subjects. She approaches the problem of mortality by tracing how humans have responded to their existential conditions in myth, literature, and history. And she focuses on the ambiguity in our fundamental relation to death, the ambivalence that is manifest when we deny this ambiguity, and the gender-coding of this denial. For Arendt also, human beings are fundamentally temporal beings who are always in the process of appearing or becoming. But the tension between finitude and infinity, between temporality and permanence, is located in the relation between the individual and the community. Instead of focusing on how existential conditions become manifest in particular historical and institutional ways, Arendt defines the political as the fundamental condition of human life. From this point of view, she investigates the struggles and conflicts that are at the heart of community, and the ways in which individual struggles with conscience reflect on their ability to live amongst a plurality of selves.

One aspect that may be striking in this discussion is the overlap between the concepts of mortality and natality, the ways in which these concepts achieve somewhat similar effects. I will try to specify the common ground that joins the notions of mortality and natality. Here it is necessary to acknowledge how material life presents themes for conscious reflection, though neither Beauvoir nor Arendt discussed birth or death as an organic event. First, the notion of change is implicit in both the concepts of mortality and natality. Death on a material level is the return of a living being to an inanimate state (Freud 1961: 32). As such, mortality is a guarantee that what we are now is not what we always will be. Hence, consciousness about the role of death in life focuses both on the transitoriness of human existence and on the process of change within the temporal span of our lives. Change is also implicit in natality. Each new life expresses a coming-into-being, though children often cannot fathom that there could be some prior state of nonexistence, and may imagine themselves as always already in their mother's belly waiting to be born. Moreover, material life is always embedded in a process of growth, development, and decay. Second, the concepts of separation and difference are implicit in both mortality and natality. The death of one's beloved implies the radical difference between him and oneself, when he has left life and grief and memory remain for those who survive him. One's own approaching death brings the awareness that one's children's time span will continue into the future without one's participation or witnessing. Difference is implicit in natality as well, since each new life marks a unique beginning. Third, the concept of vulnerability is explicit in mortality, as the fragility one confronts in injury, illness, loss, and death. Vulnerability is implicit as well in natality, in the dependence of each new life on that which precedes it. Fourth, the notion of plurality is implicit in mortality, since the surrounding world sustains itself in mourning, indifference, or ignorance in the face of each passing death. Arendt was aware of this role for plurality, when she considered the ongoing life of the community in the face of an individual's death. And natality makes explicit the plurality that is the precondition for each new life. The concepts of (1) change, (2) separation and difference, (3) vulnerability, and (4) plurality imply a fifth concept as well, that of conflict. For in the dynamic and fragile lives in a heterogeneous group, conflict recurs as a means of negotiating differences.

These five concepts also characterize ancient tragic thought, as Vigdis Songe-Møller argues in her chapter, "Antigone and the Deadly Desire for Sameness." In the writings of the pre-Socratic philosophers such as Anaximander, one finds a focus on strife as constitutive of community. And the Greek tragic poet Sophocles explores the deadly fate of the ideals of unity, sameness, homogeneity, and harmony. It is far better to accept the heterogeneity of human life than to immobilize oneself and one's society, as Sigridur Thorgeirsdottir also argues in her interpretation of the ambivalent features of Nietzsche's thought.

These concepts of ancient tragic thought provide one common frame of reference for this book and for a discussion of mortality and natality. Faced with unbearable loss, one may protest with Canetti that death is evil. And yet our protestations won't release us from the hold death has on us; rather they attest to its hold on us. Faced with the prospect of new life, one rejoices at this miracle—unless it is unwanted, coerced, and violently imposed. Even in their most personal sense, the concepts of mortality and natality show the force of human vulnerability, interdependency, conflict, and freedom; in other words, they are marked by the ambiguity of human existence. From this point of view, it is wrong to identify the concept of conflict with a death-fixation in philosophy. Instead, conflict and the related notions of ambiguity, ambivalence, and paradox travel through reflections on both death and birth.

Since it is important to analyze the concepts of mortality and natality within a common frame of reference, then by implication an exclusive focus on either mortality or natality may have the consequence of making certain features of each concept recede into the background. For example, an exclusive focus on mortality might lead to bypassing the role of plurality in death. For existential philosophy, the core meaning of mortality is constituted in relation to one's own eventual death, which becomes conceptually prior to understanding the meaning for me of the death of other persons. But it is also crucial to understand the plurality of death, in the sense that death becomes manifest in a plurality of ways: one's own death, the death of the other, the death of animals, the death of plants, and the small deaths in life that occur with each individual parting or separation. My relation to my own mortality is linked not only to the plurality of the forms of death, but to the plurality of births as well. Natality brings into focus the birth of the other, and my own temporal horizon is transformed by the birth of the other, whose life will continue beyond my own death, and who brings the dimension of something radically unexpected to my life as well as to their own. Moreover, natality is often addressed with an optimistic enthusiasm about new beginnings. As such, the implications of the vulnerability of these new beginnings may recede from view. Yet it is important to remember that new beginnings are also fraught with vulnerability—with the potential failure of one's actions, with the closing off of other options, with the risk of choosing wrongly. Reflections on mortality keep these dimensions from receding into the background. It is in this context that the authors of this book argue for the importance of a common frame of reference for understanding mortality and natality.

One might object that an attempt to find such a common frame of reference risks reducing the one to the other. The death of one's beloved is radically irreducible to anything else. And birth is irreducible in quite another way, as the uniqueness of new beginnings. Yet neither as experience nor as concept can these events be apprehended in isolation from other concepts in human existence. This book suggests that the concepts of ambiguity, ambivalence, and paradox provide conceptual tools for addressing these complex events.

The task here is not to develop a philosophy of mortality or a philosophy of natality on this basis. Rather, the task is to consider what the concepts of mortality and natality bring to philosophy. One of the contributions is methodological. For these concepts point out a field of questions, including the question of origins, the nature and role of genealogy, the nature of change, the relation of destructive and creative elements, the expectation of and obligation to the future, the nature of time and its implications for the human body and for relations between generations. In other words, the concepts of mortality and natality together present a new way of organizing a field of philosophical questions that cut across subdisciplines, for example, of ontology, philosophy of history, psychoanalytic theory, bioethics, and political theory. In this way, the approach in this book challenges the dominant discourses of death and birth today that are narrowly focused debates in contemporary metaphysics on personal identity and continuity, or in bioethics on the extent and limits of technological control. Biotechnologies have added a new dimension to birth and death by their very capacity to alter these phenomena. This capacity calls for a new way of thinking about the meaning of birth and death in a broader framework.[8]

Not only do the concepts of mortality and natality bring about a new way of organizing philosophical inquiries, but they also bring with them a reflection on sexual difference. As Beauvoir demonstrated, death is coded as female not because men and women are biologically different in relation to death (though there are systematic differences in patterns of longevity), but because men's ambivalent relation to death projects the evils of death onto woman. Similarly, birth has been coded as feminine, and the philosophical concept of natality viewed as an obviously feminine and *feminist* topic, since women give birth. But since men and women equally are born (if not born equally), this projection of birth onto women is also an ambivalent gesture. Seyla Benhabib notes that many philosophers do not acknowledge in their theories that individuals have been born. Writing about social contract theorists, she describes the strange world presumed by these philosophers, in which "individuals are grown up before they have been born; in which boys are men before they have been children; a world where neither mother, nor sister, nor wife exists" (Benhabib 1978: 85). Not only do death and birth become sexually coded, but their associated concepts may become so as well. Plato, for example, associated the procreancy of the body, which precipitated humans into a world of change and mortality, with the feminine. And Kant identified the fickleness of emotion and passion with feminine nature. In a related vein, some feminist philosophers have identified the concepts of conflict and opposition with the masculine and with a necrophilic relation to death. In each of these examples, the concepts variously associated with embodiment, change, death, emotion, conflict, and opposition are treated with ambivalence, with philosophers projecting the negative features onto the gender of the other. Reflections on mortality and natality can contribute to a decoding of the role of gender in this ambivalence toward mortality and natality.

More Reflections on Methodology

I have suggested that reflections on mortality and natality lead to a new way of organizing the philosophical field of questions. Here it is relevant to consider not only what kinds of questions one poses, but one's relation to the questions that one poses. What effect may be obtained by one's philosophical labors?

Some philosophers endow their critical work with considerable powers, and see in philosophy the power to liberate or transform the world, through the capacity to transform one's way of thinking. The transformative possibilities of philosophy may be linked with a therapeutic conception of philosophy, by which the philosopher can bring the repressed dimensions of culture to the fore in order to release the hidden sources of well-being. Or the transformative possibilities of philosophy can become imbued with a religious language in which the task of philosophy is to redeem the present from its self-imposed destruction.[9]

This book, *Birth, Death, and Femininity,* has more modest goals. This work does not aim at changing the world by disentangling traditional conceptual links about mortality and natality. But it does seek to renew philosophical thinking on these questions. The book contributes to a reorientation of philosophical questions around the themes of mortality and natality; it widens the lens of analysis so that birth and death are not treated in isolation from each other or from the broad family of concepts to which they properly belong; and it explores the significance of ambiguity, ambivalence, and paradox for a philosophical framing of these matters. Although this study will not change the world, it has changed our thinking about human existence. The tools each of us brings to this study are drawn from continental philosophy, including the traditions of hermeneutics, philosophy of life, phenomenology, existentialism, and political theory.

Since methodology incorporates the moment of self-reflection about how one interrogates the world, the methodology of this book also includes a reflection on our shared process. Each of us offers her individual analysis of death and birth and introduces a set of concepts and methods to discuss these topics. And yet, every word in the book also has been read, reread, and discussed by each of the others. In some sense, the methodology of this group can be said to reflect its central concepts. For during the repeated discussions of every chapter, each of us has been vulnerable and exposed to the critical gaze of the others. And with each new attempt, we have come to rely on and trust in the response of these others. Both vulnerability and plurality have been the hallmarks of this working process, and have attested to the significance of mortality and natality in philosophical reflection.

Yet one voice is missing from this book. At the time of writing this essay, it is just months since the death from cancer of Eva Gothlin, who was an original participant of this project. Her philosophical interests are represented here in the discussions of psychoanalysis, of Beauvoir's philosophy, and in the topics of relationality and friendship. Another death, the death of Markus Songe-Møller Soleim, has affected us throughout the work on this book. Hence, mortality in the factual sense has been part of the experiential background for this collaborative philosophical inquiry.

I will add one more note about methodology, and that is about the order of presentation. As the reader will observe, this book is structured in reverse chronological order. The first section of the book discusses issues of sexual violence and sexual violence during war, issues that have gained a measure of public awareness since the war rapes in Bosnia and Rwanda in the 1990s. I analyze these issues in part through the work of Simone de Beauvoir and Hannah Arendt, writers who are significant for contemporary theorizing about gender and politics. The second section of the book, by Sara Heinämaa, explores phenomenological accounts of mortality and generativity through the work of Beauvoir, and also through the work of Edmund

Husserl, Martin Heidegger, Emmanuel Lévinas, and Søren Kierkegaard, key thinkers in the shaping of phenomenology. The third section of the book, by Sigridur Thorgeirsdottir, focuses on nineteenth-century philosophy with an analysis of Nietzsche's philosophy of birth, which Thorgeirsdottir links to Hannah Arendt's philosophy of natality. And the final section of the book, by Vigdis Songe-Møller, moves back in time to ancient philosophy and Greek tragedy for a study of Antigone.

This reverse chronological order may seem counterintuitive, but it reflects both pedagogical and conceptual considerations.[10] From a pedagogical perspective, it is often useful to move from material that is more familiar to the reader, as the work of Beauvoir and Arendt may be, to work that is less familiar. One follows the path of curiosity from what is close at hand to what is more distant, and often discovers that what is distant opens new perspectives on what is close. This is so not because discovering the origins of a concept or problem is a clue to its future development, as presumed by an evolutionary approach to history. Foucault, in his essay "Nietzsche, Genealogy, History," warns against a search for origins, as opposed to a study of how unique events happen and different interpretations emerge (Foucault 1977: 140–52). The reverse chronological order of the book helps avoid the view that the past gives the essence of the present, and brings to light the specific variations in the concepts of birth and mortality that have emerged in the interstices of history.

More on Contemporary Problems

I began this essay by noting that the themes of death and birth may be the most intense concerns of personal life and also the subject of quite abstract philosophical reflections about the self, one's relation to other persons, to a community of individuals, and to the world in which community exists. Before concluding, I will also call attention briefly to some of the ways in which death and birth are the focus of many contemporary social problems.

As Zygmunt Bauman argues, one of the fundamental features of the project of modernity is the attempt to master and control the natural world and our bodies as part of nature. Since all things should be subject to rational control, the human body has become an intense object of medical concern, and consequently death is not viewed as a human condition but as a medical condition to be solved. He writes, "We do not hear of people dying of mortality. They die only of individual *causes*, they die *because* there *was an individual cause*" (Bauman 1992: 138). Death is always viewed as contingent, as caused by a specific disease that we failed to prevent, or through inadequate diet, stress, or injury. Since we ultimately cannot control death, we compartmentalize death and distance ourselves from it and from those who are in the throes of mourning. So while on the one hand the representation of death is omnipresent in the media both in fiction and in news coverage, on the other hand, the practices that orient our relation to dying and death in modern urban societies tend to marginalize death from everyday routines.

Although we cannot eliminate death, we can exercise control over it by inflicting it, as is done by the judiciary and penal institutions in countries, such as the United States, that condone capital punishment; by systematic racism that precipitates gang violence on the streets—such as the December 2006 killing of a fourteen-year-old black girl in Los Angeles by a Latino gang member (Altman 2007); by inflicting war on civilians, who in contemporary warfare constitute the vast majority of casualties.[11] And one can also exercise power over death by criminalizing the voluntary choosing of death, as with the legal prohibitions against euthanasia. The myriad ways in which judicial, penal, and medical institutions regulate, inflict, criminalize, and sanction death contribute to what Michel Foucault has called "bio-power"—the power of the sovereign state over the life and death of its subjects.

Birth is also treated to juridical, penal, and medical technological regulations. Denmark has the highest percent of births from in vitro fertilization (IVF) in the world, with 2,031 IVF-assisted births per million inhabitants (Skaarup 2006), and in 2006 lesbians received for the first time the right to receive artificial insemination with the assistance of a doctor. Debates rage in Denmark over whether it is fair to set an age limit of nine months less than forty-five years for a woman's access to reproductive technologies, when there is no such restriction for men; these debates were inflamed on both sides by the birth of twins to a sixty-seven-year-old Spanish mother (Sørensen 2007). This controversy will not be assuaged by the death of this woman in 2009. While there are debates about who is entitled to assisted reproduction, other women are prevented from receiving assistance to terminate pregnancy where countries have criminalized abortion, and where women have been systematically raped during war for the purpose of impregnation. With birth as well one sees the intersection of biological life and the institutions of political power.

Can the philosophical studies in this book address birth and death as contemporary problems? Some of the chapters do so explicitly, as in my discussion of war rape. More generally, this study also offers conceptual tools that are productive for these contemporary debates. For example, the concepts of ambiguity and ambivalence can be highly instructive method-ological concepts when analyzing ethical and political debates about abor-tion. It is typical for activists, both anti-abortion and pro-choice, to argue in terms of rights, as in a fetus's right to life or a woman's right to decide about her body. Activists on both sides of the debate often invoke stark oppositions between good and bad, innocence and guilt, in defending these rights, with-out considering the ambiguity of birth and death. When anti-abortion activ-ists focus on birth as wholly positive, they overlook the negative possibilities of birth, which are starkly apparent when pregnancy results from rape or forced impregnation in wartime, or when poverty makes it impossible for a mother to provide housing, food, and a decent quality of life for a child. And when pro-choice activists focus on abortion rights as wholly positive, they risk overlooking the negative dimensions of abortion, as when multiple abortions become a substitute for the adequate use of contraception. Moral absolutism on either side of the debate exemplifies the logic of ambivalence, by which the ambiguity of both birth and abortion are denied.

Approaching the problems of birth and death with concepts such as ambiguity, ambivalence, paradox, vulnerability, plurality, and conflict does not provide simple and clear paths. More often than not, such an approach adds complexity to the understanding of problems in private and institu-tional life, and brings with it an element of risk and uncertainty. Nonetheless, this may be the best path available. As Simone de Beauvoir reminds us, it is necessary to assume these fundamental conflicts in order to draw the strength to live and the reason to act (Beauvoir 1962: 9).

NOTES

1. I discuss this in Schott 2003: 230.

2. The material for the following paragraph is drawn from the *Historisches Wörterbuch der Philosophie,* entry on "Tod," which Vigdis Songe-Møller has summa-rized in a working document.

3. Hence, the challenge raised by hermaphroditism (Foucault 1978).

4. The Lebensborn ("source of life") organization was founded in 1935 as a response to declining birth rates in Germany. In September 1936 Heinrich Himmler described the program under his personal direction as "an aid to racially and biologically-hereditarily valuable families." http://en.allexperts.com/e/l/le/lebensborn.htm, accessed March 9, 2010.

5. Jan Egeland, the UN emergency relief coordinator, spoke with one woman, who told him "how she had been raped repeatedly for more than a week by a group of soldiers who kept her bound so tightly through the week that she had permanently lost the use of her hands." There is only one specialized rape clinic in the Congo, which has dealt with more than ten thousand cases in the last seven years.

6. "UN Troops Face Child Abuse Claims," *BBC News,* Nov. 30, 2006, http:// newsvote.bbc.co.uk/mpapps/pagetools/print/news.bbc.co.uk/2/hi/americas/61905.stm, accessed December 1, 2006.

7. U.S. Department of Justice, *Bureau of Justice Statistics,* http://www.ojp.usdoj .gov/bjs/cvict.htm, accessed January 22, 2007. This figure is down from the 1995 statistics, where 354,670 women were victims of rape or sexual assault. Sixty-eight percent of these victims were raped by partners, acquaintances, or other relatives. "American Rape Statistics," http://www.paralumun.com/issuesrapestats.htm, accessed January 22, 2007.

8. Julia Kristeva and Catherine Clément write, "[T]he technological progress of our advanced democracies, which has the ambition simply to 'manage' life in complete innocence, is laden with the same totalitarian threat: the threat of destroying life after having devalued the question of meaning" (Clément and Kristeva 2001: 13).

9. Jantzen uses both therapeutic and redemptive language in describing her philosophical project.

10. I am grateful to Claudia Card's suggestion about the order of presentation, which she included in her referee report.

11. In the context of war, funerals may be a too common appearance on civilian streets. But they also may be made invisible altogether, as when the prevention of funerals is part of a policy of genocide. Card 2007.

BIBLIOGRAPHY

Altman, Larry. 2007. "Latino Gang in Harbor Gateway Agrees to Truce." *Streetgangs.* January 16, 2007. http://www.streetgangs.com/topics/2007/011607peace.html, accessed January 25, 2007.

Arendt, Hannah. 1958. *The Human Condition.* Chicago: University of Chicago Press.

———. 1973. *The Origins of Totalitarianism.* New York: Harcourt Brace Jovanovich.

———. 1978. *The Life of the Mind.* New York: Harcourt Brace Jovanovich.

Bauman, Zygmunt. 1992. *Mortality, Immortality and Other Life Strategies.* Stanford, Calif.: Stanford University Press.

Beauvoir, Simone de. 1962. *The Ethics of Ambiguity.* Trans. Bernard Frechtman. Secaucus, N.J.: Citadel Press.

———. 1974. *The Second Sex.* Trans. H. M. Parshley. New York: Vintage Books.

———. 2004. *All Men are Mortals.* Trans. Euan Cameron based on the original translation by Leonard M. Friedman. London: Virago.

Benhabib, Seyla. 1978. "The Generalized and the Concrete Other." In Benhabib and Cornell 1978.

Benhabib, Seyla, and Drucilla Cornell, eds. 1978. *Feminism as Critique.* Minneapolis: University of Minnesota Press.

Card, Claudia, ed. 2003. *The Cambridge Companion to Simone de Beauvoir.* Cambridge: Cambridge University Press.

———. 2007. "Genocide and Social Death." In Schott 2007.

Clément, Catherine, and Julia Kristeva. 2001. *The Feminine and the Sacred.* Trans. Jane Marie Todd. New York: Columbia University Press.

Foucault, Michel. 1977. *Language, Counter-Memory, Practice.* Trans. Donald F. Bouchard and Sherry Simon. Ithaca, N.Y.: Cornell University Press.

———. 1978. *Herculine Barbin.* Paris: Gallimard.

Freud, Sigmund. 1961. *Beyond the Pleasure Principle.* Trans. James Strachey. New York: W. W. Norton.

Hesiod. n.d. *Works and Days.* Trans. Hugh G. Evelyn-White (1914). http://www.sacredtexts.com/cla/hesiod/works.htm, accessed January 30, 2007.

Hitt, Jack. 2006. "Pro-Life Nation." *New York Times.* April 6, 2006. http://www.nytimes.com/2006/04/09/magazine/09abortion.html, accessed April 11, 2006.

Jacobs, J. 1899. "The Dying of Death." *Fortnightly Review,* n.s., 72: 264–69.

James, P. D. 1992. *Children of Men.* London: Faber and Faber.

Jantzen, Grace. 2004. *Foundations of Violence.* London: Routledge.

Kristeva, Julia. 1980. *Desire in Language.* Trans. Thomas Gora. New York: Columbia University Press.

Langer, Monika. 2003. "Beauvoir and Merleau-Ponty on Ambiguity." In Card 2003: 87–106.

Leopold, Evelyn. 2006. "UN Calls Rape a 'Cancer' in Congo." *Boston Globe.* September 16, 2006. http://www.boston.com/news/world/africa/articles/2006/09/16/un_calls_rape_a_cancer_in_congo/, accessed September 19, 2006.

Malpas, Jeff, and Robert C. Solomon, eds. 1998. *Death and Philosophy.* London: Routledge.

New American Bible. United States Conference of Catholic Bishops. http://www.nccbuscc.org/nab/bible/genesis/genesis3.htm, accessed January 30, 2007.

Plato. 1961. *The Collected Dialogues of Plato.* Ed. Edith Hamilton and Huntington Cairns. Trans. Lane Cooper. Princeton, N.J.: Princeton University Press.

Rich, Adrienne. 1976. *Of Woman Born; Motherhood as Experience and Institution.* New York: W. W. Norton.

Rosen, Ruth. 2006. "A Wave of Sexual Terrorism in Iraq." *Alternet.* July 14, 2006. http://www.alternet.org/module/printversion/38932, accessed July 18, 2006.

Scheper-Hughes, Nancy. 1992. *Death without Weeping: The Violence of Everyday Life in Brazil.* Berkeley and Los Angeles: University of California Press.

Schott, Robin May. 1993. *Cognition and Eros; A Critique of the Kantian Paradigm.* University Park: Pennsylvania State University Press.

————. 2003. "Beauvoir on the Ambiguity of Evil." In Card 2003: 228–47.

————, ed. 2007. *Feminist Philosophy and the Problem of Evil.* Bloomington: Indiana University Press.

Skaarup, Gertie. "Født 3 mio. børn med kunstig befrugtning." *DR Videnskab.* June 23, 2006. http://www.dr.dk/Videnskab/Videnskab/2006/06/23100220.htm, accessed March 6, 2007.

Songe-Møller, Vigdis. 2002. *Philosophy without Women.* Trans. Peter Cripps. London: Continuum.

Sørensen, Anne M. 2007. "Ældre kvinder får fertilitetsbehandling i udlandet." *Politiken.* January 1, 2007. http://politiken.dk/indland/article219914.ece, accessed January 25, 2007.

Steiner, Reinhard. 1998. "Against Death." In Malpas and Solomon 1998: 16–21.

Villa, Dana R. 1996. *Arendt and Heidegger: The Fate of the Political.* Princeton, N.J.: Princeton University Press.

Young, Iris Marion. 1990. *Throwing Like a Girl and Other Essays in Feminist Philosophy and Social Theory.* Bloomington: Indiana University Press.

PART 1
Politics of Community

TWO
Sexual Violence, Sacrifice, and Narratives of Political Origins

ROBIN MAY SCHOTT

In the present era, we have become familiar with the coupling of sexual violence and political conflicts. When Serbian paramilitary soldiers committed mass rapes against Bosnian Muslims during the wars in the 1990s, it was part of a project of Serbian nation building. And when Hutus raped a quarter-million Tutsi women during the genocide in Rwanda, the violence was also fed by a passion to "sanitize" the country from Tutsi (Power 2002: 334). In both of these recent genocides, sexual violence was used as a tool for a perverted form of nation building. In the history of political narratives, one also finds ample evidence of the coupling of sexual violence with the founding of a new kind of political community. For example, the story of the rape of Lucretia portrays her rape and subsequent suicide as motivating the overthrow of tyranny and the introduction of republican rule in Rome.

Why do some narratives portray sexual violence as providing a crucial dynamic for the founding of new political communities? Is this pattern of thinking one that still affects us today? Do such narratives rationalize the wartime use of sexual violence as necessary for political change (Matthes 2000: 168–69)? Are media representations of atrocities and the response of international bystanders also influenced by the assumption that political beginnings take place over the dead bodies of women? What logic underpins stories in which a woman who is a member of a community is portrayed as suffering violence so that her community can take new shape? We have become used to thinking of sexual violence as a phenomenon that takes place between warring parties, so that rape is understood as an attack on the enemy who is unable to protect its women and its territory. It was this bit of wisdom that was encapsulated in the Cheyenne Indian saying, "A nation is not conquered until the women's hearts lay on the ground" (Arcel 1998: 184). But with this habit of thought, we overlook the ways in which sexual violence within a community also may play a decisive role for political transformations. If we focus on the narrative logic that links sexual violence with political foundations, can we loosen the grip that this pattern has on our imagination? Or do these narratives loosen progressive impulses in the minds of contemporary interpreters?

The relation between sexual violence and political transformations can be placed against a cultural, literary, mythical, psychological, and religious background of views about the relation between birth and death. In ordinary understanding, we often treat birth and death as opposites. They are at opposite ends of the life-cycle, with the concept of birth marking beginnings and origins, while the concept of death marks endings and separation. Yet scholars of myth and religion have long since pointed to the ways in which these concepts are deeply embedded in one another. As the classical scholar Jane Harrison has pointed out, certain Greek festivals, such as the wine festival of Anthesteria, which celebrated the opening of new wine, reveal both the positive and the threatening dimensions of death. During this festival, the spirits of the dead were believed to rise up for three days and fill the city with pollution. An offering of seeds to the souls of the dead was prepared for the dual purpose of appeasing them and also allowing the dead to take the seeds below the earth and then give them back to the living in the autumn. The role of the dead in nurturing the seeds is familiar to us in the function of the earth mother. Aeschylus writes of "Earth herself, that bringeth all things to birth, and, having nurtured them, receiveth their increase in turn." While death plays a life-giving role in the cycle of life for the community, death is also life-threatening, since it brings the end of the life of the individual (Schott 1993: 28–29). The ancient view that birth and death are embedded in each other is echoed in religious views more familiar to the contemporary reader. In Genesis, chapter 3, of the Hebrew Bible, Adam's and Eve's eating the fruit of the tree of knowledge and life is the cause of human mortality. And in Christianity, the sacrifice of God in the figure of Christ connects death to new life (Spielrein 1912: 491–92).

Twentieth-century psychoanalysts have also explored the interrelation between birth and death. Sabina Spielrein (1885–1942), one of the first women to become a psychoanalyst, explores in her article "Die Destruktion als Ursache des Werdens" the interrelation of processes of destruction and creation, which many consider to be seminal for Freud's understanding of Eros and Thanatos, of the drives toward life and toward death. Drawing on examples from biology, dream interpretation, psychological pathologies, myth, philosophy, religion, and literature, she argues that becoming or creation is a result of, and conditioned by, processes of destruction (Spielrein 1912: 489). On the cellular level of biological reproduction, when single cells are united to produce new life, the unity of each single cell is negated. In simplest forms of life, for example with certain flies, the parent dies with the production of new life (Spielrein 1912: 466–67). Although in human beings the reproduction of new life does not literally entail the death of the parent, Spielrein argues that there is a sense in which sexual reproduction negates the separateness of each individual in the process of reproducing new life. Thus, the sexual life that connects the individual with a collectivity that endures over time is also a certain form of death for the individual. Spielrein adds that it is really more a question of taste whether one emphasizes the existence of a new product or the disappearance of the old life (Spielrein 1912: 476).

The central implications of Spielrein's approach are as follows. (1) Destruction and becoming are inseparable moments, and they are both present in beginnings and endings. (2) Destruction involves the dissolution of individual separateness or differentiation. Thus, the experience of bonding and continuity in the experience of personal love or collective community also expresses a form of negation of self. (3) Creation involves the processes of separation, individuation, and differentiation.[1]

Spielrein's focus on the perpetuation of creation through processes of destruction can be placed in the same conceptual universe as Hegel's view that negativity—which is ultimately the negativity of death—is the motor of history, as Terry Eagleton observes (Eagleton 2003: 41).[2] In fact, this bent to look for value released by the processes of destruction provides William James with one definition of the tragedy of life. "Doesn't the very 'seriousness' that we attribute to life mean that ineluctable noes and losses form part of it, that there are genuine sacrifices somewhere, and that something permanently drastic and bitter always remains at the bottom of the cup?" (James 2000: 129; Eagleton 2003: 26). This hospitality to tragic insights characterizes dominant intellectual trends in the twentieth century. The socialist literary critic Raymond Williams considers Marxism, Freudianism, and existentialism all to be essentially tragic ideologies (Williams 1966: 189; Eagleton 2003: 10). They all probe the tension between the need for radical remaking and the terrible cost of it, a cost that some see resolved or redeemed in political transformation or revolution (Eagleton 2003: 58–60). For Williams, the tragic crisis revolves around the paradox between the need to make a choice and the unbearable loss that this choice will bring. One of the most poignant figures of this tragic crisis is the idea of sacrifice, where one is forced to yield up what is precious in the name of some greater value. And notable figures of tragic sacrifice in Western culture include the sacrifice of Iphigenia by her father Agamemnon (where according to earlier sources she was killed, but according to later sources replaced by an animal) and Abraham's sacrifice of Isaac, who miraculously also was replaced by a ram at the moment of sacrifice. Hence, one strain of this inquiry leads to a discussion of sacrifice, and I will consider the degree to which the concept of sacrifice is useful for interpreting political narratives that have sexual violence as their founding moment.

A second strain of this inquiry will probe the sexual character of the violence in these founding narratives. How is political meaning given to the cultural representation of woman as the repository of both birth and death? In *The Second Sex*, Simone de Beauvoir has pointed out ample evidence in myth, literature, ritual, and religion that attributes this doubleness to woman. The Woman-Mother is the "chaos whence all have come and whither all must one day return; she is Nothingness" (Beauvoir 1974: 166). That which is before and after life is undifferentiated, unformed, and feminine. Woman's womb is the origin of all life, but this origin also condemns man to death. "From the day of his birth man begins to die: this is the truth incarnated in the Mother" (Beauvoir 1974: 187). Because of the cultural association of woman with death, Chaucer can put the following words into the mouth of an old man unable to die: "I strike on the ground, my mother's doorway, And I say: Ah, mother dear, let me in." Both the early Greeks and the tribes of the Highland New Guineas associate the womb with the tomb. If women possess graves in their vaginas, it is because sexual intercourse for men involves reentry into that from which they emerged (Schott 1993: 29). In Christianity too, women are the gateway to death. Since the Church Fathers insisted that Eve led Adam into mortal sin, Tertullian writes, "Woman! You are the gateway of the devil. . . . Because of you the Son of God had to die" (Beauvoir 1974: 189). Yet both woman and death are also associated with fertility. Women manifestly give birth to new life, and death gives birth to new life, as in the concept of resurrection. What are the implications of the political form that narratives of foundation give to the representation of woman as the source of both birth and death?

Rape, Death, and Narratives of Foundations

I will give here four examples of narratives of the founding or reconfiguring of political communities that have at their kernel stories of sexual violence against women: (1) the rape of the Sabines and the founding of Rome, (2) the rape of Lucretia and the founding of republicanism in Rome, (3) the rape of the concubine in Gibeah in the Book of Judges, and (4) the myth about the founding of the city on the Bojana river, now in Albania.

Livy gives the following account of the rape of the Sabines in *The Early History of Rome*. After Romulus obtained the sole power over the new city, he was able to fill up his new big town by opening it to refugees and slaves, and he was able to establish a social organization. But due to the shortage of women, the greatness of Rome seemed likely to last only for a generation. Romulus sent envoys to various people to establish alliances and the rights of intermarriage. But these overtures were turned down, since the neighboring people feared the strength of this new power. Romulus then made preparations to invite neighboring peoples to a lavish festival. At the appointed time, all able-bodied men of Rome burst through the crowd to seize young women. The family of the girls escaped, with bitter comments about the treachery of their hosts. Romulus sought to convince the women, however, that their parents were to blame by refusing the right of intermarriage and that they would share all the privileges of community. Livy writes, "The women in course of time lost their resentment; but no sooner had they learned to accept their lot than their parents began to stir up trouble in earnest" (Livy 1978: 43). When the Sabines finally attacked, the Sabine women, "the original cause of the quarrel," played a decisive role. They parted the combatants, their husbands on one side and their fathers on the other, and said, "We are mothers now. If our marriage . . . is hateful to you, turn your anger against *us*. *We* are the cause of strife . . . and we should rather die ourselves than live on either widowed or orphaned" (Livy 1978: 48). Cicero's narration emphasizes instead that the Sabine women were well-born and well-educated, and were ruthlessly violated, and calls Romulus's plan for the capture of the women "rather boorish" (Matthes 2000: 42). The legend gives an account of a political community securing its future through the abduction of women for sexual relations, and the positioning of women between two hostile communities as a mediating link between them.

In *The Early History of Rome*, Livy also provides one of the earliest accounts of the rape of Lucretia, which he considers the first dreadful crime in Rome (Livy 1978: 231). Lucretia's husband was drinking with a group of men, including Sextus Tarquinus, the son of the ruling tyrant. In a rivalry about whose wife was superior, Collanatus proclaimed his wife Lucretia's incomparable superiority, and suggested that they ride to Rome to see with their own eyes what kind of women their wives were. While the other men's wives were enjoying themselves luxuriously in their husband's absence, Lucretia was hard at work at her spinning. Sextus Tarquinus was inflamed with lust for her, and determined to debauch her. A few days later, he returned to the house as a guest, and made his way to Lucretia's room in order to rape her. When she refused to submit to him, he threatened to kill both her and a slave boy, and lay his naked body by her side so that others would believe she had been caught in adultery with a servant. Lucretia yielded under this threat. The next day she recounted her rape to her father, her husband, and Brutus, a family friend, and then plunged a dagger into her heart as witness to her innocence. When Brutus drew the bloody knife from her body, "a miracle had happened—he was a changed man." Under his command, he led the populace to take up arms against the tyrants who had treated them as a vanquished enemy. Brutus became the Liberator of Rome, and Tarquin and his sons were expelled (Livy 1978: 97–101). When Rome was liberated, Brutus was named the founding father of the republic. In this account, the rape and suicide of Lucretia occasions the "miracle" that enables men to liberate Rome and found the republic.

The third rape narrative is drawn from the Hebrew Book of Judges, chapter 19. A Levite man took a concubine, who then left him and returned to her father's house. The husband went to bring her back, and on the return journey they were forced to overnight in the Israelite town of Gibeah, inhabited by the Benjamites. They could not find lodging, until an old man residing in the town came upon them in the street and gave them food and lodging. That night, the men of Gibeah surrounded the old man's house and demanded that the Levite man be sent out so that they could "know him." The man grabbed his concubine and sent her out to them instead. "They knew her and raped her all night till morning and sent her away as the dawn was rising." The woman returned to the house at dawn, dying. The Levite man rode home with the corpse of the concubine. And when he arrived home he "cut her through the bones into twelve pieces" and "sent her through the whole territory of Israel." There had never been such a deed done since the children of Israel came out of Egypt. In rage, the Israelis were united for the first time since they came from Egypt. But this unity was achieved by many more deaths—slaughtering twenty-five thousand Benjamite men—and by many more rapes—including the abduction of two hundred virgins of Shiloh.[3] In this story, the rape, death, and mutilation of a woman become a substitute for acts of sexual violence against a man, and an incitement to unite the peoples of Israel into a nation.[4]

The fourth narrative, "The Legend of Rozafa," narrates the story of the building of the Rozafa castle by the rivers Buna (or Bojana in Serbo-Croatian), Drini, and Kiri in Illyrian times.[5] According to this legend, three brothers were building a castle. But the walls that they were building during the day were ruined every night. A wise man passing by told the brothers what they must do. "Tomorrow, the wife that comes with your food must be buried alive in the walls of this castle. In this way the walls will stay strong forever." Although the brothers promised to keep this secret from their wives, the two older brothers broke their promise. The next morning, the wives of the oldest and of the middle brother both found an excuse for not taking food to the men. Rozafa, the youngest daughter-in-law, brought the food instead. When she arrived, her husband dropped his hammer and started cursing the wall. The oldest brother jumped up and said, "We have to bury alive the woman that brings us our food this day. Only this sacrifice will make the walls of the castle strong forever." Rozafa, who had a baby boy, calmly complied with her fate, but she had one request. "When you put me in this wall you must leave out my right eye, my right hand, and my right foot and my right breast. When my son cries I will be able to see him, with my hand I can stroke him, with my foot I can rock him and with my breast I can feed him. I pray that my son will be brave and become king of this land." So the brothers put Rozafa in the foundations of the castle and its walls never collapsed again. But at the base of the castle, the walls are wet from the tears that she shed and from the milk that she provides for her son.[6] Here it is the sacrifice of a breastfeeding woman that is necessary to strengthen the foundation of the nation.[7]

In many ways, these four stories are very different from one another. The story of the Sabines refers to the abduction and rape of women to ensure the future of a political community. The story of Lucretia tells of her rape and suicide, which led to the miracle that inaugurated the founding of the republic. The story from the Hebrew Bible refers to the rape, killing, and cutting up of a woman that enables the Israelis to unite as a nation. The story of Rozafa recounts the burying alive of a nursing mother. In the first three stories, rape and its consequences are central dynamics. In the last three stories, a woman must die—by her own hand, by the hand of an enemy, or by the hand of her family. And in two of the stories, it is woman's role as mother that is decisive for her fate and for the fate of the community. But in all cases, it is the violation of a woman's body that becomes the transformative moment for the community. Her fate thereby ensures the future of the community, and her violation is told as a necessary moment for securing this future. A woman is raped or killed, and the community to which she (now) belongs is reborn. Although some of these stories have been analyzed extensively elsewhere,[8] I am interested in focusing on the question whether the concept of sacrifice—only explicitly stated in the story of Rozafa—is a useful interpretive tool. If so, how can one understand the role of the figure of woman in sacrificial logic?

An Approach to Sacrifice

On one view, the idea of sacrifice characterizes ancient societies—such as the ancient Greeks or the ancient Israelis. In these contexts, sacrifice is intended to harness the power of the gods, or of Yahweh in the Hebrew Bible. From this perspective, the concept of sacrifice can have at most historical interest, or can attract the interest of anthropologists who study "primitive" forms of society. Yet on another view, sacrifice reveals some basic dynamics of human society that also have contemporary concern. Sacrifice points to the potential of violence that is *immanent* in society, as opposed to approaches to violence that view it as stemming from external threats. One might suggest, as Walter Benjamin does in his essay "Critique of Violence," that violence is in fact central to the character of law in a social order. Typically violence is viewed as a means to either a just or an unjust end, and the end adjudicates the legitimacy of violence. But a deeper understanding of violence shows that violence is implicit in the making of laws. It is because violence has both a lawmaking and law-preserving function that the community fears violence in the hands of the individual (Benjamin 1986: 283–84). When for example an individual criminal uses violence, not only does he/she violate the law, but an individual's act of violence challenges the legitimacy of the state's monopoly on violence. In this way, Benjamin understands violence as inherent in the establishment and justification of law as such. In addition to the lawmaking and law-preserving function of violence, Benjamin's reflections on the concept of sacrifice point to a third dimension of violence: the transformative function of violence. In his discussion of tragedy, Benjamin writes that sacrifice is also "the representative deed in which new contents of the life of a people announce themselves" (Benjamin 1977: 107; Eagleton 2003: 276). Sacrifice in this sense not only announces a new social order, but is a collective action that brings this new social order into being. In this sense, one may wonder whether sacrificial violence is similar to revolutionary violence. Benjamin describes revolutionary violence as outside the cycle of lawmaking and law-maintaining violence, whereby decaying laws are merely replaced by new forms of lawmaking violence. Instead, revolutionary violence founds a "new historical epoch," in his view, the abolition of state power altogether (Benjamin 1986: 300).

In the examples of "sacrificial" violence that I will be looking at here, it is evident that this violence does have a transformative function. Less clear, however, is whether these "sacrifices" break with the violence that establishes a social order, or whether they are the medium for re-establishing a new order based on new forms of violence.[9] Each of the four narratives presented above has the character of a narrative of positive political transformation, bringing political longevity, or republicanism, or national unity, or bringing into existence a new city and people. Should one ask whether the good political end justifies the violence of sacrifice? Or should one ask what the violence of sacrifice tells us about the logic of the political?

In what follows I will present five characteristics that I have gleaned about central features of sacrifice,[10] and then evaluate the different degrees to which some or all of these characteristics illuminate the political narratives under discussion. In doing so, I am not seeking to develop a theory of sacrifice, nor to claim that there is a unity of sacrifice and that one overarching theory can explain all forms of sacrifice. As Dennis King Keenan notes, sacrifice is always a concrete action in a particular context, and it is not possible to possess one meaning of sacrifice (Keenan 2005: 29). Nonetheless, I point to some common patterns among different theories of sacrifice.

One central feature for understanding sacrifice is that there is a *collective* subject of sacrifice, in contrast to an individual's arbitrary use of violence. By the focus on the collectivity, I mean that when an individual makes a sacrifice, as opposed to a random killing, it is done in the name of the community. When Agamemnon sacrifices Iphigenia, it is to appease the wrath of Artemis so that the Aegean fleet can sail and participate in the Trojan War.[11] And when violence is not done in the name of the collective, then it cannot be sacrificial violence, but at most sacrificial violence gone wrong.[12] The collective subject is indirectly the agent in the act of sacrifice; the collective is the beneficiary of sacrifice, as in the sacrifice of Iphigenia. And one might even suggest that it is through sacrificial violence in which a scapegoat is pointed out that a community temporarily comes into being. René Girard writes, "Where only shortly before a thousand individual conflicts had raged unchecked between a thousand enemy brothers, there now reappears a true community, united in its hatred for one alone of its number" (Girard 1995: 79).

A second central feature of sacrifice is that it is *beneficial* and in some sense also *transformative* for the community. Girard emphasizes the distinction between sacrificial violence that is beneficial to the community because it is preventive and harmful violence. Sacrificial violence is a form of internal violence that functions in a regulative manner. Girard writes, "The function of sacrifice is to quell violence within the community and to prevent conflicts from erupting" (Girard 1995: 14). Sacrificial violence can be one means of addressing violence without entering into a cycle of vengeance. Hence for Girard, sacrificial violence is "good violence" that must be "carefully distinguished from harmful violence" (Girard 1995: 37). Hence it is important to understand the dual nature of violence, and to situate sacrificial violence as the positive face of violence. In Girard's view, the nature of the benefit in sacrificial violence is its contribution to reinstating distinctions in the social order. When cultural differences are lost—when for example there are insufficient differences in family relations, as the relation between mother and son and wife and husband in the Oedipus cycle—then violence and chaos proceed (Girard 1995: 51, 62).[13] Sacrifice has the function of re-establishing difference and distinction, and enabling order to emerge. As Shakespeare wrote in *Troilus and Cressida*, "Take but degree away, untune that string / And, hark, what discord follows!" (Girard 1995: 49–50).[14] In Hubert and Mauss's account, the benefit of sacrifice lies in its transformational character. The basic pattern of sacrifice in their view is that it transforms the moral person who sacrifices—the sacrificer—and it transforms the victim/ object of sacrifice as well. In this process, the sacrificer is stripped of his temporal identity and is reborn in an entirely new form (Hubert and Mauss 1964: 13, 20). As such, sacrifice contains an element of new birth. Eagleton's interpretation of sacrifice focuses not just on the ritualistic and temporal transformations in sacrifice, but in its signifying the potential for radical transformation. He writes, "If a situation is dire enough, it must be broken to be repaired." His interpretation of sacrifice rests in large degree on the nature of the viewer's response to the one who is sacrificed. If one is afraid of the sacrificial victim, this response consolidates the status quo. But if one pities the victim and feels horror at the failure of the social order that is represented by this victim, then one can find the traces of revolutionary agency (Eagleton 2003: 275, 279).

Third, sacrifice is characterized by its *repetitive* character. Hubert and Mauss point out that sacrifices, whether they are occasional sacrifices that accompany the solemn moments of life or periodic sacrifices that occur at fixed moments of time, occur repeatedly. The repetition is also part of the controlled character of this violence, as opposed to random violence.

Fourth, sacrificial acts involve *sacrificial victims*. In Girard's account of sacrifice, including human sacrifice, the identity of the victim is relatively indifferent; its function is that it allows society to deflect upon a victim the violence that would otherwise be directed against its own members. The sacrificial victim is not, in Girard's view, a substitute for a particular member of the community who is in danger. Rather, the victim is a substitute "for all members of the community, offered up by the members themselves. The sacrifice serves to protect the entire community from *its own* violence; it prompts the entire community to choose victims outside of itself" (Girard 1995: 4, 8). What characterizes the sacrificial victim is that he/she stands in ambiguous relation to the community. Girard writes, "neither outside nor inside the community, but marginal to it: slaves, children, livestock. This marginal quality is crucial to the proper functioning of the sacrifice" (Girard 1995: 271). Only someone who is sufficiently removed from the community can prevent the sacrificial violence from spiraling into the negative violence of vengeance. And only somebody who is sufficiently close to the community can be enough like other members of the community to serve as an effective substitute for the community itself. Hence, the sacrificial victim is neither too foreign nor too familiar, but a bit of both.

Fifth, sacrifice *pays*, and in this manner becomes a coinage by which values are established. In other words, in the economy of sacrifice, the benefits of sacrificial violence (referred to above) are worth their costs. Or as Dennis King Keenan writes, "Most theories of sacrifice are predicated on an economy of debts and credits in which one gets a return on one's sacrificial investment" (Keenan 2005: 10).[15] The sociologist Georg Simmel argued that economic exchange makes clear the literal economic character of sacrifice. In economic exchange, one is always sacrificing a useful good for some other gain. And hence he writes, "Sacrifice is not only the condition of specific values, but the condition of value as such" (Simmel 1978: 85, Keenan 2005: 11). Georges Bataille also stresses that sacrifice is a sacrifice of "what is useful" and that it would make no sense to think of sacrificing luxury objects. It is by this means that the sacrificer can withdraw from the world of things and of utility (Bataille 1992: 43, 49). But different theories of sacrifice emphasize quite different gains from sacrifice. For Hubert and Mauss, the gains of sacrifice are the social legitimation of individuals' needs. In the personal renunciation of their property, individuals "confer upon each other, upon themselves, and upon those things they hold dear, the whole strength of society" (Hubert and Mauss 1964: 102). For Girard, the gain of sacrifice is the unanimity of the community and the containment of destructive violence. For Horkheimer and Adorno's analysis of Odysseus's self-renunciation, the gain of sacrifice is the negation of mythic power and the move toward Enlightenment rationality (Horkheimer and Adorno 1972). In James George Frazer's account, sacrifice secures the future of the state and of the culture (Frazer 1990: 119, Keenan 2005: 17). And in Christianity, the rewards of sacrifice are celestial not terrestrial, and future-oriented, as God sacrifices himself in order to redeem man. Anselm of Canterbury wrote, "[T]he restoration of human nature . . . could not be done unless man paid what he owed to God for his sin. This debt was so great that only God was able to pay it" (Anselm of Canterbury 1976: 129–30; Keenan 2005: 12)

Although Hubert and Mauss define sacrifice as a religious act carried out in a religious atmosphere by religious agents, they also highlight "how many beliefs and social practices not strictly religious are linked to sacrifice" (Hubert and Mauss 1964: 19, 103). In turning to the narratives of political foundations, my interest is also to see how some of the patterns of sacrificial thinking are present in different degrees in these narratives. Then I will consider the implications of this pattern for the sexual dimension of these narratives.

In each of these narratives, the collective subject or community is either directly or indirectly both the agent and the beneficiary of violence. The rape of the Sabines is a story of abduction and rape ordered by the ruler of the city and carried out by his men, in order to ensure that there would be progeny to sustain the future of the city. In Livy's version of the rape, the Sabine women take on the identification with the male community of Rome: "*We* are the cause of strife." This narrative move is crucial to making this story recognizable as sacrifice, since the Sabine women were not part of the original community that committed violence against them. By identifying with their new husbands they literally transform the community of Roman men who carry out violence against an external community into a community of Roman men and their wives, whose women have accepted violence done to them for the sake of their family's futures. In the narrative of the rape of Lucretia, it is the men in the drinking party, who want to test their wives' virtue, who become indirectly the agent of her death, as their actions lead ultimately to her brutal rape and subsequent suicide. Looming behind these men are the unwritten rules of the patriarchal order that the women should uphold or be held up to shame. And Lucretia's self-sacrifice is an oath of obedience to these rules, which becomes the propeller for the transformation of the polity from tyranny to a republic. The narrative of the rape of the concubine in Gibeah is also a story of group violence. However, the story does not illustrate the collective subject of sacrificial violence, but is closer to an act of random violence. The men who rape and murder her are not themselves the beneficiary of this violence, but instead they become subjected to subsequent acts of violent revenge. But the transformative effects of the concubine's rape and dismemberment bear a trace of the sacrificial pattern, as her body becomes the literal messenger sent out to the whole territory of Israel in order to achieve its unification. The legend of Rozafa fits most closely the sacrificial pattern of thinking. Here it is the brothers who, in part through conniving and deception, choose the victim to be built into the castle wall. This act of violence enables the building of the castle to be completed, and the founding of a city and a people to be surely laid.

All of these stories, by virtue of their belonging to canonical texts that tell the stories of political origins, also take on a repetitive character that is one of the features of sacrificial thinking. Each of the narratives refers to a unique, founding act, and in that sense is not part of repeated acts of violence. But what is repeated is the retelling of the acts of violence as morally exemplary stories. Melissa Matthes, in *The Rape of Lucretia*, stresses the importance of the repetition of the stories, even if there is no stable original act or event that is being recounted (Matthes 2000: 2–8). This retelling of origins is a way of constructing a shared public meaning, constructing a "we" through the act of recollecting a story of origins. This retelling is a reminder of the temporality of what is past and an attempt to hedge off the deterioration of community through time by an emphasis on the continuity with the past. Not only are these stories retold as part of the oral history of a community, but in some cases they are also rewritten or revisualized. The rape of the Sabines has attracted the interest of artists (including the painting by Nicolas Poussin from 1637–38), makers of low-budget films, and pornographers who advertise videos about rape, incest, zoo bestiality, and more.[16] The rape of Lucretia has been variously retold by Livy, Machiavelli, and Rousseau (Matthes 2000: 20). The story of the concubine in Judges is revisited in analyses of early Israeli political history.[17] And the legend of Rozafa still has great popularity in Albania, and has been immortalized in a poem, carved in stone beneath a sculpture of a nursing woman walled into the Rozafa castle, and in film.

In each of these stories a victim suffers some form of violence. The question to consider here is whether the victim can be considered a sacrificial victim. If one takes the marginal character of the victim as the defining feature of a sacrificial victim—one who is not too distant and not too near, but who belongs to both the interior and the exterior of the community—then a trace of this pattern also appears in these stories. The Sabine women belonged to a neighboring community—and as Girard points out, sometimes the most suitable victim is the neighbor.[18] Though they are originally outside the community of Roman men, their kidnapping, rape, and subsequent marriage brings them inside this expanded community. They thus have crossed borders between communities, between the Sabines and Rome, in contributing to this new enlarged collective. The story of Lucretia seems less apparently to fit this pattern. For as the perfectly virtuous wife, who sits chastely at home with her spinning while other men's wives are enjoying debauchery, she incarnates the virtue that is at the heart of the patriarchal home. But while she is central to the qualities of the home, she is marginal to the qualities of the political sphere. She herself can be no agent of political change. It is only by virtue of her death that she can serve as a catalyst to the men who are political actors in this story. She belongs to the interior of the community in its home, and is necessarily exterior to the political life of the community. The concubine who was gang-raped and murdered in Gibeah also crosses several borders. As a concubine, she was recognized as a wife but nonetheless was marked as coming from a different class (she would have paid no dowry). She was described as unfaithful to her husband, though whether her betrayal lay in her returning to her father's home or in sexual relations with other men is unclear. And she (as well as her husband) was treated as a hostile foreigner, instead of as a fellow-countrywoman deserving protection and hospitality. In all of these ways, borders of class, sexuality, and identity were crossed. The cutting up of her corpse seems to indicate that her death had been equivalent to human sacrifice, and her carcass was used, like the carcasses of animals that were sacrificed, to send a message throughout Israel. The legend of Rozafa presents what is, amongst these four narratives, most explicitly a sacrificial victim. The wife of the youngest brother, like Lucretia, seems to embody the feminine virtue that is at the heart of this social order. She nurses her baby boy as she bears food to the men, and she accepts her fate calmly. Yet her position is also in-between, half walled-in and half exposed, she remains with a breast in one world and the other given over to the world of nonhuman powers.

Each of these stories also establishes values through the relation between loss and gain. In all of these stories, something important is gained—a future, a republic, a united nation, a new people. And in three of these stories, a woman's life is lost. Although the rape of the Sabines does not result in their death, it does involve a certain form of loss for them and their families—loss of home and honor. In relation to these various characteristics of sacrifice, I have tried to show that there are traces of sacrificial patterns of thinking in these stories. I am not arguing that any of these stories is a narrative of ritual sacrifice. But I am suggesting that patterns of sacrificial thinking that are most obvious in ritual or religious spheres are visible in these stories of political origins as well. Some of these stories carry over this pattern most clearly, as in the legend of Rozafa. Others of the narratives seem to be at odds with key features of sacrificial violence. The story from the Book of Judges recounts the random and brutal violence of the men in Gibeah that is far from the contained violence of sacrifice. And the rape and death of the concubine unleashes new waves of violence as the Israelis unite against the Benjamites. Yet ultimately, her rape and death is a decisive step on the way to the re-establishment of central authority in Israel that could enforce standards of justice and morality. In this story, clear distinctions between random and controlled, destructive and constructive, violence become blurred. One may speculate whether sharp distinctions between sacrificial and nonsacrificial violence are sustainable.

The Question of Sex

Having established credibility for analyzing these narratives of political origins in terms of patterns of sacrificial thinking, the question returns: What does it mean that the community is established over the raped or dead bodies of women? How are we to understand the sexual component of these stories, that sexual identity marks the victim of violence, and rape is the medium of violence in three of these stories? Girard rejects the view that women are more often sacrificial victims than men. Although not a topic of his investigation, he expresses doubts that empirical investigations would provide evidence that women are more closely linked to the sacrificial victim than men (Reineke 1997: 84). Moreover, he argues that sexual violence can never be "collective in nature" (Girard 1995: 34). Since sacrificial violence is ultimately collective violence, and since he defines sexuality as noncollective, he excludes sexual violence from the category of sacrificial violence. Nonetheless, some feminist theorists, specifically Luce Irigaray and Julia Kristeva, disagree with Girard about the sacrificial status of woman. Irigaray suggests that the fundamental sacrifice that society does not acknowledge is the sacrifice of the mother: the failure to symbolize the maternal-feminine, and specifically the bypassing of the mother-daughter relation in the work of symbolization (Whitford 1991: 145, 75–76).

Kristeva's theory of the maternal also helps us understand why "the female body is a favored trope in discourses of sacrifice that create and secure the social order" (Reineke 1997: 102). Sacrifice is directed both toward the maternal and to women who bear her sign. Her work on abjection and the coding of the maternal as the abject is particularly important here. In *Powers of Horror*, she describes abjection as the feeling of horror or disgust that is caused by that which "disturbs identity, system, order. What does not respect borders, positions, roles. The in-between, the ambiguous, the composite" (Kristeva 1982: 4). Abjection calls to mind a condition that is prior to being, and hence prior to differentiation and individuation, a condition that reminds the individual that its existence is under perpetual threat (Kristeva 1982: 9). Rituals about defilement are based on the feeling of abjection, and they converge on the maternal. Kristeva writes, "The function of these religious rituals is to ward off the subject's fear of his very own identity sinking irretrievably into the mother" (Kristeva 1982: 64). The mother in Western culture, she argues, represents the condition of continuity—continuity with the body, continuity with nonlanguage—despite the fact that women's own identity during pregnancy and in motherhood is split and multiple. Woman is represented as marking the threshold between nothingness and being (Kristeva 1980: 238). And this representation is ambivalent. On the one hand, the mother represents the threat of the return to a nondifferentiated state, to a state of existence that precedes entry into the symbolic order of language. On the other hand, the mother represents a protection or barrier against this threat. Since the boundaries that emerge in the struggle for subjectivity and differentiation are fragile, the emergence of subjectivity is always haunted by the possibility of failure. Hence, any threat to subjectivity is marked by both sensory and psychic experience as a threat by the maternal to the order and structure of subjectivity.

Kristeva's theory gives a complex answer to the question, why are threats to individual subjectivity represented by woman? Her answer draws on psychoanalytic and linguistic theories to explain the decisive and ambivalent role of the mother in the development of individual subjectivity, and the way in which this ambivalence becomes projected into a cultural arena. In some sense, Kristeva's trajectory provides an account of the origin of Western culture's marking out of women and mothers as threatening and ambivalent. The four narratives above are also accounts of origins. But they can be read as answers to different kinds of questions: How are political communities founded? How are sexual differences necessary for constructing political communities? How is sacrifice used to establish political order? In other words, these narratives lead us to understand representations of sexual difference and of women not in terms of individual psychological development, but in terms of human community. What is decisive in this genre are the links drawn between human sexuality, internal violence, and collective transformations—the latter being central features of sacrifice.

Musing on the relationship between sexuality, sacrifice, and the political suggests that the logic of sacrifice appears both in interpretations of political life and in sexuality. First, the logic of political community is analogous to the logic of sacrifice. By this I mean that one can read each of the five elements of sacrifice that I sketch above as analogous to decisive moments of the political. What is fundamental to political community is the establishment of a collectivity, its ability to sustain and reproduce itself, its ability to control internal violence, its ability to establish values, and its possible renewal or transformation. These qualities echo aspects of sacrifice such as the collective subject, the role of repetition, the economy of loss and benefit, the role of transformation. What is less visible in political life is whether there is a structural role that corresponds to the sacrificial victim. Here I would suggest that political communities also define what or who is inside and outside the community. But the polarity inside/outside invariably involves another category, that of the in-between, which is neither wholly external nor wholly internal to the community, and which is structurally analogous to the role of the sacrificial victim. In political community, the in-between or marginal position is sometimes marked by the role of the resident foreigner.[19] Eagleton draws on a sacrificial paradigm to explain the necessity to destroy in order to create a fundamentally new political order and to understand the sacrificial victim as potentially the revolutionary agent.

Second, certain interpretations of sexuality also display a sacrificial logic. Recalling Sabina Spielrein's interpretation of human sexuality, one can view sexuality as necessarily navigating between the individual and the collective, as the individual is in some sense negated by biological reproduction and by feelings of love. Hence, through sexuality the collectivity at least intermittently emerges as central. Sexuality is also transformative, through both the creation of new unions and the creation of new life. Sexuality involves repetition through the ongoing nature of sexual desire, which does not end with a momentary satisfaction. Sexuality leads to the creation of values, through the investment in a sexual partner as the loved one or in the offspring of this union. Through the temporary negation of the individual, erotic unions also involve an unstable movement between being inside and outside the couple.

It may be that the echoes of sacrificial logic both in political community and in sexual life provide one reason that the sexual body in these stories becomes a suitable analogy for the political body. Mary Douglas argues that the body becomes the mirror of social system. She notes:

> The body is a model which can stand for any bounded system. Its boundaries can represent any boundaries which are threatened or precarious. The body is a complex structure. The functions of its

different parts and their relation afford a source of symbols for other complex structures. We cannot possibly interpret rituals concerning excreta, breast milk, saliva and the rest unless we are prepared to see in the body a symbol of society, and to see the powers and dangers credited to social structure reproduced in small on the human body. (Douglas 1966: 115, Schott 1999: 177–82)

These stories suggest that not only is there a general mirroring of the social order in representations of the body, but there is a mutual mirroring of the particular logic of sacrifice in representations both of the human body and of the social order. But it is not only a neutral human body that mirrors this logic; it is a woman's body that takes on this role. In this sense, these narratives display the pattern of asymmetry analyzed by Beauvoir by which only one sex—women—becomes identified with the powers of birth and death. By virtue of this identification with birth and death, one might add, women become marked as in-between—both inside and outside human life, both inside and outside the community. As such, their bodies become suitable markers for the sacrificial logic displayed in the political community.

These reflections on sacrifice have been in some sense unwilling. The concept of sacrifice remains loaded with negative or problematic connotations, such as primitiveness, a religious denial of the world, the self-sacrifice called upon by militarism (Schott 2008), the false altruism attributed to ideals of motherhood. What does it mean to show a close connection between the logic of political community and the logic of sacrifice? Does it not merely reinforce cultural patterns that should have been discarded long ago? What do we risk if, as Eagleton proposes, we take the notion of sacrifice seriously in our time?

The usefulness of the concept of sacrifice remains in exactly what makes us most uncomfortable: (1) its emphasis on the internal nature of violence in community and (2) its focus on the in-between or marginal position in the social order. Benjamin queries whether it is possible to establish a new order that is not merely a repetition of the old, relying as it does on establishing and maintaining law through violence. Does the concept of sacrifice keep us tied to the inevitability of violence? Or does it give us the possibility of imagining and enacting something radically outside this order of violence, as Eagleton suggests? And does recognizing the position of the in-between in society merely reinforce existing patterns of subordination, gendered and xenophobic as they may be? Or does this recognition give us critical tools for transforming these patterns?

These questions are made no easier through the virulent forms of collective violence to which we are witness today, where sexual violence against women's bodies is a recurring and abhorrent pattern, as in Darfur and the Congo. The United Nations undersecretary general for humanitarian affairs, John Holmes, has said that "[t]he sexual violence in Congo is the worst in the world. . . . The sheer numbers, the wholesale brutality, the culture of impunity—it's appalling."[20] Does a focus on the concept of sacrifice in general, and the sacrifice of women's bodies in particular in the history of political thought, reinforce the view that sexual violence is inevitable during political transitions?

And if the idea of radically transforming these patterns and negating structures of violence seems utopian or too closely tied to religiously inspired images of redemption, does this look at the structure of sacrifice reinforce the tendency toward tragic philosophy that Raymond Williams has diagnosed? And with the emphasis on negative dimensions of human existence, do such tragic propensities result in pessimistic assessments of the inevitability of violence and conflict in human affairs?

Furthermore, one may well worry that focusing on the pattern of sacrifice leads one to view it as a trans-historical dynamic, impervious to the concrete particulars and institutions of social life, unmoving in its role in human history. But this would be to turn sacrifice into a metaphysical notion that inheres in the essence of political structures. Such is not my intention. Nonetheless, focusing on historical and social structures as opposed to natural ones is no guarantee that one thereby brings to the fore radical transformations. As Terry Eagleton noted, "*longues durées* are quite as much part of human history as pastoral verse and parliaments." When critics fail to grasp this, it is because they operate with the dualism between contingence and essentialism, or change and permanence, and fail to grasp that these dualisms are not the same as the contrast between culture and nature. Eagleton adds, "It is proving rather more feasible in our age to alter certain genetic structures than it is to tamper with capitalism or patriarchy" (Eagleton 2003: xii–xiii).

These stories illustrate how narratives of sacrifice are entrenched in the constitution of identities of political communities, and how women's bodies are deemed as suitable to mark a position that is neither fully interior to the community nor fully exterior, but in-between. There is some sense in which sacrifice functions in a constructive manner, in that it constructs the narratives of belongingness to a community. It may be for this reason that sacrificial language is so readily invoked in moments of militaristic nationalism.

But sacrifice is destructive as well, seen from the point of view of the victim or eventually of victim groups. In this sense, it partakes of its own logic that construction and destruction are inextricably entwined. Sacrifice negotiates the ambivalent relation between death and birth, so that it is death that becomes the origin of new birth.[21] Bearing in mind the worries about the concept of sacrifice voiced above, I want to stress that analyzing these patterns is not to endure or endorse them, but to see their diagnostic potential. Sacrificial patterns may be useful in diagnosing some contemporary forms of collective evil. Arne Johan Vetlesen suggests that the "ethnic cleansing" in Bosnia can be understood as directed against a sacrificial victim (Vetlesen 2005: 182–88, 211).[22] Moreover, there is a critical potential in the analysis of sacrifice, which alerts one to the dangers of ideologies that link sexual violence with political transformations in periods of crisis. Finally, sacrificial patterns highlight the centrality of intracommunity—not just intercommunity—conflict. In light of that, analyzing these patterns may keep alive the search for alternative resources to negotiate internal violence and positions of marginality in community.

NOTES

1. This interrelation between processes of destruction and becoming may explain the very different theoretical views about the terms "separation" and "individuation." On the one hand, for Hannah Arendt, individuation is the key to the natality, to the possibility of new beginnings that is inherent in the creation of each new life. On the other hand, for some feminist psychoanalysts, individuation is based on a form of separation that is characteristic of male psychological development—a form of individualism based on the denial of relatedness. According to Nancy Chodorow, female psychological development is built on the relational self and is a potential strength (Chodorow 1989: 7).

2. In the following I draw on Terry Eagleton's survey of tragic thought in Eagleton 2003. I would like to thank Marc Etlin at Book Culture in New York City for recommending this and other useful sources for me.

3. Only 600 men of the tribe of Benjamin remained alive after the battle. Although the virgins from the tribe of Benjamin were not slaughtered, there were 200 too few to provide wives for each surviving man. Hence, the Israeli elders condoned the abduction of the virgin daughters in Shiloh. Although the Israelite men had promised not to *give* their daughters to the Benjamites, this does not mean that the daughters could not be *taken* (Frymer-Kensky 2002: 118–38).

4. Note that this story is preceded by an explicit story of human sacrifice. In Judges 11, Jephthah had vowed to sacrifice whatsoever came to greet him, if he returned home from battle victorious. His virgin daughter came to greet him, and he carried out the sacrifice two months later. Annual lamentations are offered to commemorate this atrocity.

5. The castle is near Shkodra in Albania. When I was giving a talk at the University of Shkodra in March 2007, my hosts coincidentally took me to this castle.

6. Alba Elezi, "The Legend of Rozafa," *EMAS Portsmouth,* http://www.blss .portsmouth.sch.uk/resources/dlstories/rosafah/rosafah.shtml, accessed August 16, 2007. This story is repeated to visitors to the castle when they pass a wet area on the walls where lime water leaks, purportedly Rozafa's breast milk. This legend is the same as referred to in the poem "Building of the City on the Bojana River." See Arsic 2002: 263. The legend still has a powerful place in Albanian culture. On an Albanian forum, readers repeated how much they loved the story, "one of my favorites," and noted similar stories referring to bridges in Mirdite and Prizren. In this case too, a woman was placed in the foundation to produce a stronger foundation for the structure. See http://www.albanian.com/community/vbl/archive/index.php/t-8950.html, accessed August 16, 2007.

7. In the Serbian version, the brothers are noblemen and one of the brothers is king. Hence it is the foundation of the kingdom that is at stake. During my visit to Rozafa castle, Entela Lako, my host and program officer at UNDP in Tirana, told me that she often uses the myth to illustrate the importance of women's activities in community sustainability.

8. See in particular Matthes's analysis of the rape of Lucretia. Matthes focuses on the relation between the narrative of rape and the securing of fraternal bonds, on how the story is a reminder of failed masculinity, on how the masculine appropriation of feminine reproductive powers shows both the desire for masculine autonomy and its need for the supplement of female power (Matthes 2000: 1–59).

9. One could pose this question to Benjamin's concept of revolution as well. Can revolutionary violence, in idea if not in practice, break truly with the cycle of lawmaking and law-maintaining violence?

10. There is a large body of research on theories of sacrifice, which I in no way seek to provide a summary of here. My focus on these five characteristics is gleaned from a range of sources, including Bataille 1992, Girard 1995, Horkheimer and Adorno 1972, Hubert and Mauss 1964, Keenan 2005, and Reineke 1997, as well as Benjamin's and Eagleton's texts referred to above.

11. On Iphigenia see http://www.stanford.edu/~plomio/iphigenia.html, accessed March 10, 2010.

12. Euripides gives an example of this in *Heracles,* when Heracles returns home after his labors and finds a usurper preparing to offer his wife and children as sacrificial victims. Driven temporarily mad by Hera, he mistakes them for his enemies and sacrifices them himself (Girard 1995: 40).

13. In Vigdis Songe-Møller's analysis of *Antigone,* it is the *sameness* that arose from the violation of the incest taboo that causes tragic destruction.

14. The argument that it is sameness rather than differences that provokes crisis seems to be counterintuitive in a xenophobic worldview. Girard's explanation is that different persons are reproached not for their difference, but for not being different enough. For example, in seeing that another person's difference (e.g., disability) is not as different as expected, the fragility and mortality of one's own world is brought into view.

15. Keenan's overview of sacrificial theories in his chapter "A Genealogy of Theories of Sacrifice" makes evident the pattern that there is a return on one's

sacrificial investment. My references here draw on his chapter. His own approach, however, moves away from the predominance of an economic theory of sacrifice.

16. Poussin accepts the Roman concept of *raptus* as "carrying off by force," and hence views it as a crime of property against the women's husbands or guardians (Wolfthal 1999: 9).

17. See Daniel J. Elazar, "The Book of Judges; The Israelite Tribal Federation and its Discontents," *Jerusalem Center for Public Affairs,* http://www.jcpa.org/dje/articles/judges.htm, accessed November 30, 2007.

18. Vetlesen uses this model to analyze the "ethnic cleansing" in Bosnia in terms of the notion of the sacrificial victim (Vetlesen 2005: 211).

19. Kristeva also addresses this problem in *Strangers to Ourselves* (Kristeva 1994). Bonnie Honig, in *Democracy and the Foreigner,* focuses on the ambiguity of the figure of the foreigner, which becomes especially important during vulnerable moments of founding or refounding. Instead of asking, "how should we solve the problem of foreignness?" we should ask, "what problems does foreignness solve for us?" (Honig 2001: 3). She writes, "Foreignness will signify different things depending on what work it is being made to do, depending on what goal the community is trying to achieve through the foreigner" (Honig 2001: 71). Sometimes the foreigner signifies the danger to which a community is subject; sometimes the foreigner provides a positive resource, as in the story of Moses. Moses as Egyptian was marked as a foreigner, though his foreignness was concealed. Thus, he could pass on the law with which the Israeli people must identify, though it was alien to them (Honig 2001: 31). Ruth the Moab is another example of a foreigner whose alien character became a positive resource for rejuvenating the people of Israel, since she became mother to a line of kings.

20. André Bourque, a Canadian consultant working with aid groups in the area, said, "Sexual violence in Congo reaches a level never reached anywhere else. It is even worse than in Rwanda during the genocide" (Gettleman 2007: 1, 11).

21. I argue in the next chapter, by contrast, that the radical experiment of genocidal rape is that birth becomes the origin of death.

22. Vetlesen, however, overlooks the fact that Girard views sacrificial violence as essentially beneficial.

BIBLIOGRAPHY

Anselm of Canterbury. 1976. *Why God Became a Man.* In *Anselm of Canterbury.* Vol. 3. Ed. and trans. Jasper Hopkins and Herbert Richardson. Toronto: Edwin Mellen Press.

Arcel, Libby Tata. 1998. "Sexual Torture of Women as a Weapon of War—The Case of Bosnia-Herzegovina." In *War Violence, Trauma and the Coping Process,* ed. Libby Tata Arcel. Copenhagen: International Rehabilitation Council for Torture Victims.

Arsic, Branka. "Queer Serbs." 2002. In Bjelic and Savic 2002.

Bar On, Bat-Ami, ed. 2008. *Hypatia: Special Issue on Just War.* Bloomington: Indiana University Press.

Bataille, Georges. 1992. *Theory of Religion.* Trans. Robert Hurley. New York: Zone Books.

Beauvoir, Simone de. 1974. *The Second Sex*. Trans. H. M. Parshley. New York: Vintage Books.

Benjamin, Walter. 1977. *The Origin of German Tragic Drama*. Trans. John Osborne. London: Verso.

———. 1986. "Critique of Violence." In *Reflections*. Trans. Edmund Jephcott. New York: Schocken Books.

Bjelic, Dusan I., and Obrad Savic, eds. 2002. *Balkan as Metaphor*. Cambridge, Mass.: MIT Press.

Card, Claudia, ed. 1999. *On Feminist Ethics and Politics*. Lawrence: University of Kansas Press.

Chodorow, Nancy. 1989. *Feminism and Psychoanalytic Theory*. New Haven, Conn.: Yale University Press.

Douglas, Mary. 1966. *Purity and Danger*. London: Routledge and Kegan Paul.

Eagleton, Terry. 2003. *Sweet Violence; The Idea of the Tragic*. Oxford: Blackwell.

Frazer, James George. 1990. *The Golden Bough: A Study in Magic and Religion*. New York: St. Martin's Press.

Frymer-Kensky, Tikva. 2002. *Reading the Women of the Bible*. New York: Schocken Books.

Gettleman, Jeffrey. 2007. "Savage Rapes Stoke Trauma of Congo War." *New York Times*. October 7, 2007.

Girard, René. 1995. *Violence and the Sacred*. Trans. Patrick Gregory. London: Athlone Press.

Honig, Bonnie. 2001. *Democracy and the Foreigner*. Princeton, N.J.: Princeton University Press.

Horkheimer, Max, and Theodor W. Adorno. 1972. *Dialectic of Enlightenment*. Trans. John Cumming. New York: Continuum Press.

Hubert, Henri, and Marcel Mauss. 1964. *Sacrifice: Its Nature and Function*. Trans. W. D. Halls. Chicago: University of Chicago Press.

James, William. 2000. *Pragmatism and Other Writings*. London: Penguin.

Keenan, Dennis King. 2005. *The Question of Sacrifice*. Bloomington: Indiana University Press.

Kristeva, Julia. 1980. "Motherhood According to Bellini." In *Desire in Language*. Trans. Leon S. Roudiez. New York: Columbia University Press.

———. 1982. *Powers of Horror*. Trans. Leon S. Roudiez. New York: Columbia University Press.

———. 1994. *Strangers to Ourselves*. Trans. Leon S. Roudiez. New York: Columbia University Press.

Livy, Titus. 1978. *The Early History of Rome*. Trans. Aubrey de Selincourt. New York: Penguin Books.

Matthes, Melissa M. 2000. *The Rape of Lucretia and the Founding of Republics*. University Park: Pennsylvania State University Press.

Power, Samantha. 2002. *A Problem from Hell*. New York: Basic Books.

Reineke, Martha J. 1997. *Sacrificed Lives*. Bloomington: Indiana University Press.

Schott, Robin May. 1993. *Cognition and Eros: A Critique of the Kantian Paradigm*. Boston: Beacon Press; paperback, University Park: Pennsylvania State University Press.

————. 1999. "Philosophical Reflections on War Rape." In Card 1999.

————. 2008. "Just War and the Problem of Evil." In Bar On 2008.

Simmel, Georg. 1978. *The Philosophy of Money.* Trans. Tom Bottomore and David Frisby. London: Routledge and Kegan Paul.

Spielrein, Sabina. 1912. "Die Destruktion als Ursache des Werdens." *Jahrbuch für psychoanalytische and psychopathologische Forschungen* 4, no. 1: 465–503.

Vetlesen, Arne Johan. 2005. *Evil and Human Agency.* Cambridge: Cambridge University Press.

Whitford, Margaret. 1991. *Luce Irigaray: Philosophy in the Feminine.* London: Routledge.

Williams, Raymond. 1966. *Modern Tragedy.* London: Chatoo and Windus.

Wolfthal, Diane. 1999. *Images of Rape: The Heroic Tradition and Its Alternatives.* Cambridge: Cambridge University Press.

THREE
Natality and Destruction: Arendtian Reflections on War Rape

ROBIN MAY SCHOTT

Sex crimes are perpetrated against women civilians around the world, and appallingly the number of these crimes is increasing rather than decreasing. Amnesty International reports that forty thousand women and girls were raped in the Congo in the period 1999–2005. Sexual torture has been documented in Rwanda, the Sudan, Yugoslavia, Iraq, and East Timor (Booth 2005: 118).

For those of us interested in the safety of women and girls, and their economic and political rights, addressing the issue of war rape is high on the agenda. This issue has recently attracted active engagement by international lawyers as well as by scholars working in political science, anthropology, and psychology, to name a few fields. The question that motivates me here is whether sexual violence also puts a claim on philosophical reflection.

My starting point is that sexual violence does demand the engagement of philosophers. Just as Hannah Arendt argued that twentieth-century totalitarianism and the Nazi death camps placed a demand to reflect on the fundamental problem of evil, so I argue that sexual violence in wartime puts a demand on us to reflect anew on the fundamental relation between the human body and the body politic. In this essay, I will be thinking with Hannah Arendt on the relation between the body and the body politic, though I will arrive at some non-Arendtian conclusions.[1]

Sexual violence in wartime is not new to the twentieth century, though I will discuss below features that are specific to the twentieth century. We find references to it in Homer's *Iliad,* as well as references to capturing women in war in the Hebrew Bible. Not until the fourteenth century did European leaders announce standards of chivalry to forbid rape, though these rules were rarely enforced. The license to rape was considered a major incentive for being a soldier (Niarchos 1995: 660–62).[2] Not until the nineteenth century did humanitarian law protect noncombatants, including women. In the twentieth century, mass rape occurred during the Rape of Nanking, which refers both to the rape of 20,000–80,000 Chinese women by Japanese soldiers in 1937 and the killing orgy that took 350,000 lives in a few weeks. During World War II, up to two million women were raped by soldiers in the Soviet army (Beevor 2002).[3] The French army allowed Moroccan soldiers to rape Italian women. And there was evidence of major Nazi sexual crimes against French women, though the Nuremburg tribunal did not mention rape in the final judgment.[4] Rape did take place in Auschwitz, though there has been a conspiracy of silence about it, and the victims of rape in the camps were psychologically the "sickest" after liberation (Krystal 1968: 342). In the 1990s, not only did war rape take place in Europe (with an estimated 20,000–50,000 women raped in the former Yugoslavia), but during the genocide in Rwanda when 500,000 to 800,000 Rwandans were massacred, the majority of them Tutsi, at least a quarter-million women were raped. In the Congo, every armed group has discovered that rape is a cheaper weapon of war than bullets (Goodwin 2004: 8–22). A Human Rights Watch specialist noted that women have had their lips and ears cut off and eyes gouged out after they were raped, so they cannot identify or testify against their attackers (ibid.).

Until recently, sexual violence in wartime has been characterized by physical invisibility—in the double sense that civilian casualties are often invisible in official casualty statistics and that rape does not always leave visible signs on the bodies of the victims. With this physical invisibility has been a political invisibility. What is new in the late twentieth century is the *political visibility,* of war rape which has had decisive consequences for international law. The United Nations resolution leading to the establishment of the Yugoslavia Tribunal contained the Security Council's first condemnation ever of war rape. Richard J. Goldstone, chief prosecutor of the United Nations International Criminal Tribunal for the former Yugoslavia and Rwanda (1994–96), notes that despite the fact that rape is a war crime that has been occurring for centuries, it had never received sufficient attention even to justify definition. The Rwanda Tribunal took a major step by defining rape as "a physical invasion of a sexual nature committed on a person under circumstances which are coercive."[5] In the Rome Statute of the International Criminal Court (1998), gender crimes are no longer subsumed under outrages to personal dignity, but are expressly named as crimes against humanity and as war crimes in both national and international armed conflict.[6]

This legal shift from treating war rape as an offense to personal dignity to treating it as a violation of human rights is also based on the changed character of conflict in the sociopolitical, religious, and ethnic civil wars of the twentieth century. These conflicts involve the politicization of daily life, the centrality of the body as a physical and symbolic object of strife, and often a familiarity with the enemy (Van Boeschoten 2003: 43).

Following the war rapes in the former Yugoslavia and Rwanda, and their judicial recognition as crimes against humanity,[7] there has been a rapid growth of research in the issue of war rape. Much of the research focuses on causal explanations, from a wide variety of social and psychological perspectives. Some scholars have argued that war rape should be understood primarily from the point of view of psychohistory, by which war rape is understood as arising from abusive child-rearing practices, in which maternal abuse is considered central for the mentality of rapists (Demause 2002: 371). Others have argued that war rape should be understood primarily in terms of patriarchy's oppression of women. And still other scholars emphasize the role of nationalism in the escalation of sexual violence both during and after wartime conflict.[8] My purpose here is not to adjudicate causal explanations of war rape, but to explore the meaning of the body that is implicit in war rape, and its implications for theory of political community. The relation between the individual body and the political community has been much discussed recently, with focus particularly on the role of discourse in constituting subjects as "heterosexual" or "homosexual." Here I will raise different questions about the relation between the body and the political by focusing on the concept of birth and its transformation in sexualized violence.

I will analyze the phenomenon of war rape by tracing the concepts of the "body" and the "political" in the work of two thinkers: the German-born philosopher Hannah Arendt and the Italian philosopher Giorgio Agamben. Arendt introduced the concept of natality—referring to new beginnings in human life—which plays a vital role in her understanding both of the human condition and of political life. For Arendt, the metaphorical meaning of birth as new beginnings—as opposed to death and endings—is decisive for political thought. By contrast, Giorgio Agamben views life's subjection to a power over death as a key for reflecting on political power (Agamben 1998: 83). I will study the implications of war rape—not mentioned by Arendt, but discussed briefly by Agamben—for their reflections on the relation between the body and the concept of the political. If one follows Arendt's analysis of natality, war rape appears as an event that *violates* the fundamental qualities of political life. If one follows Agamben's focus on the power over death, war rape appears as a phenomenon that *discloses* the fundamental workings of political power. I will consider which path is most productive for an analysis of war rape.

Arendt on Natality

Arendt is a peculiar thinker to draw on to study the relation between bodies and politics. On the one hand, she did not develop an analysis of birth for societal reproduction, as Karl Marx and Friedrich Engels did, or as Marxist- and socialist-feminists after them have done.[9] Indeed, she is often chastised for the "missing body" in her work. Following the traces of ancient philosophy and the city-state, Arendt viewed the natural, biological body as an unquestioned condition of life, but decidedly not as a topic for political life. And to the chagrin of many contemporary feminist philosophers, she treated the body as a genderless form of existence, leading Mary Dietz to remark, "It is certainly curious that Arendt never makes this central feature of the human condition an integral part of her political analysis" (Dietz 1991: 240; Zerilli 1995: 174). Her disinterest in the category of gender is accompanied by a disinterest in the concepts of maternity and femininity. On the other hand, Arendt's concept of natality arguably makes a revolution in philosophical thought, with its inherited focus on mortality as the horizon on which meaning takes place. The concept of natality is rooted in the lived body in relation to its life-history, and in Arendt's view natality is one of the fundamental conditions of political life. Here I will consider Arendt's concept of birth and of natality as a feature of the human condition and consider what happens to this feature when it becomes the site of extreme destruction. Interrogating Arendt's concept of natality through a discussion of war rape sheds light on her understanding of the relation between the human body and political life.

Arendt writes of natality under three aspects: as a natural category, as part of the human condition, and as a political category. As a natural category, Arendt used the term "birth" to refer to the coming into being of individual life and the maintenance of the life of the species. In *The Human Condition* she suggested that this sphere is strictly pre-political, and she lamented the way in which under modernity "the life process itself . . . has been channeled into the public realm" (Arendt 1958: 45). As a feature of the human condition, natality signifies the principle of beginning—the beginning of something unique—in the world (Arendt 1958: 177–78). As a political category, natality refers to the fundamental conditions of life in political community. It is the loss of natality that marks the loss of genuinely political life under totalitarianism and in the death camps.

For Arendt, biological life and the sphere of necessity belong to the private sphere of the household, whose purpose is the maintenance of life.

In her view, force and violence are involved in order to master necessity. But since violence cannot be justified in the political sphere, Arendt viewed biological life as pre-political. In the private sphere, human beings exist "only as a specimen of the animal species man-kind" (Arendt 1958: 46). By implication, the natural life of the body is private and does not display features of the political, including communication, which is central for political life. For example, Arendt describes extreme bodily pain as the most private and least communicable of experiences (Arendt 1958: 50).[10] The public sphere, by contrast, is not bound by nature. In order to establish a public sphere of relations between equals, it is necessary that the body's natural needs are satisfactorily met in the household, so that they do not impinge on political life. In view of this dichotomy between private and public spheres, some feminist philosophers map a gender dichotomy onto Arendt's text, arguing that Arendt fulfills a "phallocentric desire for release from the realm within which 'Woman' has been traditionally figured: bodily maintenance, necessity, and life" (Brown 1988: 180; Dietz 1995: 26).

Arendt introduced the term "natality" when writing about the most general conditions of human existence: "birth and death, natality and mortality" (Arendt 1958: 8). The most general conditions of human existence also include "life itself . . . worldliness, plurality, and the earth" (Arendt 1958: 11). Her notion of the human condition emphasizes the fact that human beings are *conditioned* and that they act out of these conditions in order to create new conditions by either accepting or rejecting this facticity. This notion of givenness, which Arendt develops in her book *Love and Saint Augustine*, is central for her analysis of natality, for natality implies that human beings are created and not just creators. Arendt views natality as the "principle of beginning" in the world, in which the three forms of activity—labor, work, and action—are rooted (Arendt 1958: 177).

For Arendt, action is the human initiative of beginning something new and is the political activity par excellence. Natality is the quality in the human condition that makes possible human action. She writes, "[T]he new beginning inherent in birth can make itself felt in the world only because the newcomer possesses the capacity of beginning something anew, that is, of acting. In this sense of initiative, an element of action, and therefore of natality, is inherent in all human activities. Moreover, since action is the political activity par excellence, natality, and not mortality, may be the central category of political, as distinguished from metaphysical, thought" (Arendt 1958: 9). She later describes both action and speech as a kind of "second birth, in which we confirm and take upon ourselves the naked fact of our original physical appearance" (Arendt 1958: 176–77).[11]

What do Arendt's concepts of birth and natality indicate about her understanding of the relation between the human body and the political world? One view that she expresses is that the relation between the body and the political world is similar to the relation between nature and transcendence. She writes, "The fact is that the human capacity for life in the world always implies an ability to transcend and to be alienated from the process of life itself" (Arendt 1958: 121). Arendt implies that the immediacy of natural life must be both conserved and transcended in order for human beings to construct meaning in the world. In this model of immediacy/transcendence, the realm of natural birth and death appears as hidden from the public realm. As with the Eleusinian Mysteries, birth and death is common to all, yet unknowable and unspeakable. Hence, the crucial moments of entering and exiting life could appear as "non-political and perhaps antipolitical by definition" (Arendt 1958: 63).

But as Peg Birmingham notes in her book *Hannah Arendt and Human Rights,* Arendt is not consistent in treating natality as a strictly physical event. Arendt also explains that the birth and death of human beings "are not simple natural occurrences but are related to a world in which single individuals, unique, unexchangeable, and unrepeatable entities, appear and from which they depart" (Arendt 1958: 96–97). The embodied dimension of birth is inseparable from its linguistic dimensions. For birth implies, as Birmingham points out, the birth of a unique "who" that gives voice to the unexpected word and can tell her/his story. In other words, birth is also the birth of a political self (Birmingham 2006: 23–24). By implication, the body is not transcended by the political world, but its full meaning is an accomplishment of the political world.

Arendt develops her notion of natality out of her reading of Saint Augustine. For Augustine, one of the primary questions for human beings is: "What kind of existent am I?" The answer to this question, according to Augustine, is achieved through memory, which he equates with self-consciousness (Arendt 1966: 46). Hence, the question of self-knowledge is not the future-oriented sense of "*whither* shall I go, but about origins and *whence* I come" (Arendt 1966: 48). Arendt notes that "the decisive fact determining man as a conscious, remembering being is birth or 'natality,' that is, the fact that we have entered the world through birth. The decisive fact determining man as a desiring being was death or mortality, the fact that we shall leave the world in death" (Arendt 1966: 51–52). Natality reveals four features of human existence: createdness, temporality, memory, and newness.

In relation to one's origin, one discovers that one is created, and is not the creator of one's own existence. In Arendt's words, there is a deep and fundamental "mode of human dependence" "on something outside the human condition as we know it" (Arendt 1966: 49). As a created being, one is dependent and necessarily related to a being outside of oneself. Hence, life "exists in the mode of relation" (Arendt 1966: 53). For Augustine, the createdness of human existence is rooted in the idea of a divine Creator. Arendt extracts this notion from a religious and theological perspective and places it in her analysis of the human condition. Recognizing that human beings are not self-created emphasizes our origins in birth.

Since human beings are created, they are also temporal beings. Arendt writes that "everything that began exists in the mode of becoming" (Arendt 1966: 54). For Augustine, time is the mode by which finite human beings understand the whole of which they are a part. The temporality of human existence is linked to its perishability and mortality, whereas the whole is imperishable. In Arendt's adaptation of Augustine's philosophy, temporality and becoming point both backward—to one's origins—and forward—to change and newness in human life.

Natality also indicates the decisive role of memory for human existence. Since we are created, it is only through memory that we can return to the origin of life on which we are dependent. For Augustine, memory is the way in which human beings become a question to themselves and realize that their essence lies outside of their existence; hence, memory provides the path for achieving self-consciousness. Memory reconnects us to our origin and is thus the only way in which a created thing can "*be* truly" (Arendt 1966: 51). Arendt emphasizes that memory not only recalls the past, but makes the past into a future possibility that we may approach with hope or fear. She writes, "[I]t is memory and not expectation (for instance, the expectations of death as in Heidegger's approach) that gives unity and wholeness to human existence" (Arendt 1966: 56).

Finally, natality represents the principle of beginnings. It highlights the aspect by which human beings are able to "act as a beginning and enact the story of mankind" (Arendt 1966: 55). It is the character of all beginnings to bring something unexpected, unpredictable, and startling into the world. Hence, Arendt's comment that "the new therefore always appears in the guise of a miracle" (Arendt 1958: 178). Temporal existence has the possibility of enacting something radically new, of creating a rupture and not just a continuity with that which precedes it.[12] In Arendt's account, this capacity for newness is fundamentally a source of faith and hope. "The miracle that saves the world, the realm of human affairs, from its normal, 'natural' ruin is ultimately the fact of natality" (Arendt 1958: 247). Hence, natality is both the source of our origin and the source of our possibilities.

When Arendt turned her attention to the analysis of the political world, she took the concept of natality that she had developed from Augustine's thought with her as the central category of political thought.[13] According to Arendt, political life is fundamentally characterized by these four features of createdness or dependency, temporality, memory, and newness. Plurality, which Arendt considered "*the* condition . . . of all political life," refers to the fact that unique individuals live among others (Arendt 1958: 7). Plurality as a concept for political life expresses the view that human beings are neither self-created nor self-sufficient, but have a deep dependence on something outside themselves—the world of a plurality of individuals.

Temporality or the process of becoming is also central for Arendt's account of political life, since it is the constant "influx of newcomers" that makes a demand on us to "preserve the world" and provide for newcomers (Arendt 1958: 9). Only through temporality can we understand ourselves as a finite part of the world that is "common to all of us," the public world.

Arendt also identifies memory as a crucial aspect of the political. Political bodies create the condition for remembering by transforming private acts into a public reality through storytelling, discourse, and historical narratives. Although Arendt frequently uses the term "storytelling," she uses it to refer to a wide range of phenomena that include artistic narratives but are not limited to them. Storytelling in its widest sense refers to the public bearing witness in the presence of others (Arendt 1958: 50). Storytelling refers to communicability, and includes both the communicability of our private sorrows and joys and the public accounting of the history of a community. Historical narratives are themselves part of the political life of a community, as is evident, for example, in the changing character of the commemoration of the Holocaust in Israel. Whereas a generation ago, the Israeli documentaries detailed the horrors of the victims' nails clutching the walls of the gas chambers as they died, today they document Jewish resistance and heroism. Memory has been refashioned so as to create a political identity suitable for a warrior community.[14]

For Arendt, the fourth quality of natality, that of newness, is also a crucial aspect of the political. The constant striving for newness is evident in the *agonal* spirit that she saw in the *polis*, "where everybody had constantly to distinguish himself from all others, to show through unique deeds or achievements that he was the best of all" (Arendt 1958: 41). The polis in this sense was the arena for the flourishing of individuality. The meaning of such action is found not in its motivation or consequences, but in the performance of the action itself (Arendt 1958: 206). Hence, political action is unique; it is never wholly determined by that which precedes it, and it can never be understood as merely a repetition of past events. Nor is political action primarily instrumental, since its integrity lies within the action itself, and not in its intended consequences.

Arendtian Reflections on War Rape

Arendt's work *The Origins of Totalitarianism* was a groundbreaking achievement that addressed the historical and political preconditions of totalitarianism, and its destruction of the sphere of the political as exemplified in the Nazi death camps. But Arendt did not reflect on the question of war rape. Although rapes did occur in the Nazi camps, the first studies of sexual violence in the camps did not begin to appear until the 1960s. However, Arendt's reflections could offer several possibilities for investigating the meaning of war rape.

One strategy is to emphasize the similarity between the Nazi death camps and the rape camps in Bosnia in the 1990s. The death camps were enabled by the historical act of depriving an entire population of their civil rights, creating a situation of being effectively stateless and homeless (Arendt 1973: 451).[15] Similarly, one could argue that war rape in Bosnia was used to displace a population, severing their ties to home and community. One observer noted that "we could recognize refugees in Zagreb for a long time afterward because *other people's clothes* on them were so obvious" (Nicevic 2004: 111). And just as the camps transformed human beings into "specimens of the human animal" (Arendt 1973: 455), so too the rape camps deprived women of the most basic aspects of individuality, such as deciding when to go the bathroom, when to sleep, whether to engage in sexual acts, or how to care for their children. Arendt also pointed out that the Nazi death camps sought to eliminate memory traces even during military defeat. One of the witnesses in Claude Lanzmann's film *Shoah* explained how the Germans tried to eradicate any trace of dead bodies. He reported that the head of the Vilna Gestapo told the prisoners, "There are ninety thousand people lying there, and absolutely no trace must be left of them." The plan was to leave no trace of the crime of historical mass murder, and no trace of those who witnessed the crime (Felman and Laub 1992: 226). In war rape, the weapons of erasure are not just bullets and graves, but also the shame and fear of ostracism that often accompany the silence of survivors. Hence, it is a major achievement to establish a historical record of this material for use in judicial proceedings.[16] The Nazi camps also annihilated the uniqueness of the individual, both of the victim and of the executioner (Arendt 1973: 453), in an experiment in total domination designed to transform human nature itself. Similarly, war rape eliminates the uniqueness of each person. One twenty-two-year-old Serbian man, condemned to death by a military court in Sarajevo, said that he did not know how many girls he had raped, how many were killed, or what their names were. He described all his victims as the same, "[t]all, dark-haired, and between twenty and twenty-five years of age." And he always raped the girls in the company of other soldiers (Stiglmayer 1994: 155).

Other possible Arendtian strategies crowd the mind as well. The radicality of evil, in Arendt's use of the term, points to the attempt to undermine human nature as such, to eliminate spontaneity and plurality. Since war rape undermines the raped women's freedom and their place in community, war rape can be understood as a manifestation of radical evil. War rape could also be understood in light of the banality of evil, a term Arendt introduced in her book on Adolf Eichmann's trial. Banal evil suggests that it is thoughtlessness and not diabolical motivation that may characterize the actions of a mass murderer. Similarly, sadism or a diabolical motivation is not useful for characterizing the perpetrators of mass rape. One could also enlist Arendt's notion of narrative and its role in moral judgment for exploring the significance of survivors' stories.

Hence, Arendt's analysis of the death camps may be well suited for understanding other instances of mass atrocities. It points to the eradication of freedom; it provides an account of the concept of evil; and it provides an account of narrative that is an important part of moral education after atrocities. But my goal here is not to apply the concepts that Arendt introduces in her analysis of the Nazi death camps to the phenomenon of war rape. Rather, my interest is to ask how the phenomenon of war rape leads one to reflect on Arendt's political philosophy. In particular, how does war rape lead one to revise her reflections on the relation between the human body and the political body?

As argued above, the most compelling interpretation of Arendt's reflections on birth understands this event not merely as a physical process that can be viewed as a natural category, but as the birth of a political self. Hence, both the terms "birth" and "natality" carry a political meaning for Arendt, by referring to the birth of embodied, linguistic individuals who speak and act in the world. Death then is also the death of a political self. To speak of the processes of birth and death as meaningful in the context of a political horizon does not mean that one must follow an organic tradition in political thought, "by which power and violence are interpreted in biological terms" and where violence is justified on the grounds of life's alleged creativity. Arendt argues explicitly against such a tradition, which reduces politics to biological terms and glorifies violence with the view that "in the household of nature destruction and creation are but two sides of the natural process" (Arendt 1970: 75). Instead, in focusing on birth and death in the context of political community, Arendt contributes to a political phenomenology (Caygill 1997: 26–30). In this approach, birth and death are understood not merely as being individual events but as having a collective dimension. Arendt notes that although death is "the most anti-political experience there is," "faced collectively . . . death changes in countenance." In one sense, the collective meaning of death includes the "potential immortality of the group we belong to and, in the final analysis, of the species" (Arendt 1970: 68). But in another sense, the collective threat of death as in wartime violence includes the potential mortality of the group.

Reflecting on war rape lends support to Arendt's focus on the *political* character of birth and death. In light of this focus, it is tempting to compare Arendt's approach with Agamben's notion of biopower, which interrogates the relation between biological life and political strategies. Agamben notes that Arendt's work has been important for understanding how biological life has come to occupy center stage in political modernity. She analyzed the "unnatural growth" of the natural in mass society (Arendt 1958: 47), in which the tasks of survival spill over into the public realm and in which communities are transformed into mere "societies of laborers and jobholders." Agamben puzzles over the fact that Foucault, who introduced the term "biopower," never referred to Arendt's work, which preceded his own by more than twenty years. He explains this puzzle by the difficulties and resistance encountered by thinking about the relation between biological life and the political. Western philosophy since Aristotle has excluded natural life from the polis; hence an analysis of their relation in modernity demands a radically new analytic approach. The difficulties in developing a new approach to biological life and politics may also explain Arendt's failure to develop a biopolitical perspective in her analysis of totalitarian power. And similar difficulties may account for Foucault's failure to connect his analysis of modern biopolitics with the concentration camps in the twentieth century (Agamben 1998: 4–5).

For Foucault, the notion of biopower refers to the historical phenomena by which "the species and the individual as a simple living body become what is at stake in society's political strategies" (Agamben 1998: 3). What we take to be simple biological, pre-political processes are themselves the subject of political interventions. Drawing inspiration from Foucault's analysis both of political techniques and of technologies of the self, Agamben argues that the *original* activity of political sovereignty is the production of bare life; hence, bare life is not merely a feature of political modernity. Agamben uses the term "bare life" to refer to the "simple fact of living common to all living beings" (Agamben 1998: 1). He claims that the "politicization of bare life" has been the driving force in Western thought (Agamben 1998: 4). He takes the Nazi death camps as the paradigm of this political production of bare life. He writes, "[T]he camp—as the pure, absolute, and impassable biopolitical space . . . —will appear as the hidden paradigm of the political space of modernity" (Agamben 1998:123). And he explains the emergence of Serbian racism in the Yugoslav war by reference to biopolitics, "in which the only real question to be decided was which form of organization would be best suited to the task of assuring the care, control, and use of bare life" (Agamben 1998: 122). From the perspective of biopolitics, the traditional distinctions between Right and Left dissolved into a politics characterized by a program of ethnic cleansing.

Agamben argues that although Arendt's analysis could have led her to analyze biopower, in fact her work reveals the absence of a biopolitical perspective. As noted above, Arendt analyzed the concentration camps as an experiment in total domination. Agamben comments, "Yet what escapes Arendt is that the process is in a certain sense the inverse of what she takes it to be, and that precisely the radical transformation of politics into the realm of bare life (that is, into a camp) legitimated and necessitated total domination" (Agamben 1998: 120). In other words, for Agamben the biopolitical perspective implies that the production of bare life is the internal telos of the political, which necessitates certain political strategies to achieve this goal.

In Agamben's theory, war rape must be viewed as the production of bare life, where the biological body and the political body become indistinguishable. There seem to be least four consequences of this position. First, in an Agambenian reading, the production of the raped body in war is yet another manifestation of the telos in Western thought and politics that reduces the body to bare life. As such, there is nothing radically new or different in this phenomenon. It is yet another example of the biopolitical body, like the body of the Muselmänner in the Nazi camps, or the body of Karen Quinlan—whose biological body was maintained only by legally prescribed life-support technology (Agamben 1998: 186). In other words, biopolitics in some sense is the production of the *same,* the same fundamental reduction of life, regardless of whether it is by rape, starvation, torture, or technology. There is no possibility within this frame to analyze the differentiation and specificity of experiences.

Second, since the biopolitical body of the rape camp continues the historical trajectory of the Nazi death camps, it would be meaningless to explore the specifically *sexual* dimension of this torture. The specifically sexual dimension of this torture consists not in sexual pleasure—which is nonexistent for most perpetrators, and absolutely nonexistent for the women who are the victims. The sexual dimension of torture refers instead to the way in which sexual difference becomes used as an instrument of torture. In this case, torture involves the sexual violation of women's bodies and the violent use of their reproductive capacities. Indeed, certain historical conditions made the development of the rape camps possible. Agamben notes that since WWI, the fiction that birth guaranteed one's identification with the nation has been challenged, as evident in the mounting refugee crisis in the twentieth century (Agamben 1998: 131).[17] And Agamben writes, "If the Nazis never thought of effecting the Final Solution by making Jewish women pregnant, it is because the principle of birth that assured the inscription of life in the order of the nation-state was still—if in a profoundly transformed sense—in operation" (Agamben 1998: 176).[18] So these historical changes enabled—or in Agamben's framework, necessitated—the use of war rape today to produce the biopolitical body. But in Agamben's account, this historical shift is primarily related to shifts in concepts of the nation-state, rather than to changes in the violent uses of sexual difference in wartime.

Third, since the biological and the political body are indistinguishable, all bodily experiences can be understood within the framework of the biopolitical body. Hence, in an Agambenian approach, war rape can be understood exclusively in terms of the political formation of modernity. In this account, there is little room to reflect on the implications of rape for the *subjectivity* of a woman. It is because Agamben's account bypasses the attempt to understand the subjective dimension of war rape that he can claim, "there is certainly nothing shameful in a human being who suffers on account of sexual violence" since one can speak of shame only if one takes pleasure in one's own suffering, if one is moved by one's own passivity (Agamben 1999: 110). Here he indicates an astonishing ignorance of the narratives of the survivors of war rape, many of whom wrestle with feelings of shame, in marked contrast to his close assessment of the narratives of survivors of the concentration camps.[19]

Fourth, Agamben's analysis of biopolitics overlooks the role of political mediations, institutions, and juridical proceedings (Kalyvas 2005: 117). This approach is explained by his view that politics "appears as the truly fundamental structure of Western metaphysics" (Agamben 1998: 8). In other words, metaphysics is the lens through which Agamben approaches the political, in contrast to philosophers such as Arendt who clearly distinguish between the metaphysical and the political. With his metaphysical interest in the political, Agamben overlooks the widely different ways in which war rape actually has functioned in war—from its prohibition under Mao Tsetung to its specific incitement in the genocide in Bosnia.

An Arendtian reflection on war rape reveals very different commitments about how to analyze war rape as political violence. First, politics cannot be understood as teleological, as it is in Agamben's account of the production of the biopolitical body. Hence, political violence does not realize an internal trajectory of the political. In her study of the death camps, Arendt analyzed the uniqueness of the experiment in total domination, which transformed human beings into specimens of the human animal (Arendt 1973: 455). An Arendtian approach to the rape camps in Bosnia would similarly ask what is unique and unprecedented in this experiment. War rape cannot be understood as a repetition of a trans-historical political trajectory; it cannot be understood as *like* other forms of political manipulation and torture. Instead, it must be understood as a distinct political strategy.

Second, Arendt's approach would make room for an analysis of the *sexual* violations of women's bodies in war rape. She acknowledges the fundamental role of sexual difference as the ground for human plurality. She invokes Genesis, "We know only 'male and female created he them'" (Arendt 1958: 8). Sexual difference is also the unquestioned precondition for the new beginnings inherent in birth. And it is necessary to focus on the specifically sexualized nature of the violence in war rape in order to catch sight of the strange paradox at its heart: that the generative dimension of human sexuality is transformed into an instrument of death. In war rape, death is indeed at stake—as Agamben's focus on "life's subjection to a power over death" would indicate (Agamben 1998: 83). In cases where the woman is forcibly impregnated, the woman may wish for her own death and the death of the baby. One Bosnian woman who gave birth to a child from rape said, "[I]f anyone had tried to show it to me after it was born, I'd have strangled them and the baby too" (Stiglmayer 1994: 131–33). The raped woman may be threatened with death by her own family, as when a Muslim father gave his raped daughter a rope to hang herself. And war rape may aim at the destruction of a community, as in the case of the genocidal rapes in Bosnia (Allen 1996: 62). But what is unique with forced impregnation in war rape is that *birth* itself becomes a *weapon of death*. In this context, the fundamental meaning of birth becomes radically transformed. Arendt noted that "men, though they must die, are not born in order to die but in order to begin" (Arendt 1958: 246). It is the transformation of birth for the purpose of death that, in Arendtian terms, represents the radical experiment of war rape.[20] War rape aims to bring death and destruction to individual women and to political communities; and it aims as well to destroy a fundamental feature of the human condition.

Third, Arendt's emphasis on memory opens the possibility for exploring the subjective experience of war rape. Memory, as noted above, makes the past into a future possibility that we may approach with hope or fear. The memory of war rape brings with it a memory of trauma and shame that may destroy a woman's hope for the future. This may be the case if a woman bears a child born of rape, who indelibly bears the mark of her enemy. And her hope for the future may also be destroyed, if she is physically or psychologically unable to have a child because of the trauma of the rape.

Fourth, Arendt's approach to history focuses on its interruptions and ruptures, instead of viewing history as an unfolding of its internal dynamic. This means that war rape cannot be analyzed merely in general terms, but must be analyzed in its historical specificity. And it means that resistance to war rape is a present possibility. Resistance can take the form of individual soldiers' refusal to follow orders to rape, of military leaders' refusal to condone sexual violence, of judicial judgments condemning rape, or of grassroots organizations documenting sexual violence and demanding recognition and compensation for the victims.

Thus, Arendtian reflections provide us with the following insights. (1) War rape, as with any form of political domination, must be understood in terms of specific political projects and not in terms of metaphysical or trans-historical dynamics, as Agamben might suggest. (2) Sexualized violence, when coupled with forced impregnation as in the Bosnian case, represents a radical experiment and transformation of the concept of human birth. (3) The past traumas of war rape are never just past for survivors, but have ongoing repercussions for their future. (4) Resistance to war rape by all possible means becomes an urgent priority.

Here I will consider briefly the implications of war rape for Arendtian reflections on natality. Arendt described the human condition as being conditioned by "life itself, natality and mortality, worldliness, plurality, and the earth" (Arendt 1958: 11). The question I would like to consider here is whether the phenomenon of sexual violence leads one to revise Arendt's understanding of the concept of natality. Natality, as discussed above, implies dependency, temporality, memory, and newness. All of these features are present in war rape as well. It is the dependency on others that becomes a source of violation and abandonment. It is the perishability of life-forms that puts individuals' ability to care for and feed their families at risk. It is traumatic memory that destroys an individual's openness to the future.[21] And it is the capacity to begin something new that can be a source either of hope or of despair at breaking with the cycle of violence that has marred one's life. Here one can note that societies with chronic conditions of war or intergroup conflict also experience a marked increase in family violence (Minow 2002: 64). These examples illustrate that Arendt's concept of natality can be applied to study essential issues of war rape. But at the same time these examples put into relief Arendt's habit of using the concept of natality to emphasize the positive aspects of human existence, rather than the negative possibilities. It may be this tendency to idealize the human condition that provides the background for Seyla Benhabib's criticism that Arendt relies on normative presuppositions that she does not justify (Benhabib 2005: 195–96). To counteract this tendency to idealize, one needs to add another concept to these fundamental conditions put forth by Arendt—the concept of vulnerability. Vulnerability derives from the Latin word *vulnus,* which means wound. Vulnerability refers to my injurability—and hence points to the limits of the view of the subject as an autonomous agent. Instead, vulnerability implies the risk that one's capacities and one's weaknesses will be used against oneself, against one's consent. Vulnerability points to the risk of becoming an unwilling instrument of violence against others and of losing those whom one loves.[22] Vulnerability points to the uncertainty that permeates human life and to the dissymmetry in human relations in terms of trust and empowerment. Hence it is not just a physical vulnerability, as in one's capacity for pain, illness, or injury, but is existential as well, as in one's capacity to be wounded by the contingency of events, as in the illness or death of those whom one loves. In Bryan Turner's view, the vulnerability of the human body is mirrored in the precariousness of social institutions. A question to discuss in another context is whether the shared vulnerability in the human condition can provide the basis for normative rights to protect all individuals from suffering and indignity, as Turner argues (Turner 2006: 25, 9). My focus here is how emphasizing vulnerability as a dimension of natality brings to the fore both the destructive and constructive dimensions of new beginnings. Hence, this concept develops Arendt's project further and is necessary to account for the destructive and violent dimensions of human coexistence.[23]

Thus, war rape shows some of the complex relations between the human body and the political world, and the futility of the view that birth and death are natural events that represent strictly nonpolitical moments. Raising Arendtian questions to war rape leads us to examine the specificity of political projects that work on the human body and to grasp the radicality of the political experiment to transform human birth into a form of death. With this lens, we can also glimpse the ways in which human beings incorporate political projects into their own life histories, both through the work of survival and through practices of resistance on individual and institutional levels. I have also indicated that bringing the phenomenon of war rape into the heart of Arendt's thought leads us to develop more than she did the notion of vulnerability in the human condition, and to pursue the implications of vulnerability for justifying and protecting political rights.

I have argued that the concept of natality contains both positive and negative possibilities for experiencing dependency, temporality, memory, and newness, although Arendt's own account tends to focus on their positive dimensions. It is through the concept of vulnerability that we bring to mind the negative risk in human natality. Nevertheless, we should remember the positive dimensions of natality, the capacity for new beginnings even in the darkest of times. And Arendt invokes this term in the closing pages of *The Origins of Totalitarianism.* She notes that the crisis of our time has brought forth "an entirely new form of government which as a potentiality and an ever-present danger is only too likely to stay with us from now on." And she adds, "But there remains also the truth that every end in history necessarily contains a new beginning. . . . 'that a beginning be made man was created' said Augustine. This beginning is guaranteed by each new birth; it is indeed every man" (Arendt 1973: 478–79). Natality also represents the possibility of resistance and hope that is missing in Agamben's analysis, and that is crucial for individuals and societies recovering from atrocities.

NOTES

1. In this spirit, Seyla Benhabib writes that "we must leave the pieties of textual analyses and ask ourselves Arendtian questions and be ready to provide non-Arendtian answers" (Benhabib 1996: 198).

2. Niarchos cites Theodor Meron, *Henry's Wars and Shakespeare's Laws: Perspectives on the Law of War in the Later Middle Ages* (Oxford: Oxford University Press, 1993), 111–12.

3. One should note that some historians oppose the numbers game, in which the highest possible figure is systematically cited.

4. "Rape and Genocide in Rwanda: The ICTR's Akayesu Verdict," http://home pages.uc.edu/thro/rwanda/RwandaRapeCase2.htm, accessed October 27, 2003, 4.

5. Goldstone considers this a progressive definition, though notes that it might go too far in not requiring penetration by a sexual organ to constitute rape (Goldstone 2002: 278, 283–85).

6. Kelly Dawn Askin is critical of this subsumption of rape under the category of crime against humanity. She writes, "Thus, while it is of great significance that rape was specifically listed as a crime against humanity, it is nevertheless troublesome that a vicious and devastating act of sexual assault would need to be committed for a particular reason before redress might be rendered" (Askin 1997: 349). Hence, Askin argues for the need to add gender to the list of protected target groups, and thus eliminate the problem of determining why a sexual assault occurred (Askin 1997: 355).

7. In February 2001, the ICTY sentenced three Bosnian Serbs for committing acts of rape and sexual torture. This is the first time that an international court has convicted offenders solely on the basis of sexual offenses (Schiessl 2002: 208).

8. Patricia Albanese argues for both factors, insisting that nationalist ideologies revive archaic gender relations, and that nationalist politics have put women backward by at least 50 years (Albanese 2001: 1002, 1008).

9. For examples of feminist analyses of birth and societal reproduction, see Barrett 1980 and O'Brien 1981. O'Brien considered Arendt to be a "female male supremacist" (Dietz 1991: 19).

10. The difficulty in communicating extreme pain is the subject of Elaine Scarry's book *The Body in Pain* (Scarry 1985).

11. Arendt began to address the notion of beginnings in her doctoral dissertation, *Love and Saint Augustine*, which was published in German in 1929. She introduced the term "natality" in *The Human Condition*, published in 1958. When she set about revising her dissertation for English publication in the 1960s, she inserted the term "natality" in the earlier text to clarify her discussion of beginnings (Arendt 1966). In the first translation of this passage from her dissertation Arendt writes, "Because the world, and thus any created thing, must originate, its being is determined by its origin (*fieri*)—it becomes, it has a beginning." In the revised version Arendt writes instead, "To put it differently, the decisive fact determining man as a conscious, remembering being is birth or 'natality,' that is, the fact that we have entered the world through birth" (Arendt 1966: 132–33).

12. In this context, Arendt departs from Augustine's conception of time as the human mode of perceiving the relation of parts to whole.

13. Scott and Stark write, "Arendt entered the public world of academic political theory, taking Augustine with her. In 1951 (*Origins of Totalitarianism*) Arendt applied the *Existenz* of *caritas*-inspired new beginnings to political life" (Arendt 1966: 183).

14. Moriya Kariv described these memorial practices to me in a conversation in Copenhagen on May 4, 2006.

15. See also my use of Arendtian concepts for an analysis of war rape in Schott 2009. In that article, I focus on how war rape undermines political rights and the concept of the political.

16. See, for example, Birte Weiss, "Den Tavse Forbrydelse" *Weekendavisen,* March 17–23, 2006. The article tells the story of Bakira Hasesic, herself a victim of rape and the mother of a teenager who was also raped, who has founded the NGO Women, Victims of War to provide information for the police and the courts.

17. Arendt was also deeply concerned with the phenomenon of refugees. She herself was a refugee from Germany who lived stateless in the United States for ten years. See her chapter, "The Decline of the Nation-State and the End of the Rights of Man" (Arendt 1973: 267–302).

18. Agamben does not mention that Jewishness is traditionally passed on through the mother. Given the traditional Jewish practice of matrilineal descent, the children born to raped Jewish women would also be Jewish. Mass rape of Jewish women in Roman times was one of the reasons that the rabbis replaced patrilineal with matrilineal descent. Note that Agamben's comment also assumes that Jewishness is functionally equivalent to national identity, which is a presupposition that Arendt debunks.

19. Erik Vogt discusses a different tension between Agamben's analysis of biopolitics and his invocation of poetic testimony, when he suggests that the latter sustains Agamben's transcendental orientation (Vogt 2005: 99–100).

20. There is still a sense in which new beginnings take place for the child of war rape—whether the child lives with the mother, in an orphanage, or with adoptive parents abroad. But the narrative of their birth can never be separated from this traumatic start of life.

21. Rudolf Bernet writes, "Aside from this brief moment of activity and lucidity which is nonetheless inseparable from the instant of repression and misrecognition, the traumatised subject finds itself given over to a foreign alterity which concerns it most closely and which monopolises its life: at first under the form of the mute and insistent trace of the first shock and then under the form of the inhibition of its entire adult life by an incomprehensible symptom" (Bernet 2000: 163).

22. See my review of Judith Butler's *Precarious Life* (London: Verso, 2004) in *Forum,* December 22, 2004, http://www.forum.kvinfo.dk/forskning/?id=3350201.

23. One related question is, what is a politics of vulnerability? Here one might also consider how discourses of vulnerability are used politically. Under conditions of sexual dissymmetry, one is more apt to consider certain people, i.e., women, as vulnerable. Hence, the politics of protection undermine the acknowledgment of the shared condition of human vulnerability. But to include vulnerability in the political domain means including discourses of pain as political, and challenging Arendt's claim that "pain is the most private and least communicable" of experiences (Arendt 1958: 50). Expanding an Arendtian frame to consider the political discourses of pain implies not only examining the role of narratives of pain for moral judgment (Lara 2007), but understanding how these testimonies operate both in the court of law and in other forms of public reconstructions of history.

BIBLIOGRAPHY

Agamben, Giorgio. 1998. *Homo Sacer.* Trans. Daniel Heller-Roazen. Stanford, Calif.: Stanford University Press.
———. 1999. *Remnants of Auschwitz.* Trans. Daniel Heller-Roazen. New York: Zone Books.

Albanese, Patricia. 2001. "Nationalism, War, and Archaization of Gender Relations in the Balkans." *Violence against Women* 7, no. 9: 999–1023.

Allen, Beverly. 1996. *Rape Warfare*. Minneapolis: University of Minnesota Press.

Arendt, Hannah. 1958. *The Human Condition*. Chicago: University of Chicago Press.

———. 1966. *Love and Saint Augustine*. Ed. Joanna Vecchiarelli Scott and Judith Chelius Stark. Chicago: University of Chicago Press.

———. 1970. *On Violence*. New York: Harcourt Brace.

———. 1973. *The Origins of Totalitarianism*. New York: Harcourt Brace Jovanovich.

Askin, Kelly. 1997. *War Crimes against Women*. The Hague: Kluwer Law International.

Barrett, Michele. 1980. *Women's Oppression Today*. London: Verso.

Beevor, Antony. 2002. *Berlin: The Downfall, 1945*. New York: Viking.

Benhabib, Seyla. 2005. *The Reluctant Modernism of Hannah Arendt*. London: Sage.

Bernet, Rudolf. 2000. "The Traumatized Subject." *Research in Phenomenology* 30, no. 1: 160–79.

Birmingham, Peg. 2006. *Hannah Arendt and Human Rights*. Bloomington: Indiana University Press.

Booth, Cherie. 2005. "Sexual Violence, Torture, and International Justice." In Roth and Worden 2005, 117–30.

Brown, Wendy. 1988. *Manhood and Politics*. Lanham, Md.: Rowman and Littlefield.

Caygill, Howard. 1997. "The Shared World—Philosophy, Violence, Freedom." In Sheppard, Sparks, and Thomas 1997, 19–31.

Demause, Lloyd. 2002. "War as Righteous Rape and Purification." *Journal of Psychohistory* 27, no. 4 (Spring 2002): 356–445.

Dietz, Mary G. 1991. "Hannah Arendt and Feminist Politics." In Shanley and Patement 1991, 232–52.

———. 1995. "Feminist Receptions of Hannah Arendt." In Honig 1995.

Felman, Shoshana, and Dori Laub. 1992. *Testimony: Crises of Witnessing in Literature, Psychoanalysis and History*. New York: Routledge.

Goldstone, Richard J. 2002. "Prosecuting Rape as a War Crime." *Case Western Reserve Journal of International Law* 34, no. 3 (Summer 2002): 277–85.

Goodwin, Jan. 2004. "Silence=Rape." *Nation*. March 8, 2004.

Honig, Bonnie, ed. 1995. *Feminist Interpretations of Hannah Arendt*. University Park: Pennsylvania State University Press.

Kalyvas, Andreas. 2005. "The Sovereign Weaver." In Norris 2005, 107–34.

Krystal, Henry, ed. 1968. *Massive Psychic Trauma*. New York: International Universities Press.

Lara, María Pía. 2007. *Narrative Evil: A Postmetaphysical Theory of Reflective Judgement*. New York: Columbia University Press.

Minow, Martha. 2002. *Breaking the Cycles of Hatred*. Princeton, N.J.: Princeton University Press.

Niarchos, Catherine N. "Women, War and Rape: Challenges Facing the International Criminal Tribunal for the Former Yugoslavia." *Human Rights Quarterly* 17 (1995): 649–90.

Nicevic, Sanja. 2004. "Rape as War Strategy: A Drama from Croatia." *PAJ: A Journal of Performance and Art* 77, no. 1: 110–14.

Norris, Andrew, ed. 2005. *Politics, Metaphysics, and Death: Essays on Giorgio Agamben's Homo Sacer*. Durham, N.C.: Duke University Press.

O'Brien, Mary. 1981. *The Politics of Reproduction.* London: Routledge.

Roth, Kenneth, and Minky Worden, eds. 2005. *Torture.* New York: New Press/Human Rights Watch.

Scarry, Elaine. 1985. *The Body in Pain.* New York: Oxford University Press.

Schiessl, Christoph. 2002. "An Element of Genocide: Rape, Total War, and International Law in the Twentieth Century." *Journal of Genocide Research* 4, no. 2: 197–210.

Schott, Robin May. 2009. "War Rape and the Political Concept of Evil." In Veltman and Norlock 2009.

Shanley, Mary Lyndon, and Carole Pateman, eds. 1991. *Feminist Interpretations of Political Theory.* University Park: Pennsylvania State University Press.

Sheppard, Darren, Simon Sparks, and Colin Thomas, eds. 1997. *On Jean-Luc Nancy.* London: Routledge.

Stiglmayer, Alexandra, ed. 1994. *Mass Rape: The War against Women in Bosnia-Herzegovina.* Lincoln: University of Nebraska Press.

Turner, Bryan. 2006. *Vulnerability and Human Rights.* University Park: Pennsylvania State University Press.

Van Boeschoten, Riki. 2003. "The Trauma of War Rape: A Comparative View on the Bosnian Conflict and the Greek Civil War." *History and Anthropology* 14, no. 1: 41–44.

Veltman, Andrea, and Kathryn Norlock, eds. 2009. *Evil, Political Violence and Forgiveness: Essays in Honor of Claudia Card.* Lanham, Md.: Lexington Books / Rowman and Littlefield.

Vogt, Erik. 2005. "S/Citing the Camp." In Norris 2005, 74–106.

Zerilli, Linda M. G. 1995. "The Arendtian Body." In Honig 1995, 167–93.

PART 2
Phenomenologies of Mortality and Generativity

FOUR

The Sexed Self and the Mortal Body
SARA HEINÄMAA

Simone de Beauvoir's *The Second Sex* (*Le deuxième sexe* 1949) includes a strong and influential argument about the associative link between femininity and death. Beauvoir points out that both men and women tend to associate women with finitude and mortality, and correspondingly, men with infinitude and eternal life. This holds for laymen and their common sense as well as for writers and scholars and their scientific, theological, and philosophical accounts of human life. In respect to death, our thinking is still mainly mythical: "Death is a woman, and it is for women to bewail the dead because death is their work" (Beauvoir [1949] 1993: 247/179).

Beauvoir uses a major part of the first book of *The Second Sex* to demonstrate that the association between femininity and death has a great influence on our thinking and a central role in our self-understanding. She surveys a great amount of various textual materials, from anthropological and historical sources to theological interpretations and scientific and philosophical explications, and shows how the association recurs in different forms in different contexts. Instead of simply rejecting or contesting the association, Beauvoir sets out to study how it originated and what motivates its emergence and recurrence.

Ultimately Beauvoir tracks the association down to habituated, repeated acts of projection and introjection: through centuries men have struggled emotionally and intellectually to deal with their finiteness and mortality. They have tried to reject and suppress their true condition and have ended up projecting it onto women (Beauvoir [1949] 1993: 249/180, 297/213–14, 318–19/229). Women, for their part, have accepted, and at times even embraced, this projection. They have assumed that men take responsibility for their shared spiritual tasks and common striving for the eternal, and they have abandoned their own aspirations for the infinite (Beauvoir [1949] 1993: 242/175, [1949] 1991: 522–93/639–87). In these projections and introjections, both men and women are motivated by fear and anxiety. To face the human condition in its ambiguous and paradoxical openness is demanding for any individual (cf. Kierkegaard [1843] 1950: 49–51).

Beauvoir's account is based on her existential interpretation of the duality of human life: All human beings, both men and women, live between two existential poles: finitude and infinitude, mortality and eternity. We all are bound by space and time in our individual histories and environments, but we are also able to transcend these limitations by imagination, creation, reflection, and language. Incessantly, we move from one pole to the other and then back. We may live long periods and even pass through whole phases of life focusing on one aspect and neglecting the other, but eventually we have to embrace both opposites.

This condition cannot be escaped, for it is in the core of our human existence; it can only be endured and maintained in different ways.[1] The back-and-forth movement is necessary, and cannot be arrested. The state of this duality and indecision, however, is terrifying and generates anxiety, and so both men and women try to escape it by abstracting one aspect from their lives and by identifying themselves with the other: men have denied their mortality and projected it onto women, and women have relinquished their spirituality and abandoned it to men. Beauvoir describes the unhappy results of such projections as follows:

> The truth is that if the vicious circle is so hard to break, it is because the two sexes are each the victim at once of the other and of itself. [...] woman is pursuing a dream of resignation, man a dream of estrangement. Authenticity does not pay: each blames the other for the unhappiness he or she has incurred in yielding to the temptations of easiness; what man and woman hate in each other is the evident failure of each one's own self-deception and cowardice. (Beauvoir [1949] 1991: 647/728)

Later feminist studies have confirmed Beauvoir's basic thesis about the recurring association between femininity and death even if they have rejected the moral conclusions that Beauvoir draws from her analysis. The association has been documented in the fields of anthropology, psychology, theology, and the history of ideas and sciences, and this indicates that the phenomenon has deep roots and that it can perhaps be illuminated only by interdisciplinary investigations.

The analyses of the nature and basis of the connection greatly vary. Some scholars claim that the link is conceptual, inscribed on the conceptual system of human thinking and reasoning; others argue that the connection is symbolic and common to linguistic and nonlinguistic symbol systems. Genevieve Lloyd, for example, argues in her often-cited work *The Man of*

Reason (1984) that the link between femininity and death is conceptual and metaphorical, mediated by the concepts of matter, body, and sensibility (1984: x–5, 106, cf. 1993: 72; cf. Reuter 2006), whereas Grace M. Jantzen suggests that the connection is symbolic and independent of the conceptual-linguistic form (1998, 2003, 2004: 4–20).

Beauvoir's account differs from such later developments in a crucial respect.[2] What is specific and important is that she tracks the femininity-death connection down to its preconceptual and presymbolic motivations in our emotional and perceptual life. This must not be misunderstood: even though Beauvoir proceeds from concepts and symbols to their experiential basis in affects and desires, her argument is not psychological. She does not discuss emotions and perceptions as worldly processes but studies them as our very basic ways of having the world given to us (Beauvoir [1949] 1993: 105–109/91–93). Her account is experiential but not empirical-inductive.

In order to understand Beauvoir's argument about femininity and death, and to evaluate its validity, we need to study her understanding of human existence as well as its starting points in the existential and phenomenological traditions of modern philosophy. I will begin by introducing the basic ideas of Kierkegaard's existential account of human life as paradoxical, and then show how Beauvoir connects the phenomenological explication of the living body to this framework. I will then proceed to study alternative existential-phenomenological discourses on death and life, and at the end will return to Beauvoir's explication to assess the resources that it provides for understanding the gendered nature of mortality and death. My three chapters thus aim at deepening our understanding of the association between femininity and mortality, but they also provide an overview of the existential-phenomenological discussion on finitude and death. We will see how the death of the other can be differentiated from my own death and how the different meanings of ending and beginning contribute to our understanding of the interconnectedness of life, death, and birth—my own demise and rise, and the other's death and nativity, his passing and advent.[3]

Ambiguous and Paradoxical Existence

Kierkegaard characterizes the duality and paradoxicality of the human condition most clearly in *Sickness unto Death* (*Sygdommen til døden* 1849). Human life is a difficult struggle in which man tries to find a balance between the different aspects of his existence, between finitude and infinitude, temporality and eternity, freedom and necessity, psyche and body (Kierkegaard [1842–43] 2001: 79–83, [1844] 1980: 81, 195, [1849] 1950: 242/43). The different factors of our lives do not emerge in any successive, developmental manner, but are simultaneous or contemporary. In our thoughts, we can unify them by subjecting them to some one principle or category, but in existence we cannot accomplish such an operation: "As soon as I must actually exist, the distinction is there, and the existence-consequence of canceling the distinction [. . .] is suicide" (Kirkegaard [1844] 1980: 343–48).

Kierkegaard does not offer any clear, univocal answer to the question whether the opposition between finitude and infinitude can be synthesized or whether the synthesis can be completed. Neither does he provide any simple normative account of the best way to endure or mediate between the opposites. Instead he gives us several different models and possible prognoses. On the one hand, there is the positive model in which the synthesis can be sustained and completed, not by any intellectual or purely rational activity, but with the help of God. On the other hand, it seems that God cannot help us to overcome or transcend the opposites, but can merely assist our attempts to juxtapose them and to endure their tension. Instead of proposing a Hegelian synthesis, Kierkegaard argues that we must struggle to bear the opposition, affirm our "double nature,"[4] and let go of the fantasy of unification and fulfillment.[5] He asks: "What is existence?" and answers: "Existence is the child that is born of the infinite and the finite, the eternal and the temporal, and is therefore a constant striving" ([1846] 1960: 85).

Thus Kierkegaard argues that the continuous movement between the opposites is necessary for our existence. We cannot resolve or undo the paradox, but we can live it in different ways. In *Sickness unto Death*, he describes several unhappy possibilities, but he also insists that it is possible to find an equilibrium between finitude and infinitude ([1849] 1950: 242–43/44).[6] This is the task of the human being.

To reject one's finitude is one of the unbalanced ways of living the duality of human existence (Kierkegaard [1849] 1950: 273–74/60–62). Instead of accepting the paradox of his existence, a human being tries to resolve it by denying his corporeality and finiteness. This is the attitude of a person who aspires to abstract pure infinity and aims at identifying with it. In Kierkegaard's account, such a person creates a fantastic idealization by using the infinite within himself:

> By means of this infinite form, the self wants in despair to rule over himself, or create himself, make this [infinite form] the self he wants to be, determine what he will have and what he will not have in his concrete self. His concrete self, or his concreteness, had indeed

necessity and limits, [. . .] [his concrete self] is this quite definite
thing, with these aptitudes, predispositions, etc. in this concrete set
of circumstances. But by means of the infinite form [. . .] he wants
first to undertake to refashion the whole thing in order to get out
of it a self such as he wants [. . .] He does not want to see his task
in the given self, he wants, by virtue of being an infinite form, to
construct himself. (Kierkegaard [1849] 1950: 273–74/99)[7]

Both men and women can live in such a desperate mode of consciousness,
but in Kierkegaard's understanding, this attitude is typical of men. Women
for their part seem to suffer from the opposite form of despair, forgetting
the infinite and identifying with the finite (Kierkegaard [1849] 1950: 260/80,
273–78/98, 276–78/103–104, cf. [1844] 1980: 61).[8] In Kierkegaard's account,
both these attitudes involve an oblivion of the meaning of existence.

Beauvoir accepts and affirms the Kierkegaardian notion of human existence as essentially paradoxical: the subject is in constant indecision between
inwardness and externality, finitude and the infinite, temporality and eternity,
solitude and bonding (Beauvoir 1947: 11–15/7–19). Following Kierkegaard,
Beauvoir also argues that the paradoxes of human existence cannot be
resolved (Beauvoir 1947: 186–87/133–34), they can only be endured, and
executed in different ways. In her ethical essays *Pyrrhus and Cineas* (*Pyrrhus
et Cinéas* 1944) and *The Ethics of Ambiguity* (*Pour une morale de l'ambiguïté*
1947), Beauvoir describes several alternatives: the infantile, the narcissistic,
the serious, and the artistic-critical. In *The Second Sex*, she distinguishes
between two main attitudes, one typical of men and the other characteristic
of women. She argues that women tend to identify with the finite and the
temporary, whereas men identify with the infinite and the eternal. These
typical identifications have wide-ranging implications for our emotional,
moral, and intellectual lives. In the case of men, the one-sided identification leads to a heavily charged notion of one's own embodiment. Beauvoir
describes the masculine attitude and self-understanding as follows:

[H]e [man] sees himself as a fallen god: his curse is to be fallen
from the bright and ordered heaven into the chaotic shadows of his
mother's womb. This fire, this pure and active inhalation in which
he wishes to recognize himself, is imprisoned by woman in the mud
of the earth. He would want to be necessary, like a pure Idea, like
the One, the All, the absolute Spirit; and he finds himself shut up
in a finite body, in a place and time he never chose, where he was
not called for, useless, cumbersome, absurd. The contingency of

flesh [. . .] also dooms him to death. This quivering jelly which is elaborated in the womb [. . .] evokes too clearly the soft viscosity of carrion for him not to turn shuddering away. (Beauvoir [1949] 1993: 245–56/177–78, cf. 273–74/197)[9]

And further: "[W]hat man cherishes and detests in woman—loved one and mother—is the fixed image of his animal destiny; it is the life that is necessary to his existence but that condemns him to the finite and to death" (Beauvoir [1949] 1993: 273–74/197).[10]

So on the basis of Kierkegaard's account of the human condition, Beauvoir develops an interpretation of the relations between the sexes. She argues that we have come to divide the double task of being human between ourselves, as if we could take care of our existential duties by a division of labor: "if you handle the infinite, then I take care of the finite," "if you identify with what is eternal, I identify with what is transitory and changing." But such a division is impossible, for we all are beings that live between the opposites, and each of us has to reinterpret the opposition in the context of his or her own situation and history. The task of enduring the opposition between the finitude and the infiniteness, or maintaining oneself in it, is not a task that somebody else can perform, execute, or carry out for us. Kierkegaard expresses this by saying that only God can assist us here; Beauvoir points to the same existential fact by describing the absolute responsibility that we have for our own lives.

Throughout *The Second Sex,* Beauvoir emphasizes that men and women share the same existential condition. Both live their lives as bodies and souls, as active and passive, as dependent and independent, as free and bound. Each person has to decide his own life and find his individual unique way of mediating between these opposites. At the end of *The Second Sex,* Beauvoir again states: "[T]hey [both men and women] live in their different ways the strange ambiguity of existence made body. [. . .] In both sexes is played out the same drama of the flesh and the spirit, of finitude and transcendence; both are gnawed away by time and laid in wait for death, they have the same essential need for the other; and they can gain from their liberty the same glory" (Beauvoir [1949] 1991: 658/737, cf. [1949] 1993: 400/286).[11]

Body Lived and Objectified

In Beauvoir's reading, Kierkegaard's existential thinking comes close to Nietzsche's in two crucial respects that help to understand the association between femininity and death. Both argue that Western theorizing, to a great degree, is characterized by the neglect or disregard of the body, and both agree that this neglect is reflected in our conceptions of the sexes and in the idolization and mystification of women. The predominant focus of Western thinkers has been on the faculties of the intellect and the reason, but the theoretization of these capacities has been motivated by bodily and sensuous experiences, experiences of passivity and power, weakness and strength, vitality and decay, which have not been acknowledged, or even noticed, but have been disguised or suppressed. At the beginning of *Gay Science* (*Die fröliche Wissenschaft* 1882), Nietzsche expresses this concern most explicitly: "The unconscious disguise of physiological needs under the cloaks of the objective, ideal, purely spiritual goals goes frighteningly far—and I have asked myself often enough whether, on a grand scale, philosophy has been no more than an interpretation of the body and *a misunderstanding of the body*" (Nietzsche [1882] 1994: 10/5).[12]

For Beauvoir, Nietzsche's and Kierkegaard's bold reflections on desires, emotions, sensations, and bodily needs were disenchanting.[13] What was lacking, however, was a systematic explication of the living body as distinct from physical things. This Beauvoir found in the works of the phenomenologists Edmund Husserl and Martin Heidegger and their early followers.

Phenomenology offered a clear distinction between the body *as it is lived* in sensations, perceptions, and emotions and the body *as it is thematized and objectified* in different kinds of activities and practices, from everyday occupations to scientific reflections. On the one hand, we have the body as an aspect of the experiencing self, and on the other hand, we have the body as the experienced object. All bodily states and processes can be considered from these different perspectives: simple sensations, such as pain, pleasure, and dizziness, as well as complex bodily states and processes, such as pregnancy, delirium, and old age. Also death can be considered in two different ways, as it is lived in the first-person perspective and as it is perceived or observed from a third-person viewpoint.[14]

Both viewpoints are implicated in the specific relation that a living body has to itself. When a living being touches itself, for example, or when it hears itself cry or laugh, it both captures itself as a perceptual thing and lives in the sensual activity of perceiving (Husserl Hua4: 96/101, 145–47/153–55). In such experiences, the body is given as the sensed objectivity and as the sensing self, and moreover these two positions are not separate but reciprocal and interchangeable, appearing as two aspects of one and the same phenomenon.[15]

In this context, objectification does not mean any negative operation—alienation or estrangement—but must be understood as a necessary structural feature of all experience of worldly, spatial-temporal things and events.

To be sure, the fact that we can objectify ourselves and each other in perception and action allows for different forms of abuse, violence, and mishandling, but objectification as such is not an act of violence (cf. Morris 1999). Even the acts of respect, love, and desire objectify their aims, but merely in the formal sense of presenting their aims as respected, loved, or desired.

Another related distinction that is crucial to Beauvoir's phenomenological reflections on femininity and mortality is the distinction between the expressive body and the physical (mechanical) body (Beauvoir [1949] 1993: 73/66, 78/69, [1949] 1991: 586/682). The original source of this distinction is in the unpublished second part of Husserl's work *Ideas* (Hua4), but Beauvoir was familiar with the distinction from the later explications of Jean-Paul Sartre (1943) and Maurice Merleau-Ponty (1945).

The starting point of Husserl's analysis in *Ideen II* is the fact that we can objectify living bodies in two fundamentally different ways. On the one hand, we can take the attitude of the natural scientist and abstract all meaning, value, and purpose away from the bodies that we study. Thus the positions and movements of the bodies appear to us as mere effects of external and internal causes. In this way, animal bodies and human bodies are given as complex biochemical mechanisms, and we can then try to explain and predict their behavior by subsuming them under general laws. On the other hand, we can—and we do—relate to living bodies as meaningful and purposeful agents, persons, in Husserl's terminology. In this case, our own activity and interest is not in explaining or predicting the behavior of others, but in responding to their movements and gestures (Husserl Hua4: 183–239/192–250; cf. Stein 1917: 44–60/41–54).

These two attitudes to the living body are not on equal footing. Husserl further argues that the primary way in which living bodies are given to us is personalistic and expressive. We do not experience animal or human bodies primarily as bio-mechanisms or as cultural artifacts, but as expressive means and as functional tools, motivated by sensations and feelings, directed by intentions and purposes, and responsive to affects and appeals.

More fundamentally, my own body is given to me not just as a sensed object, but also as the field of sensations and as the zero point of orientation and movement. It stands out from all the other things in being the only "thing" that I can move immediately and spontaneously. In the final analysis, this means that my body is not a thing among other things but is my connection to all possible thinghood (Heinämaa 2003: 27–37; cf. Stein 1917: 44–47/41–43). The bodies of others are similar to my own body in their constitutive role, but, at the same time, they express sensations, feelings, desires, and volitional acts that are irrecoverably beyond my reach. As such, our living bodies are not fully constituted things, but, as Beauvoir puts it, "our grasp upon the world and the outline of our projects" (Beauvoir [1949] 1993: 73/66, translation modified).

The natural scientific attitude and its physical body and the personalistic attitude and its expressive body represent two different ways of objectifying the body as it is lived in sensations and perceptions. On the one hand, we have the body as a mechanical physical thing theorized by the natural sciences; on the other hand, we the body as an expressive gesture involved in different kinds of practices, interpreted in them and thematized and described by the human sciences. The hierarchical relation between the two attitudes means that the natural scientific objectification is secondary and dependent on the personalistic objectification in its meaning.

Objectifying Death

In *Sickness unto Death*, Kirkegaard warns against the tendency to reduce death to an event or happening in intersubjective time. In *The Concluding Unscientific Postscript*, he refers to the fragility of our existence and writes:

> Suppose death were insidious enough to come tomorrow! Just this uncertainty, if it is to be understood and held firm by an existing person and consequently be thought into everything precisely because it is uncertainty [. . .] so that I make it clear to myself whether I am beginning something worth beginning [. . .]—this uncertainty already gives rise to unbelievable difficulties [. . .] If, however, the uncertainty of death is something in general, then my dying is also something in general. Perhaps dying is something in general for systematicians, for absentminded people. [. . .] But for me, *my* dying is by no means something in general; for others, my dying is some such thing in general. (Kierkegaard [1846] 1960: 166–67)

The idea here is that we should not assume that death is given in a similar way to all persons involved, the dying person, the mourning survivors, and the casual passersby. To be sure, all these people live in the same space-time. The witnesses of death, however, experience a temporal worldly event or a process—devastating perhaps, or unthinkable or unbearable, but proceeding in time and preceding other events.[16] Time, however, is "running out" for one person in a crucial and specific sense, or, as Heidegger put it, "the end is impending" (Heidegger [1927] 1993: §50 250/293). Kierkegaard warns that if we confine ourselves to thinking about death merely as a worldly event, we shut ourselves from death as that which might show us our singular lives "as true" ([1849] 1950: 99; cf. Heidegger [1927] 1993: §47 236–39/279–83). How should we understand this warning? What is at issue here?

The phenomenological account of embodiment helps to understand the problems involved in the tendency to objectify death and consider it merely as a worldly event. It shows that the objectifying of death can take two different forms: a natural scientific objectification and a personalistic objectification. Superficially these are very different, but from the point of view of Kierkegaard's argument about the singularity of death they function in the same way.

In the natural scientific objectification, we think about our death as a natural end of our biological or organic life, similar to the perishing of animals and the wilting and withering of plants, and comparable even to the breakdown of machines, such as the "dying" of an engine.[17] In such reflections, our death is given to us as one natural event among other natural events. One particular organism ceases to exist in objective space and time, but the world itself persists and life goes on. In the second form of objectification, we study and understand ourselves and others as spiritual or meaning-producing persons living in a common world. Accordingly, death is not just an end of an organism but also an end of a unique and original perspective to the world as a whole. Thus the personalistic objectification may seem experientially or emotionally less problematic than the naturalistic one, as it acknowledges that something irreplaceable is lost for ever.[18]

However, from the point of view of Kierkegaard's argument, the personalistic objectification equals the naturalistic one in confusing two senses of dying: own and other. In both objectifications, we insert our own death in objective time, as an event among other events, and avoid thinking through the special kind of temporality that characterizes the ending of our own subjectivity. Instead of facing our own death and understanding its relation to our life, past and present, we postulate a future event in intersubjective time, a worldly event that we ourselves cannot experience or live through but that is given to others basically in the very same way as any other event. The others see it happening, they can empathize with me, and they may mourn my absence, but afterward, when the dreadful moment has passed, they necessarily attend to other things—however senseless or insignificant such things may appear to them in relation to the loss. I however, do not experience any such loss or change, for I have ceased to exist as an experiencing subject. There is a fundamental difference between these two perspectives.

This does not imply that we as survivors are unaffected by the death of others: the loss of a beloved one may color and tone our lives till the end;

and even the death of a total stranger may change our ways of seeing and experiencing the world. Moreover, the other's death may affect our relation to our selves in a fundamental way and turn our lives to a completely new direction. Kierkegaard does not deny any of this but merely points out that the two perspectives—the perspective of the dying person and the perspective of all others—are separate and cannot be reduced one to the other. My death as it is given to me differs from my death as it appears to any other, and the other's death as it is given to him differs from what I can witness happening to him.

Emmanuel Lévinas describes the common basis of the two ways of objectifying death by saying that in both cases death is thought in the perspective of the "survivors" ([1961] 1988: 47–49/55–56; cf. Kierkegaard [1846] 1960: 154–77; Heidegger [1927] 1993: §29 237–40/281–84, 246–47/291). In the scientific objectification, death is inserted into the objective time of natural history; in the personalistic objectification, it is posited as an event in the intersubjective time of human history: "Birth and death as punctuous moments, and the interval that separates them, are lodged in this universal time of the historian, who is a survivor. Interiority as such is a 'nothing,' 'pure thought,' nothing but thought. In the time of the historiographer interiority is the non-being in which everything is possible, for in it nothing is impossible—the 'everything is possible' of madness" (Lévinas [1961] 1988: 55).

Neither form of thinking captures the special form of lived time or immanent temporality that is characteristic of the experience of mortality and the facing of one's own death. In both forms of objectification, we avoid posing the question about our own death and its meaning in the wholeness of our life and the givenness of the world. We think about some related or similar worldly phenomena, the death of animals and plants, the death of our near ones and beloved ones, and fail facing our own death as the "possible impossibility of every way of existing" (Heidegger [1927] 1993: §53 262/307).

Two misunderstandings must be clarified. The point is not that my own death is more important or more significant to me or to my life than the death of someone else. The argument is about the meaning of death, but here "meaning" does not denote worth, valency, or importance, but the intentional structure of experience. So the claim is not that my own death affects me or my life in a more fundamental way than the death of the other, but rather that in order to understand what the other's death means to him, I need to have a relation to my own dying. So an eternal consciousness or an immortal person, such as Virginia Woolf's Orlando or Simone de Beauvoir's

Fosca,[19] can be affected by the deaths of others, even greatly and deeply, but insofar as such persons cannot die, they cannot experience what it means to live with the possibility of dying and thus cannot understand what death means to us humans.

Another possible misunderstanding confuses the question of meaning with the question of knowledge. I may come to realize that I will eventually die, not by reflecting on the processes of my own life, but by experiencing the death of someone else. Children, for example, usually start asking questions about death and mortality when exposed to dead animals; and in adult life, the death of a parent is often an awakening and disenchanting experience. However, the Kierkegaardian argument is not about the way in which we come to realize a possibility, but is about the meaning of this possibility. The argument does not include a stand on the question of how one comes to realize that one dies, but concerns the meaning of this possibility.

So the argument is not that my own death or life is more important or more significant to me than someone else's death or life, but that I can understand the meaning of death only by facing the possibility of my own death, and by studying what implications this "impossible possibility" has to my life here and now.

Kierkegaard's emphasis on one's own death and its significance to the meaning of human life was reinterpreted and elaborated by Martin Heidegger in *Being and Time* (*Sein und Zeit* 1927). Both Beauvoir and Emmanuel Lévinas launched a harsh critique against Heidegger's concept of living-towards-death, Beauvoir in her ethical essays and Lévinas in his early work *Time and the Other* (*Le temps et l'autre* 1947).[20] Neither proposed, however, that we could substitute the other's death for our own death as the basis of meaning constitution. Rather than proposing that the other's death is equal to mine, both argued that the other's life—a newcomer's life—adds an existential dimension to my being-in-the-world and opens a new horizon in inner temporality. Thus both suggested that it is not the other's death but his or her birth and life that is the key to the unlocking of the "Heideggerian trap." The future, the ultimate possibility, which gives meaning and structure to our lives, is not in the horizon of our own finitude and death but in the horizon of the other's appearance, his advent. Whereas Heidegger emphasized that one can take responsibility for one's life—identify one's possibilities and distinguish them from the general possibilities of being human— only by facing the possibility of one's own end, Beauvoir and Lévinas argued that in order to live a human life, we must, necessarily, reach beyond our own time.[21] Lévinas put his main thesis in the beginning of his essay simply:

"[T]ime is not an achievement of an isolated and lone subject, but [...] is the very relationship of the subject with the Other" (Lévinas 1947: 7/39). For Beauvoir the human subject was a freedom but essentially dependent on future others: "[T]o be free is not to have the power to do anything you like; it is to be able to surpass the given toward an open future; the existence of others defines my freedom and is even the condition of my own freedom" (Beauvoir 1947: 127/91).

Beauvoir and Lévinas saw and described the intersubjective character of human futurity in very different ways, but they agreed that this aspect of existence was neglected in Heidegger's interpretation of time and temporality. Neither rejected Heidegger's account of mortality as simply mistaken or wrong; rather both claimed that it was inadequate: it rightly affirmed and explicated Kierkegaard's understanding of the singularity of death but wrongly concluded that our ownmost being is being-towards-death. In order to understand this dispute and the differences between these conceptions of temporality and futurity, it is necessary to be familiar with the basic results of the phenomenological analysis of inner temporality developed by Husserl in the 1910s.[22] The end of this chapter undertakes this task and also provides an overview of Husserl's reflections on death. This provides the background for the explication of the dispute between Heidegger and his critics.

Inner Time and the Impossibility of Dying

The core of Husserl's analysis of time is in the argument that lived time, time as we experience it in sensations, perceptions, and cognitive and volitional acts, is not a series of punctual moments but a unity with a complex inner structure (see esp. Husserl Hua10, Hua11: 125–45/170–92; cf. Lévinas [1940] 1998: 77–78; Merleau-Ponty [1945] 1993: 100/84, 469–79/410–19). Each moment bears internal references to all other moments, and each opens up into two directions, the past and the future.[23] Thus understood, no moment of our lives is a self-enclosed point, but each moment has a complex internal structure and each is intertwined with other moments, forming a multidimensional texture of living. The objectivistic notion of time proves to be illusory or else a dependent notion: fundamentally time is not given to us as a series of discrete moments without any cross-references but constitutes itself as a unified continuity in which every moment refers to all other moments.

Husserl distinguished this inner time or lived time from the objective time that is shared equally by all conscious beings and includes all entities and facts that can be experienced by any conscious self. Moreover, he argued that the constitution of all experience and all experienced objects, practical and theoretical, natural and historical, is based on the constitution of inner time. Thus no object can be given to us unless time constitutes itself for us in the stream of our experiences. The exact time of the natural sciences is based on the shared time of intersubjective communion, and this, in turn, is based on the internal time of lived experience. Lévinas explains the main idea in an illuminative way: "[Inner] time, which Husserl distinguishes from objective time [...], is thus not the form of a stream of consciousness which would be like another being facing the being of the world. The intentions and sensations which are immanent to the stream of consciousness are not a sort of psychological reality [...]; they are implicated in the meaning of this deep subjectivity, about which one can no longer say that is a being" (Lévinas [1940] 1998: 77–78).[24]

Husserl's account of the constitution of time and of the structure of inner temporality has important implications for our conceptions of death. Especially, three points need to be emphasized, because they affected later existential-phenomenological discussions on death.

First, Husserl argues that birth and death are not just empirical issues— biological, medical, psychological, or moral issues—but have a transcendental significance. In the late work *The Crisis of European Sciences* (*Die Krisis der europäischen Wissenschaften und die transzendentale Phänomenologie* 1936–37, 1954), he outlined the range of transcendental-phenomenological inquiries by explaining that its problems encompass "all living beings insofar as they have, even indirectly but still verifiably, something like 'life'" (Husserl Hua6: 191/188). He then continued: "Also appearing thereby, in different steps, first in respect to human beings and then universally, are the problems of generativity, the problems of transcendental historicity [...] further there are the problems of birth and death and the transcendental constitution of their meaning as world occurrences [*Weltvorkommnisse*]" (Husserl Hua6: 191–92/187–88, cf. Hua1 169/142, Hua15: 37–38, 138, Hua27: 98, Hua34: 473–75, Ms. C 17 85b quoted in Steinbock 1995: 304; Heidegger [1927] 1993: §49 246–48/290–91).

To these Husserl added "the problem of the sexes" and "the problem of the 'unconscious.'" The task in all these cases is to explicate how the object in question can appear to us as it does. We ask, for example, how certain phenomena are constituted as singular things or singular events and others are given to us as general states of affairs or essences. Thus, the phenomenologist analyzes the meanings involved in the phenomena and shows how such meanings are constituted in the stream of experience and in the communicative relation between separate, even diachronic, streams of experience. In the case of death, the phenomenologist asks, for example, "How can my own death be given to me as a worldly occurrence?" and "How can the birth of the other extend the temporal horizons of my experience?"

Birth and death are transcendental problems for the phenomenologists, because the phenomenological method discloses the transcendental self as thoroughly temporal. The self thus discovered is very different from the universal and atemporal subject that Kant presented, and it also differs from all forms of subjectivity that presuppose an all-encompassing world soul.[25] Husserl's ego is concrete, personal; it is a temporal formation that changes and develops in internal time of flowing experiences (Heinämaa 2007). Correspondingly, the transcendental foundation of objectivity is not in any universal subjectivity but in the transcendental community of personal temporal selves. Such a foundation is not homogeneous or unitary but is multiple and heterogeneous (Heinämaa 2010).

So the transcendental self, as disclosed by phenomenology, is not a universal structure or an empty form but is a temporal person intentionally tied to its own living body and, through its body, related to other intending selves and to material things. Some of these others are contemporary, given to the self as coexisting or living "at the same time" or in the same historical situation with it; others are antecedents or successors, who have lived before or who will live later. Some others can be faced in simple perception, while other others can be reached only by the medium of language, speech and writing (Husserl Hua1: 156–63/126–36, cf. Hua15: e.g. 38, 163–164, 218, 416–18, 428–31, 613–57).[26] Husserl's main teaching about constitution is that I am dependent on all these others in the constitution of the meaning of the objective world. In a manuscript, he explains: "Transcendentally the world is a constitutive product of transcendentally awakened subjects with one another [. . .] in the unity of tradition—this tradition that constitutes itself in the world beyond the 'pauses' [of the] birth and death of the individual" (Husserl Ms. C 17 85a quoted in Steinbock 1995: 304).[27]

This means that I am not the sole source of all meaning or a solitary creator of the existing world. To be sure, I can intend another intending self only because I can intend myself as a sensing-sensed body, and in this respect my relation to myself is primary (Hua1: 121–43/89–113, Hua6: 220–21/216–18). But this does not imply that all meaning would stem from me or that the other would be merely a meaning to me. On the contrary, I need the others in order to be able to experience the objective world and my own body and soul as parts of the objective world.

Husserl's second influential thesis about death concerns the immortality of the pure transcendental self. He states: "The pure subject does not arise or vanish" (Hua4: 103/109), and again "the transcendental self cannot die and cannot be born" (Hua11: 379–81/469–71, cf. Hua29: 332–33, Hua14: 156–57). This is often misunderstood as a statement about some specific sort of object: an immortal soul or an eternal spirit residing in a nonmaterial world above the world of perception. But Husserl explicitly rejects such readings (Husserl Hua11: App. 2 §10 377/467; cf. Heidegger [1925] 1979: 315). What is at issue is not any atemporal or supratemporal object but the structure of time as the ultimate basis of all being and objectivity (Merleau-Ponty [1945] 1993: 483–84/422–23).

Husserl's thesis about the immortality of the pure self concerns the unity of inner time: every intentional experience directed to whatever object, internal or external, thingly or non-thingly, real or ideal, bears in itself a reference to other experiences, preceding and following it in inner time (Husserl Hua11 378/467–68, Hua 14: 156–57; cf. Merleau-Ponty [1945] 1993: 249/215). If every moment by necessity includes a reference to a future moment, then it is not possible to have a "last moment" that would lack all reference to subsequent moments.

Our expectations and anticipations of the future can be minor, and they can be devastating, and in the nearness of death or in the process of dying they often are: there is no time to do anything anymore, no time for goodbyes, consolation, or forgiveness, just another gasp for breath or another moment of pain. However, the idea that we could live through or experience our death is illusory; the idea of a last moment that would not include any reference to future is a construct or else derived from the experience of the other's death. Husserl's analysis of the confusion is stringent: from the thought about the possible cessation of every conceivable particular object, one illegitimately moves to the thought of a putative cessation of a stream of life that gives us all such objects. "The cessation itself as cessation of the object presupposes non-cessation, namely, consciousness to which the cessation is given" (Husserl Hua11: 377/467).

Our expectations of future can of course be disappointed; things may turn out quite different than we supposed, and our life can be much shorter than we hoped and believed. But to experience or live through our own death would mean that we could pass from a future-bound present to a last putative moment completely closed from all future and all futurity. In the light of the analysis of inner time-consciousness, this is non-sense.

Husserl's discourse on immortality explicates Epicuros's famous argument according to which death "is nothing to us, seeing that, when we are, death is not come, and when death is come, we are not" (Laertius 1925: 10 125). It shows that the basis of Epicuros's intuition is based on the structures of lived temporality.[28] Merelau-Ponty summarizes the reflection as follows: "Neither my birth nor my death can appear to me as experiences of my own, since, if I thought of them thus, I should be assuming myself to be pre-existent to, or outliving, myself, in order to experience them, and I should therefore not be genuinely thinking my birth or my death" (Merleau-Ponty [1945] 1993: 249/215; cf. 418/364, cf. Heidegger [1927] 1993: §47 237–38/281; Lévinas 1947: 59–60/71–73).

Husserl's third argument concerns our possibilities of experiencing our own deaths as worldly occurrences. He does not deny this possibility but argues that it depends on our relation to other conscious selves: I could not experience myself as a body among other similar bodies or my death as a worldly event among other events, unless I had other sensing and perceiving selves given to me in experience. Without reference to other experiencing selves, my death would be given to me merely as the unattainable limit of inner time.

This means that I can objectify my death and birth as worldly events only because I have others who can witness such events, or, in other words, I am dependent on others in being able to give the meaning "worldly event," "occurrence," and "happening" to my own death. On the other hand, this dependence also means that my experience of the event of my death is not original, but is mediated, as if "secondhand." I can think this event and imagine it thanks to the existence of others, but it is not given to me in first person, and this is by necessity.

So my death gains a richer meaning through my relations with others; the sense "worldly event" is included in it. Despite this transcendental fact, the original meaning of an immanent limit persists, remains valid, and structures my life.

Martin Heidegger reinterpreted these phenomenological and existential results with his influential concept of being-toward-death. The task of the next chapter is to explicate Heidegger's concept and to investigate through it the phenomenological idea that one's own death provides the primary horizon of life. I will argue that Heidegger's conceptualization captures an important aspect of meaning constitution and that the other's death is dependent on my own death at the level of meaning constitution.

After this constructive reading, I will turn to study three forms of critique that Heidegger's contemporary phenomenologists launched against his concept of being-towards-death: the critiques of Emmanuel Lévinas, Hannah Arendt, and Simone de Beauvoir. All these three thinkers argued that, despite the primacy of my own death, I owe to the other a certain temporal aspect or dimension of my life. However, none of the phenomenologists wanted to simply substitute the *other's death* for my own death as a foundation of meaning. Rather they all argued that it is the *other's birth or natality* that opens a new dimension into my temporality or liberates me from my own beginning. So what they all propose is a complex description of mutual dependences, and not any simply progression from a "necrophilic" philosophy to a "biophilic" one.

NOTES

1. Kierkegaard's most important distinction is between the aesthetic (egocentric), the ethical (social), and the religious (absolute). This distinction is reconceptualized by Beauvoir (1947) as the distinction between the infantile, the serious, and the authentic, and by Lévinas (1961) as the distinction between the sensible, the economical, and the ethical. For Kierkegaard's distinction, see his *The Concept of Anxiety* (*Begrebet angest* 1844) and *Concluding Unscientific Postscript* (*Afsluttende uvidenskabelig Efterskrift til de philosophiske smuler* 1846). For an illuminative overview of his arguments, see Liehu 1990.

2. Historically, Beauvoir's account belongs to the philosophical discourse prior to the so-called linguistic turn. The lack of the linguistic framework can of course be taken as a drawback, but on the other hand it also means that Beauvoir's account is free from certain assumptions about the relationship between linguistic-conceptual thinking and perceptual experience, shared by contemporary analytical and Continental schools of philosophizing. With other early phenomenologists, she recognizes and theorizes a layer of experience prior to language and linguistic representation. For this, see Heinämaa 2010.

3. I will use the pronouns "he" and "his" in the general, non-gendered sense throughout my three chapters.

4. An expression that Kierkegaard uses in his journals (1996).

5. Cf. Liehu (1990: 43–61). For Kierkegaard's account of the paradoxes of human existence, see Theunissen [1993] 2005 and Pattison 2005. For Kierkegaard's relation to Hegel, see Stewart 2003.

6. The thesis of *Sickness unto Death* is that the self cannot arrive at an equilibrium by itself, but only by relating to God ([1849] 1950: 242–43/44). It is debatable whether this captures Kierkegaard's position, for the author of the book is not given as "Søren Kierkegaard" but as "Anti-Climacus," and Kierkegaard's other works present other alternatives.

7. Françoise Dastur explains that this identification of the self with the ideal is motivated by two concerns, by the interest to capture a totality of the given at once and by the interest to transcend sensible nature (1994: 4–5).

8. Sylvia Walsh (1997) attacks Kierkegaard's distinction between feminine and masculine forms of despair on two grounds: on the one hand, she argues that the distinction does not cohere with Kierkegaard's general concept of selfhood, and on the other hand, she argues that the distinction merely repeats sexual stereotypes and fails

to capture anything of concrete human existence. For a religious, Christian, reading of the same material, see Howe 1997.

9. Compare to Aristotle's characterization of contemplation in *Nicomachean Ethics*: "Such a life as this however will be higher than the human life: not in virtue of his humanity will a man achieve it, but in virtue of something within him that is divine" (Aristotle *Nicomachean Ethics* X 7 1177b27–29; cf. Heidegger [1927] 1993: §10 49/74–75).

10. For an interpretation of Beauvoir's discussion of our detest of flesh and "the slimy," see Heinämaa 2009.

11. Compare to Luce Irigaray's religious-ethical formulation in *An Ethics of Sexual Difference* (*Éthique de la différence sexuelle* 1984): "The third era of the West might, at last, be the era of the *couple*: of the spirit and the bride? [. . .] The spirit is not imprisoned only in the Father-son duality. The spirit eludes this 'couple.' The event is announced in the Gospel itself: the female, the women partake not in the Last supper but in the Pentecost, and it is they who discover and announce the resurrection. This seems to say that the body of man can return to life when woman no longer forgets that she has a share in the spirit" (Irigaray 1984: 140/149).

12. Compare Nietzsche's proposal to Kierkegaard's diagnosis of the condition of our theological thinking, in *The Concept of Anxiety*: "If men had pursued further the ancient idea that man is a synthesis of soul and body, which is constituted by spirit, men would long since have thought more precisely with regard to sin and hereditary sin, its origin and its consequences" (Kierkegaard [1844] 1980: 195).

13. At the beginning of her philosophical carrier, Beauvoir was captivated by Hegel's rationalism and idealism, but already before the publication of her first works, *She Came to Stay* (*L'invitée* 1941) and *Pyrrhus and Cineas* (*Pyrrhus et Cinéas* 1944), she started to question Hegel's idealism and turned (back) to the fathers of existentialism, Kierkegaard and Nietzsche (Beauvoir [1930–39] 1990: 335–36, 366, 369, [1960] 1995: 537/468–69).

14. For a detailed account of these two attitudes, see Heinämaa (2003: 21–51).

15. The phenomenon is known as "double sensation" or "double apprehension" (Husserl Hua4: 147/155; Stein 1917: 47–48/43–44; Merleau-Ponty [1945] 1993: 109/93). For a discussion of the foundation of this phenomenon, see Al-Saji 2010.

16. Merleau-Ponty argues that such experiences disclose two different layers of experience, the personal and the anonymous: "While I am overcome by some grief and wholly given over to my distress, my eyes already stray in front of me, and are drawn, despite everything, to some shining object" (cf. Merleau-Ponty [1945] 1993: 100/84).

17. For a philosophical explication of the bioscientific concept of life, see Sterelny and Griffiths 1999.

18. For an illuminative account of the phenomenology of events, see Zarader 2006.

19. Fosca is the main character of Beauvoir's novel *All Men Are Mortal* (*Tous les hommes sont mortels* 1946). Orlando is Woolf's main character in the novel by the same name (1928). In addition to being immortal, Orlando also appears in different sexual forms and figures: s/he lives both as a woman and as a man.

20. Both Beauvoir and Lévinas use the French term *être pour mourir* for Heidegger's concept of being-towards-death. This is somewhat misleading as the word *pour* gives the impression that life is put in the service of death. Even though Heidegger's living-towards-death means living in the anticipation of death, it does not imply that life serves death, in any sense of the word, or that life-goals are determined

by the necessity of dying. For this reason, I translate the French *être pour mourir* into "being towards death," and not as "being for death" as some translators have decided to do (e.g. Timmermann and Keltner 2004: 146n67). Cf. Dastur (1994: 40).

21. All these thinkers can be characterized as "Judeo-Christian" in the philosophical (nonreligious) sense of thinking life in terms of the future (Derrida [1992] 1995). For the Kierkegaardian background of both these conceptions of futurity (my future death and the future of the other), see Pattison (2005: 142). For the phenomenological origin, see Husserl's account of generativity (e.g., Hua15: 171–73).

22. Husserl presented his original analysis of inner time-consciousness in his lectures in 1904–10. These lectures were edited by Husserl's assistant Edith Stein and published by Heidegger in 1928. A few years later, Lévinas explained the main results of Husserl's analysis in his study *The Theory of Intuition in Husserl's Phenomenology* (*Théorie de l'intuition dans la phénoménologie de Husserl* 1930). At the same time, Beauvoir studied the German edition of the lectures, as she says, "with great enthusiasm" (Beauvoir [1960] 1995 231/201, cf. 1981: 247/172).

23. Husserl calls these modes of consciousness *retention* and *protention*. For a good introduction into these topics see Zahavi (2003: 80–98). For the later developments of Husserl's reflections of time see Kortooms 2002, Rodemayer 2003, Zahavi 2004.

24. For a detailed account of Lévinas's complex relation to Husserl's phenomenology of time, see Bernet 2002.

25. Plotinian or Hegelian.

26. Cf. Römpp 1989; Steinbock 1995: 190. In his manuscripts, Husserl developed rich and detailed analyses of the different senses of intersubjectivity and their constitutional relations (Hua13–15).

27. Anthony Steinbock argues that in the latest phases of his thinking Husserl developed a generative phenomenology in distinction from the earlier static and genetic versions. Further, Steinbock argues that only a generative phenomenological approach can account for phenomena such as birth and death (Steinbock 1995, 1998, 2001: xxxiii–xxxiv).

28. The phenomenological reading of Epicuros's statement is different from the discussion central to contemporary analytical philosophy. In the latter the main concern is the "harm" that death causes or may cause (see, e.g., Luper 1996, 2003). The main issue for phenomenology is not the issue of harm or happiness but the internal connection of all experience in temporality.

BIBLIOGRAPHY

Note: Date in square brackets is the original publication date; the following date is the edition cited. Where two sets of page numbers are given in citations in text, the first is the cited edition in the original language, and the second is the English edition.

Al-Saji, Alia. 2010. "Bodies and Sensings: On the Uses of Husserlian Phenomenology for Feminist Theory." *Continental Philosophy Review* 43, no. 1, 13–37.
Aristotle: *Nicomachean Ethics*. Trans. H. Rackham. Cambridge, Mass.: Harvard University Press, 1994.

Beauvoir, Simone de. [1930–39] 1990. *Letters to Sartre*. Trans. and ed. Quintin Hoare from the French edition of Sylvie Le Bon de Beauvoir. London: Vitange.

———. 1941. *L'invitée*. Paris: Gallimard. In English *She Came to Stay*. Trans. Yvonne Moyse and Roger Senhouse. London: Flamingo, 1984.

———. 1944. *Pyrrhus et Cinéas*. Paris: Gallimard. In English *Pyrrhus and Cineas*. Trans. Marybeth Timmermann. In *Philosophical Writings by Simone de Beauvoir*. Ed. M. A. Simons and S. Le Bon de Beauvoir, 92–149. Beauvoir Series 1. Urbana: University of Illinois Press, 2004.

———. 1946. *Tous les hommes sont mortels*. Paris: Gallimard. In English *All Men Are Mortal*. Trans. Leonard M. Freidman. New York: W. W. Norton, 1992.

———. 1947. *Pour une morale de l'ambiguïté*. Paris: Gallimard. In English *The Ethics of Ambiguity*. Trans. Bernard Frechtman. New York: Carol Publishing Group Editions, 1994.

———. [1949] 1991. *Le deuxième sexe II: l'expérience vécue*. Paris: Gallimard. In English *The Second Sex*, ed. and trans. H. M. Parshley. Harmondsworth: Penguin, 1987.

———. [1949] 1993. *Le deuxième sexe I: les faits et les mythes*. Paris: Gallimard. In English *The Second Sex*. Ed. and trans. H. M. Parshley. Harmondsworth: Penguin, 1987.

———. [1955] 1994. *Les mandarins II*. Paris: Gallimard. In English *The Mandarins*. Trans. Leonard M. Friedman. London: Harper Perennial, 1991.

———. [1960] 1995. *La force de l'âge*. Paris: Gallimard. In English *The Prime of Life*. Trans. Peter Green. Harmondsworth: Penguin, 1981.

———. 1981. "*La cérémonie des adieux*" suivi de "*Entretiens avec Jean-Paul Sartre: août–septembre 1974*." Paris: Gallimard. In English *Adieux: A Farewell to Sartre*. Trans. Patrick O'Brian. New York: Pantheon Books, 1984.

Bernet, Rudolf. 2002. "Levinas' Critique of Husserl." In *The Cambridge Companion to Levinas*, ed. Simon Critchely and Robert Bernasconi, 82–99. Cambridge: Cambridge University Press.

Dastur, Françoise. 1994. *La mort: essay sur la finitude*. Paris: Hatier. In English *An Essay on Finitude*. Trans. J. Llewelyn. London: Athlone, 1996.

Derrida, Jacques. [1992] 1995. *The Gift of Death*. Trans. David Wills. Chicago: University of Chicago Press. Original "Donner la mort," in *L'éthique du don, Jacques Derrida et la pensée du don*.

Heidegger, Martin. [1925] 1979. *Prolegomena zur Geschichte des Zeitbegriffs, Gesamtausgabe, II. Abteilung: Vorlesungen 1923–1944, Band 20*. Ed. Petra Jaeger. Frankfurt: Vittorio Klostermann. In English *History of the Concept of Time*. Trans. Theodore Kisiel. Bloomington: Indiana University Press, 1992.

———. [1927] 1993. *Sein und Zeit*. Tübingen: Max Niemeyer. In English *Being and Time*. Trans. John Macquarrie and Edward Robinson. Oxford: Blackwell, 1992.

Heinämaa, Sara. 2003. *Toward a Phenomenology of Sexual Difference: Husserl, Merleau-Ponty, Beauvoir*. Lanham, Md.: Rowman and Littlefield.

———. 2007. "Selfhood, Consciousness, and Embodiment: A Husserlian Approach." In *Consciousness: From Perception to Reflection in the History of Philosophy*, ed. Sara Heinämaa, Pauliina Remes, and Vili Lähteenmäki, 311–28. Dordrecht: Springer.

———. 2009. "Psychoanalysis of Things: Objective Meanings or Subjective Projections." In *Beauvoir and Sartre: The Riddle of Influence*, ed. Christine Daigle and Jacob Golomb. Bloomington: Indiana University Press.

————. 2010. "A Phenomenology of Sexual Difference: Types, Styles, and Persons." In *Feminist Metaphysics: Explorations in the Ontology of Sex, Gender and Identity*, ed. Charlotte Witt. Dordrecht: Springer.

Howe, Leslie A. 1997. "Kierkegaard and the Feminine Self." In *Feminist Interpretations of Kierkegaard*, ed. Céline Léon and Sylvia Walsh, 217–47. University Park: Pennsylvania University Press.

Husserl, Edmund. Hua1. *Cartesianische Meditationen und pariser Vorträge*. Ed. Stephan Strasser. The Hague: Martinus Nijhoff, 1950. In English *Cartesian Meditations*. Trans. Dorion Cairns. Dordrecht, Boston: Martinus Nijhoff, 1960.

————. Hua4. *Ideen zu einer reinen Phänomenologie und phänomenologischen Philosophie. Zweites Buch: Phänomenologische Untersuchungen zur Konstitution*. Ed. Marly Bimel. The Hague: Martinus Nijhoff, 1952. In English *Ideas Pertaining to a Pure Phenomenology and to a Phenomenological Philosophy. 2nd book: Studies in the Phenomenological Constitution*. Trans. Richard Rojcewicz and André Schuwer. Dordrecht: Kluwer Academic Publishers, 1993.

————. Hua6. *Die Krisis der europäischen Wissenschaften und die transzendentale Phänomenologie: Eine Einleitung in die phänomenologische Philosophie*. Ed. Walter Biemel. The Hague: Martinus Nijhoff, 1954. In English *The Crisis of European Sciences and Transcendental Phenomenology: An Introduction to Phenomenological Philosophy*. Trans. David Carr. Evanston, Ill.: Northwestern University, 1988.

————. Hua10. *Zur Phänomenologie des inneren Zeitbewusstseins (1893–1917)*. Ed. Rudolf Boehm. The Hague: Martinus Nijhoff, 1969.

————. Hua11. *Analysen zur passiven Synthesis: Aus Vorlesungs- und Forschungsmanuskripten, 1918–1926*. Ed. Margot Fleischer. The Hague: Martinus Nijhoff, 1966. In English *Analyses Concerning Passive and Active Synthesis: Lectures on Transcendental Logic*. Trans. Anthony Steinbock. Dordrecht: Kluwer Academic Publishers, 2001.

————. Hua13. *Zur Phänomenologie der Intersubjektivität, Texte aus dem Nachlass, Erster Teil: 1905–1920*. Ed. Iso Kern. The Hague: Martinus Nijhoff, 1973.

————. Hua14. *Zur Phänomenologie der Intersubjektivität, Texte aus dem Nachlass, Zweiter Teil: 1921–1928*. Ed. Iso Kern. The Hague: Martinus Nijhoff, 1973.

————. Hua15. *Zur Phänomenologie der Intersubjektivität, Texte aus dem Nachlass, Dritter Teil: 1929–1935*. Ed. Iso Kern. The Hague: Martinus Nijhoff, 1973.

————. Hua27. *Aufsätze und Vorträge, 1922–1937*. Ed. T. Nenon and H. R. Sepp. Dordrecht: Kluwer Academic Publishers, 1988.

———— Hua29. *Die Krisis der europäischen Wissenschaften und die transzendentale Phänomenologie. Ergänzungsband, Texte aus dem Nachlass 1934–1937*. Ed. Reinhold N. Smid. The Hague: Kluwer Academic Publishers, 1992.

————. Hua34. *Zur phänomenologischen Reduktion, Texte aus dem Nachlass (1926–1935)*. Ed. Sebastian Luft. Dordrecht: Kluwer Academic Publishers, 2002.

Irigaray, Luce. 1984. *Éthique de la différence sexuelle*. Paris: Minuit. In English *An Ethics of Sexual Difference*. Trans. Carolyn Burke and Gillian C. Gill. Ithaca, N.Y.: Cornell University Press, 1993.

Jantzen, Grace M. 1998. "Necrophilia and Natality: What Does It Mean to Be Religious?" *Scottish Journal of Religious Studies* 19, no. 1: 101–21.

———. 2003. "The Horizon of Natality: Gadamer, Heidegger, and the Limits of Existence." In *Feminist Interpretations of Hans-Georg Gadamer,* ed. Lorraine Code, 285–306. University Park: Pennsylvania University Press.
———. 2004. *Foundations of Violence.* Vol. 1: *Death and the Displacement of Beauty.* London: Routledge.
Kierkegaard, Søren. [written] [1842–43] 2001. *Johannes Climacus, Or A Life of Doubt.* Revised and ed. Jane Chamberline, trans. T. H. Croxhall. Original unpublished manuscript *Johannes Climacus eller De omnibus dubitandum est.*
———. [1843] 1950. *Frygt og Bæven, Dialektisk lyrik.* In *Værker i udvalg II: Filosofen og teologen.* Ed. F. J. Billeskov Jansen. København: Nordisk forlag. In English *Fear and Trembling—Repetition, Kierkegaard's Writings, VI.* Trans. Howard V. Hong and Edna H. Hong. Princeton, N.J.: Princeton University Press, 1983.
———. [1844] 1980. *The Concept of Anxiety: A Simple Psychologically Orienting Deliberation on the Dogmatic Issue of Hereditary Sin.* Trans. Reidar Thome in collaboration with Albert A. Anderson. Princeton, N.J.: Princeton University Press. Original *Begrebet angest (af Vigilius Haufniensis).*
———. [1846] 1960. *Concluding Unscientific Postscript.* Trans. David F. Swenson, trans. completed by Walter Lowrie. Princeton, N.J.: Princeton University Press. Original *Afsluttende uvidenskabelig Efterskrift til de philosophiske smuler.*
———. [1849] 1950. *Sygdommen til døden af Anti-Climacus.* In *Værker i udvalg II: Filosofen og teologen.* Ed. F. J. Billeskov Jansen. København: Nordisk forlag. In English *Sickness unto Death by Anti-Climacus.* Trans. Alastair Hannay. Harmondsworth: Penguin, 1989.
———. 1996. *Papers and Journals: A Selection.* Trans. Alastair Hannay. Harmondsworth: Penguin Press.
Kortooms, Toine. 2002. *Phenomenology of Time: Edmund Husserl's Analysis of Time-Consciousness.* Dordrecht: Kluwer Academic Publishers.
Laertius, Diogenes. 1925. *Lives of Eminent Philosophers.* Trans. R. D. Hicks, Books 6–10. Cambridge, Mass.: Harvard University Press.
Lévinas, Emmanuel. [1930] 1963. *Théorie de l'intuition dans la phénoménologie de Husserl.* Paris: Vrin. In English *The Theory of Intuition in Husserl's Phenomenology.* 2nd ed. Trans. André Orianne. Evanston, Ill.: Northwestern University Press, 1995.
———. [1940] 1998. "The Work of Edmund Husserl." In *Discovering Existence with Husserl.* Ed. and trans. Richard A. Cohen and Michael B. Smith. Evanston, Ill.: Northwestern University Press, 47–87. Original "L'œuvre d'Edmond Husserl."
———. 1947. *Le temps et l'autre.* Paris: Quadrige/PUF. In English *Time and the Other.* Trans. Richard A. Cohen. Pittsburg, Pennsylvania, 1987.
———. [1961] 1988. *Totalité et infini: essai sur l'extériorité.* Paris: Kluwer. In English *Totality and Infinity: An Essay on Exteriority.* Trans. Alphonso Lingis. Pittsburgh: Duquesne University Press, 1969.
Liehu, Heidi. 1990. *Søren Kierkegaard's Theory of Stages and Its Relation to Hegel.* Acta Philosophica Fennica, vol. 47. Helsinki: Philosophical Society of Finland.
Lloyd, Genevieve. 1984. *The Man of Reason: "Male" and "Female" in Western Philosophy.* London: Methuen.
———. 1993. "Maleness, Metaphor, and the 'Crisis' of Reason." In *A Mind of One's Own: Feminist Essays on Reason and Objectivity,* ed. Louise M. Anthony and Charlotte Witt, 69–83. Boulder: Westview.

Luper, Steven. 1996. *Invulnerability: On Securing Happiness*. Chicago: Open Court.
———. 2003. *The Philosophy of Death*. Cambridge: Cambridge University Press.
Merleau-Ponty, Maurice. [1945] 1993. *Phénoménologie de la perception*. Paris: Gallimard. In English *Phenomenology of Perception*. Trans. Collin Smith. New York: Routledge and Kegan Paul, 1995.
Morris, Phyllis Sutton. 1999. "Sartre on Objectification." In *Feminist Interpretations of Jean-Paul Sartre*, ed. Julien S. Murphy, 64–89. University Park: Pennsylvania State University Press.
Nietzsche, Friedrich. [1882] 1994. *Die fröliche Wissenschaft ("La gaya scieza")*, *Werke in drei Bänden, Band 2*. Köln: Könemann. In English *The Gay Science ("La gaya scieza")*. Trans. Josefine Nauckhoff. Cambridge: Cambridge University Press, 2001.
Pattisson, Georg. 2005. *The Philosophy of Kierkegaard*. Chesham: Acumen.
Reuter, Martina. 2006. "The Significance of Gendered Metaphors." *Nora: Nordic Journal of Women's Studies* 14, no. 3: 151–69.
Rodemeyer, Lanei. 2003. "Developments in the Theory of Time-Consciousness: An Analysis of Protention." In *The New Husserl: A Critical Reader*, ed. Donn Welton, 125–54. Bloomington: Indiana University Press.
Römpp, G. 1989. "Der Andere als Zukunft und Gegenwart: Zur Interpretation der Erfahrung fremder Personalität in temporalen Begriffen bei Lévinas und Husserl." *Husserl Studies* 6, no. 2: 129–54.
Sartre, Jean-Paul. [1943] 1998. *L'être et le néant: essai d'ontologie phénoménologique*. Paris: Gallimard. In English *Being and Nothingness: A Phenomenological Essay on Ontology*. Trans. Hazel E. Barnes. New York: Washington Square Press.
Stein, Edith. 1917. *Zum Problem der Einfühlung*. Halle: Buchdruckerei des Weisenhauses. In English *On the Problem of Empathy*. 3rd rev. ed. Trans. Waltraut Stein. Vol. 3 of *The Collected Works of Edith Stein*. Washington, D.C.: ICS Publications.
Steinbock, Anthony. 1995. *Home and Beyond: Generative Phenomenology after Husserl*. Evanston, Ill.: Northwestern University Press.
———. 1998. "Liminality and Liminal Experience." *Alter: revue de phénoménologie* 6: 275–96.
———. 2001. Translator's introduction. In Edmund Husserl, *Analyses Concerning Passive and Active Synthesis: Lectures on Transcendental Logic*, xv–lxvii. Dordrecht: Kluwer Academic Publishers.
Sterelny, Kim, and Paul E. Griffiths. 1999. *Sex and Death: An Introduction to Philosophy of Biology*. Chicago: University of Chicago Press.
Stewart, Jon. 2003. *Kierkegaard's Relation to Hegel Reconsidered*. Cambridge: Cambridge University Press.
Theunissen, Michael. [1993] 2005. *Kierkegaard's Concept of Despair*. Trans. Barbara Harshav and Helmut Illbruck. Princeton, N.J.: Princeton University Press.
Timmermann, Marybeth, and Stacy Keltner. 2004. Notes [to Beauvoir's *Pyrrhus and Cineas*]. In *The Beauvoir Series*, vol. 1: *Philosophical Writings by Simone de Beauvoir*. Ed. Margaret A. Simons and Sylvie Le Bon de Beauvoir, 141–49. Urbana: University of Illinois Press.
Walsh, Sylvia. 1997. "On 'Feminine' and 'Masculine' Forms of Despair." In *Feminist Interpretations of Kierkegaard*, ed. Céline Léon and Sylvia Walsh, 203–15. University Park: Pennsylvania University Press.
Woolf, Virginia. [1928] 1998. *Orlando*. Harmondsworth: Penguin.

Zahavi, Dan 2003. *Husserl's Phenomenology*. Stanford, Calif.: Stanford University Press.
———. 2004. "Time and Consciousness in the Bernau Manuscripts." *Husserl Studies* 20, no. 2: 99–118.
Zarader, Marlene. 2006. "The Event—between Phenomenology and History." In *The Past's Presence: Essays on the Historicity of Philosophical Thinking*, ed. Marcia Sá Cavalcante Schuback and Hans Ruin, 25–54. Södertörn Philosophical Studies 3. Huddinge, Sweden: Söderntörn högskola.

FIVE

Being towards Death
SARA HEINÄMAA

Martin Heidegger presents his much-discussed and often criticized concept of being-towards-death in *Being and Time* in chapter 4, which deals with being as care and Dasein's necessary incompleteness.[1] In a well-known paragraph on the existential-ontological structure of death, he writes:

> With death, Dasein stands before itself in its ownmost potentiality-for-Being. This is a possibility in which the issue is nothing less than Dasein's Being-in-the-world. Its death is the possibility of no-longer being-able-to-be-there. If Dasein stands before itself as this possibility, it has been fully assigned to its ownmost potentiality-for-Being. When it stands before itself in this way, all its relations to any other Dasein have been undone. (Heidegger [1927] 1993: §50 250/294, cf. [1925] 1979: 317–18)

And some paragraphs later: "Death is Dasein's *ownmost* possibility" (Heidegger [1927] 1993: §53 263/307). What is characteristic to Heidegger's interpretation of death and what also comes up in these central paragraphs is the idea that primarily death must be seen as a relation to oneself and as a differentiation from others. The argument is liable to many sorts of misunderstandings, but the Kierkegaardian and Husserlian background outlined in the previous chapter helps to delineate and explicate Heidegger's main point.

Heidegger's relation to these two starting points is very different. Whereas he affirms Kierkegaard's analyses of mortality and anxiety as mainly correct even if preparatory, he explicitly rejects Husserl's understanding of personal existence and attacks his analysis of time-consciousness (Heidegger [1927] 1993: §10 45–48/71–74, §69a 363/414, 498, cf. [1925] 1979: 165–74/119–25).[2] Heidegger argues that Husserl's concept of time-consciousness, and consequently his whole account of personal existence, is preoccupied with the present and with the actual, and must be corrected by a new interpretation of being that correctly characterizes the role of future and the possible in our experience of temporality. He does not question Husserl's arguments about the interconnectedness of the three dimensions of temporality—past, present, and future—but he attacks the assumption that future can be conceived on the basis of the present. Heidegger's discussion of death gets its special character from this emphasis on the future, and the concept of being-towards-death must be understood in this light.

Individuation and Dying

Heidegger's main argument is that my death is an impossible possibility that, when faced, is able to individuate me, to give my life its singularity by distinguishing my possibilities from the possibilities of human life in general (Heidegger [1927] 1993: §53 266/310). Through the impossible possibility of my own ceasing to exist, I identify myself with my own concrete possibilities, which are historically and contextually specific. What is at issue is not any cognitive or objective situating of oneself but an affective, practical, and active engagement. The experience of facing or encountering the extreme possibility of death, the cessation of all my projects and possibilities and the end of my world, awakens me to my being-there (Dastur 1998: 26–27, 38; Carr [1986] 1991: 81–82). Thus I am liberated from the false identification with the abstract possibilities of human beings or rational beings in general. Heidegger explains: "*[A]nticipation [in Being-towards-death] reveals to Dasein its lostness in the they-self, and brings it face to face with the possibility of being itself, primarily unsupported by concernful solicitude, but of being itself, rather, in an impassioned* freedom towards death—*a freedom which has been released from the Illusion of the 'they,' and which is factical, certain of itself, and anxious*" (Heidegger [1927] 1993: §53 266/311, cf. 241–42/285–86, [1925] 1979: 429/310).

This means that in order to understand human finitude, we have to abandon the sense of being that belongs to the objects that surround us in our practical and theoretical activities, but we also have to reject the sense of being that characterizes our relations with others in our everyday dealings. Neither our concernful being-occupied with things nor our being with others can help us in our attempt to understand the fundamental meaning of human death:

> [A]ll Being-alongside the things with which we concern ourselves, and all Being-with Others, will fail us when our ownmost potentiality-for-Being is the issue. Dasein can be authentically itself only if it makes this possible for itself of its own accord [. . .] Dasein is authentically itself only to the extent that, *as* concernful Being-alongside and solicitude Being-with, it projects itself upon

its ownmost potentiality-for-Being rather than upon the they-self.
(Heidegger [1927] 1993: §53 263/308)

Heidegger's discussion of death has been attacked by several writers. As already pointed out, both Beauvoir and Lévinas questioned his concept of being-towards-death. Others after them have presented even more scathing commentaries.

Some commentators argue that Heidegger valorizes one's own death and belittles the significance of the other's death; others claim that, despite his efforts to the contrary, Heidegger offers an abstraction that artificially separates the subject from its vital connections with the others.[3] Still others claim that Heidegger's concept of death contradicts his attempt to destroy or deconstruct the tradition of the metaphysics of the presence.[4] In this reading, Heidegger repeats the most profound gesture of Western philosophy— the gesture of substituting death for birth as the meaning-giving substrate of life. In this vein, Grace Jantzen, for example, argues that Heideggerian phenomenology is preoccupied with death and, moreover, is death-loving or "necrophilic" (Jantzen 1998b: 102–103, 2001: 2, 22).[5] Further, she proposes that Western philosophy can be recuperated only by a "biophilic" or life-affirmative attitude, such as we find in the works of Hannah Arendt and Mary Daly. Finally, Jantzen suggests that the theoretical or meditative preoccupation with death is a masculine or masculinist feature of thinking, which can, and must, be corrected by feminine reflections (Jantzen 1998a, 1998b, 2001, 2003; cf. Cavarero 1990; Benhabib 1996: 104–107).[6]

We can hear echoes of Beauvoir's analysis of femininity in this "sexing" or "gendering" of philosophies of life. However, Beauvoir's existential account of the association between femininity and death differs from contemporary feminist accounts in one important respect. Whereas Beauvoir argues that men project their finitude and mortality onto women, contemporary feminists claim that men are preoccupied with death and that they substitute death for birth as a principle of life. From Beauvoir's point of view, the existential-phenomenological urge and task to face one's own death signals a historical possibility to unravel the association between femininity and mortality: insofar as men are able to accept their finiteness and affirm their true condition, they will not be disposed to project mortality onto women; and insofar as women are able to relate to the infinite in themselves, they are prepared to reject the identification of femininity with corporeality. For many contemporary feminists the existential-phenomenological concept of death is just another expression of the age-old tendency to substitute death for nativity characteristic of Western theorizing and reflection since Plato's *Phaedo;* for Beauvoir this concept, even if biased and one-sided, is a necessary step toward the understanding of the duality and plurality of human existence.

In order to evaluate these different forms of critique we need to focus on Heidegger's precise formulations and study his original wording. Only a close reading can show whether Heidegger's concept of being-towards-death can rightly or meaningfully be rejected as egocentric or androcentric.

The Heidegger quote given above ends in a perplexing statement. Heidegger claims that when Dasein stands before itself with death, "all its relations [*Bezüge*] to any other Dasein have been undone [*gelöst*]." At first glance, this one statement may seem to confirm the egocentric reading. It seems that Heidegger simply gives death the same function that Descartes assigned to God: the being of the world is constituted not on the basis of any relations that we have with finite others (for all finite others are included in the world) but on the basis of the absolute relation that we have with the Unattainable Absolute. The only difference would be that Descartes understood the Unattainable Absolute as God, but Heidegger identified it with the incompleteness of Dasein. Thus understood, there seems to be a structural similarity between Heidegger's existential account and Descartes's epistemological solipsism (cf. Arendt [1932] 1994: 46; Dastur 1994: 47).

But this isomorphism proves superficial when we recall that Heidegger's analysis operates on the transcendental ontological level on which all ontic uses of *being* have been suspended. What is at issue is not the relation between two different kinds of beings—finite and infinite, temporal and eternal—but the relation that we have to Being. In other words, the relations at issue are not any ontic relations between worldly (or otherworldly) entities but transcendental relations of meaning constitution. Thus, to say that in the face of death, Dasein finds all its relations to others "undone" is not to say that one worldly entity has detached itself from others or stepped outside the social world into another, solipsistic universe. Rather the argument is that human life involves a level or a dimension on which being does not mean being-with-others or being-in-the-world but means living in the anticipation of the end of being. Moreover, Heidegger argues that this dimension of human existence is primary and irreducible: being-towards-death is a necessary aspect of being human, and it cannot be reduced to being-with-others.

Even when read in this transcendentalist way, Heidegger's thesis is of course controversial and open to different sorts of criticism, but it is crucial to notice that the thesis cannot be disproved by any (empirical) argument that refers to our ontic relations with others—social, psychic, corporal, or deitic. This is because the thesis concerns not our inner-worldly dependencies but their conditions of possibility.

Heidegger explains that the transcendental undoing of the relations with others does not change the world in any way, but it modifies our relation toward the world. When facing his death, the human being changes in his attitude toward others as well as toward the things in his environment. Instead of just belonging to and living in an undifferentiated community of equals or alter egos, Dasein finds itself anew among *singular* and *unique* others. The others as he now encounters them cannot be replaced, they cannot be substituted one for the other in death or in life ([1927] 1993: §47 239–40/283–84).[7] They all are unique, and they have taken their unique positions in the history and tradition of being human. Heidegger states this explicitly in another paragraph of *Being and Time:*

> *[A]uthentic* disclosedness modifies with equal primordiality both the way in which the "world" is discovered [. . .] and the way in which the Dasein-with of others is disclosed. The "world" which is ready-to-hand does not become another one "in its content," nor does the circle of Others get exchanged for a new one; but one's Being towards the ready-to-hand understandingly and concernfully, and one's solicitous Being with Others, are now given a definite character in terms of their ownmost potentiality-for-Being-their-Selves. (Heidegger [1927] 1993: §60 298/344)

Thus, while authentically living in the nearness of death, both my social relations of being-together-with others and my practical relations to the utensils and instruments of my projects are radically transformed. The impossible possibility of my own death restructures all my relationships and transforms my way of life.[8] As Heidegger emphasizes, the change is not quantitative; we don't win another universe, beyond the given one, more real or more persistent, nor do we enter into relations with different things or unknown others. The change is qualitative; we relate in a new way to our fellow human beings and to our practical environment. It is as if our eyes were opened and we would see the world, others and things, in a new way. So the possibility of my own death transforms my relations with my fellowmen: I see them now as unique individuals who cannot be replaced one for the other. By confronting my own mortality, I thus come to realize the specific meaning of human death and the specificity of human life; and this confrontation is the base on which I can, in a human way, grieve and mourn the loss of others.

The Death of the Other

Heidegger's discourse also includes an explicit reflection on the other's death that, by contrast, helps to understand his thesis about being-towards-death. He argues that the deceased other, near or foreign, is never given to us as lifeless matter or as a purely corporeal thing [*pure Körperding*], but always appears as one who "has lost life" and always is characterized by a special "no-more." The survivors still *live with* the deceased other, because they shared the world with him:

> In tarrying alongside him in their mourning and commemoration, those who have remained behind *are with him*, in a mode of respectful solicitude. In such Being-with the dead, the deceased himself is no longer factically "there." However, when we speak of "Being-with," we always have in view Being with one in the same world. The deceased has abandoned our "world" and left it behind. But in terms of that world those who remain can still *be with him* (Heidegger [1927] 1993: §47 238/282, translation modified; cf. Husserl Hua4: 343/352)[9]

The dead human being is never mere matter for us and never similar to any perished animal. This is easy to accept in the case of our near and beloved ones, and sounds even trivial, insensitive, and offensive when juxtaposed with our grief and mourning: how could we even imagine seeing or touching the body of our beloved one in a similar way as we see and touch dead animal bodies? Heidegger's point, however, concerns not our personal relations to our near ones but our relations to *all* human beings, the most precious ones as well as completely unknown and anonymous. The other's dead body always and by necessity indicates his singular existence and refers back to a shared world. Even a human skeleton or skull found at the excavations of ancient ruins or in prehistorical sites indicates a human life, a human way of being, with which we by necessity share the world. This special form of givenness that belongs to the human corpse accounts for the terror that we experience when we see mass graves and human bodies lying unburied on the ground.[10]

Basing on Heideggerian insight, Françoise Dastur points out that our contemporary funeral rites are rooted in an archaic understanding and practice of living-with, which encompassed not just the ones alive, but equally the dead ones. She refers to Aristotle while explaining that humans live not just with their contemporaries but also with their ancestors, and she emphasizes that the same idea can be found in all human cultures.[11] Dastur concludes that it is exactly this mode of living-with that distinguishes human existence from animal life: the absent ones are collectively presentified by ritual and expressive acts and practices, singing, speech, prayer, and burying (Dastur 1994: 9–10, 1998: 13–16). Our funeral rites and our linguistic practices both make reference to the ones who are absent; both aim at establishing a spiritual relation to the ones who are no longer present in flesh and blood. It is this context, Dastur emphasizes, that helps us to understand and evaluate the boldness and despair of Princess Antigone, who buries her brother against the command of the king: "The world in which Antigone lives is populated both by living and by dead [...], without funeral, this process of spiritualization, could not take place [avoir lieu]. For this reason she struggles hard, to the point of risking her own death, to furnish a tomb for her brother" (Dastur 1998: 23–24, cf. 1994: 16). It is in the very concrete sense that the burying has to "take place": there must be a place that marks our relation to the absent lost other. Thus, tombs and graves are not just containers but, more fundamentally, places of communication and communion.[12]

To be sure, Heidegger does not ask or study how the death of the singular other, a unique person, affects our lives, and this clearly seems to be a weakness of his account.[13] Several commentators have interpreted this restriction as a principal defect and argued that Heidegger's discourse of death does not allow any philosophical discussion on the death of a beloved one and that it forces us to bypass the other's life and focus our reflections on our own lot. Thus the crucial critical question is whether the conceptual and methodic framework that Heidegger provides allows a discussion on the other's death or whether it, on the contrary, excludes the other's death from philosophical topics and locates it among empirical issues.

Most Heidegger scholars argue that there is no principal limitation here, and some show concretely how Heidegger's concepts can be developed to account for the trauma we experience when we lose our beloved ones or witness a tragic death of a stranger. In her two books on death, La mort (1994) and Comment vivre avec la mort (1998), Françoise Dastur offers a Heideggerian account of such experiences. She points out that the loss of the other person is not only a loss of particular possibilities, but more fundamentally a radical loss of a way of living in a natural familiar world. After such events, we find ourselves as strangers in a strange environment. Things that had full significance now present themselves as empty, futile, and barren. It is not merely that they have lost their value and importance to us, but more fundamentally that we do not recognize them anymore.

Dastur's analysis helps to understand the uncanniness of the experience of a personal loss: I remember sitting on a bench outside the hospital after my father's death and thinking that I never need to move anymore, as if the bench and the open sea by the hospital building would constitute the whole world. I wandered around in his empty apartment, touching and looking at his belongings, things that were familiar from my childhood and my youth, and found myself thinking: "What is this?" His absence trembled all things that surrounded me and shook the whole structure of my environment.

It is not simply a loss or absence of a particular person that we experience when a significant other dies; rather his death seems to restructure our whole life-world: things lose their meanings, and on the other hand, they gain new meanings; objects that have been quite insignificant now stand out in a strange way and come to the fore (cf. Husserl Hua15: 211–13).[14] So instead of experiencing an absence, a hole in the fullness of being, I experience the breakdown of my familiar world and its habitual structures of presence and absence.[15]

Moreover, the deceased person himself may appear in peculiar ways to us, not as a full person in flesh and blood but like a phantom or a shadow (cf. Husserl Hua1: 171–72/145, Hua4: 94/100). We may recognize his figure in the crowd on the street or hear his voice in someone else's speech. Complete strangers may attract our attention because they presentify familiar postures and ways of moving. We know that it is not the deceased in person, but we see something of him in others and may feel him in the postures and movements of our own body. The deceased other is not simply absent but both present and absent in an unusual way. He may appear also in our dreams in a new lively manner that is different from the symbolic function that he used to have before his death. He does not stand for anything else, not for anybody or for any aspect of ourselves, but occupies a position of his own. Thus the ambiguous presence of the deceased affects our whole life-world—oneiric and waking, own and alien (cf. Merleau-Ponty [1945] 1993: 96–101/80–85).

Dastur assigns the other's death a much more significant role than Heidegger does. As we cannot experience our own death, she argues, the only death that we encounter in experience is the death of the other. Moreover, she claims, it is the "primary experience" of the loss of a beloved one and the sorrow over his death that allows us to establish a relation to ourselves as mortal beings and to develop consciousness of our own finitude. This, however, does not cancel Heidegger's argument about being-towards-death. To make this point, Dastur refers to the story of Gilgamesh, a mythical Assuro-Babylonian king. Gilgamesh is a half-divine being who first learns about death by experiencing the perishing of his friend and companion Enkidou (Dastur 1994: 7–8, 1998: 10; cf. Heidegger [1927] 1993: §47 236/279). In the order of knowledge, the other's death is crucial and primary: Gilgamesh learns *that* he will die by witnessing the death of Enkidou. However, his understanding of the sense of death does not consist of his suffering and mourning of the loss of his friend, even though this experience certainly awakens him to reflect on his own condition. Rather the understanding of death emerges only by the encountering of the possibility of one's own death and by the realizing of this possibility's meaning to having a world and living in it.[16]

So in the epistemic order, the other's death is primary, but in the order of sense constitution, it is one's own death that is decisive and crucial. This realization of one's own mortality provides the proper meaning to the experience of the other's perishing: what I mourn is not just an absence of something that was part of my world or belonged to it, but I face the more fundamental loss of a life and a whole lived world different and separate from mine (cf. Dastur 1994: 43–44). This means that the phenomenological reflection on the other's death and on the experienced loss does not compromise Heidegger's main argument about the specific role that my own death has in our understanding of the meaning of life. On the contrary, it shows that it is completely different to lose a person and to lose life. Heidegger expresses the distinction by writing: "Death does indeed reveal itself as a loss, but a loss such as is experienced by those who remain. In suffering this loss, however, we have no way of access to the loss-of-Being as such which the dying man 'suffers.' The dying of Others is not something which we experience in a genuine sense, at most we are always 'there alongside'" (Heidegger [1927] 1993: §47 239/282).

The claim is that no reflection on or analysis of the meaning to me of the other's death can answer the question about the ontological meaning of death: what it means to die. This question can be answered only by encountering the impossible possibility of one's own death.[17] So from Heidegger's point of view, it is a confusion to claim that one understands or learns about this fundamental meaning of death by watching others perish, by empathetically accompanying them to their death, or by mourning their absence. This represents a fundamental misunderstanding, a misunderstanding about the character of the question, for the aim is not to answer any psychological, moral, or metaphysical questions, but to pose a transcendental existential question: "We are asking about the ontological meaning of dying of the person who dies, as a possibility-of-Being which belongs to *his* Being. We are not asking about the way in which the deceased had Dasein-with or is still-a-Dasein with those who are left behind" (Heidegger [1927] 1993: §47 239/282, cf.§46 237/280–81).

Birth as Limit and Death as Interruption

Another common complaint against Heidegger's discourse of death is that it neglects the phenomenon of birth or that it values mortality over "natality" and death over birth.[18] We have seen that Heidegger lays a specific emphasis on death, but it is important to notice that he binds the limits of birth and death explicitly together and argues that Dasein exists as living in care between these two limits:

> Factical Dasein exists as born; and as born, it is already dying in the sense of being-towards-death. As long as Dasein factically exists, both the "ends" and their "between" *are*, and they are in the only way which is possible on the basis of Dasein's being as *care*. Thrownness and that being-unto-death in which one either flees it [death] or anticipates it, form a unity; and in this birth and death are "connected" in a manner characteristic of Dasein. As care, Dasein is the "between." (Heidegger [1927] 1993: §72 374/426–27)

Heidegger argues, however, that death and birth do not have the same role in the constitution of meaning. This is due to the specific form of directedness characteristic of human life and its ecstatic futural temporality: every moment of life opens onto two directions, the past and the future, but the nature and role of these two openings is different. Both directions contribute to the constitution of the meaning of life: the past life already lived serves as a background for our present experiences, and the life yet to be lived gives it a directionality. But whereas our past generates and delimits our possibilities, the future constitutes the horizon for these possibilities. For this reason, birth and death, as the two limits of existence, are not equal or symmetrical in their meaning for our being. As we exist, as we already are there in the world, the impossible possibility of ceasing to exist is appalling and threatening in a different way than the thought about not being born or the possibility of never coming into being. The possibility of ceasing to exist and losing the world is not just an intellectual dilemma but is an existential threat (Dastur 1994: 33–35).[19]

Thus philosophically, existentially and phenomenologically, birth does not constitute the other "end point" of human life, equal in its meaning and in its role to death, as if this life could pass on or move in two directions.

Life is futural, and death marks the limit of this fundamental futurity; for this reason, Heidegger argues, it deserves a special place in the philosophy of human existence.

Heidegger acknowledges that the analysis of Dasein must include an inquiry of birth as a limit, but he emphasizes that this inquiry is not, and cannot be, an inversion of our reflections of death. In the framework of Dasein, birth is not a modification or variation of death, nor its opposite, but requires its own specific concepts and its own specific analyses in order to be understood as a limit of life. Philosophically, death and birth cannot be discussed in an analogous way, even if both have a place in our philosophical work (Heidegger [1928–29] 1996: 124–25; Arendt 1958: 96–98).[20]

These preparatory remarks have given some idea of the transcendental (fundamental ontological) asymmetry between death and birth, as Heidegger conceives them. We cannot, however, understand the asymmetry without clarifying how Heidegger's concept of death relates to his account of human life as an incomplete whole and as a movement exposed to radical interruptions.

The philosophical context of Heidegger's discussion of death is in his struggle to liberate thinking from the onto-theological tradition that has conceptualized life and its possibilities primarily in terms of reality, actuality, and presence.[21] This means that Heidegger's discussion of death is intrinsically interwoven with his critique of "the metaphysics of presence."[22] The aim is to question the philosophical primacy or privilege of the present and the actual. We see this already in the way Heidegger sums up his main argument about death: "The closest closeness which one may have in Being towards death as a possibility, is as far as possible from anything actual" (Heidegger [1927] 1993: §53 262–63/306–307). Françoise Dastur explains:

> But if death is for us the preeminent possibility, as Heidegger says, this implies a redefinition of the traditional concept of possibility. For in the philosophical tradition, possibility is opposed to reality. It is considered something less than reality. But here, in the light of death, possibility is defined as something more preeminent than reality [. . .] In the phenomenological perspective, possibility is the locus of excess with regards to reality. This allows us to consider possibility as a higher category than reality. Possibility is something other than a category which is a structure of things. It is a structure of existence [. . .] since the mode of being of human existence is not the mode of being of the *res* (that is, *realitas*), but the mode of being as having to be (in other words, as possibility). Because the human

being is a mortal being and, in existing, has a constant relation to its own death, it constantly remains in the mode of possibility. It remains in the mode of a structural anticipation toward its own being, which remains unrealized for as long as it exists. (Dastur [1998] 2000: 183–84, cf. 1994: 51–56)

Death has a special existential significance because it discloses our possibilities in a special way, as authentically and concretely belonging to us. The nearness of death is not the nearness of something expected, something on its way to actualization or realization.[23] The nearness of death does not make death more actual; on the contrary, the nearness intensifies death's potentiality, its nature as a possibility, a never-actualizing possibility. Thus our relation to death is not the relation of expecting something that may actualize but is a relation of anticipating something that in nearness grows greater and greater as a possibility without actualizing or giving us anything to actualize. The greatness of this possibility of not existing is "measureless" [*masslosen*] (Heidegger [1927] 1993: §53 262/307).[24] Thus human death is never an endpoint or a completion, never expected, but always comes as an interruption.[25]

The background of Heidegger's concept of death as an interruption is in his understanding of life as an incomplete whole, as a whole that necessarily remains incomplete and cannot, by definition, be carried to any proper ending. This is not just a side issue in Heidegger's destructive reading of Western metaphysics. On the contrary, his project of thinking against the onto-theological current of traditional philosophy culminates in his conception of human life. For Heidegger, the human way of being, Dasein, is a necessarily incomplete self-transcending; and he discusses its being as a counterexample to the dominant understanding that equates being with presence, completion, fulfillment, and perfection.[26] Moreover, all completion and fullness gains meaning only in relation to human life and its horizon of un-presence.[27]

Dasein's incompletion is not accidental, as if human life could in principle be completed but has been left unfinished because of contingent circumstances. Life is not like a half-finished building; it is not comparable to unfinished or uncompleted productive activities, or to production that merely accomplishes a half-ready result. Or to put it in a different way, the incompleteness of human life does not just characterize its final state but characterizes equally each of its moments, and for this reason, no prolongation of this way of being, real or imaginable, could complete it.

The main point here is that human life as such is contingent in a very specific sense, not just in the everyday sense of including unexpected happenings and unforeseen incidences. This everyday sense of an event or an interruption refers to the contents of experience: something new and unforeseen comes along and shakes our habitual modes of experiencing, but does not affect the structure of time, which functions as the basis for all forms of experiencing and happening, habitual and usual as well extraordinary and unexpected. The Heideggerian argument is different and concerns the transcendental basis of experience. Here contingency is attributed not just to worldly events and happenings but to life itself, to its temporal succession. The claim is that time as the fundamental structure of life is saturated or impregnated with contingency, so that contingency is not accidental to life but inherent in life itself.[28]

We can describe this fundamental contingency by the concepts of event and direction, but ultimately the issue is not about the unexpected occurrences or about the unforeseen direction that life can take but about the intensity and force that lived moments can get in the flow of time. Something strikes us from outside and gives a special intensity to one particular moment. This is an intrusion, not in our control and not in expectation. Its possibility, however, is given together with the futural openness of each present, and thus is intrinsic to life itself.

Death, and not birth, is emblematic of this structural potentiality of lived time exactly because death concerns the one who lives-in-the-world. Death accents the radical and fundamental unexpectedness that belongs to lived time and, as a potentiality, to each of its moments. Two factors are crucial here: first, death is conceptualized not as an end point or conclusion of life but as an interruption; second, death is understood as a radically unexpected and unforeseen interruption that necessarily escapes all our prospects and calculations. Death is not just unexpected as in the case of accidents and sudden strokes. Even in long sickness and suffering, death comes as a surprise. Its moment and its ways cannot be prepared or predicted, and its direction is definitely beyond our reach.[29]

The prominence of death should not lead us to accept any simple opposition between death and birth. Both these "events" are necessary structures of human life. Birth is the opening of life, and death is the impossible possibility of its ending. But as human life is fundamentally futural, both death and birth deserve their own *separate* analyses. Thus the oppositions between death and birth and between death and life are apparent and existentially misleading.

NOTES

1. An initial analysis was presented in the lecture course on *The History of the Concept of Time* in 1925 (Heidegger [1925] 1979: 422–42/305–20).

2. Heidegger presents Kierkegaard as the philosopher who has identified the *"existentiell* phenomenon" of the instant [existenzielle *Phänomen des Augenblicks*] and the one who "has gone the farthest in the analysis of the phenomenon of anxiety" (Heidegger [1927] 1993: 338n1/497niii, 190/235, 492, cf. 235n1/494nvi).

3. See, for example, Benhabib 1996, Cohen 2006, Critchley 2006.

4. Compare, however, to Heidegger's own emphasis on the positive sense of his destructive methodology: "In thus demonstrating the origin of our basic ontological concepts by an investigation in which their 'birth certificate' is displayed, we have nothing to do with a vicious relativizing of ontological standpoints. But this destruction is just as far from having the negative sense of shaking off the ontological tradition" (Heidegger [1927] 1993: §6 22/44).

5. The distinction between biophilic and necrophilic attitudes is part of Mary Daly's feminist critique of patriarchal theology (Daly 1984). For a good overview of Daly's use of this distinction, see Suhonen 2000.

6. Françoise Dastur gives a more refined critique of our philosophical tradition in her two books on death, *La mort* (1994) and *Comment vivre avec la mort?* (1998). She acknowledges that Western philosophy includes a form of meditation for which death is the privileged object and which seeks to conquer death by thought, contemplation, and meditation. She stresses, however, that there is a parallel tradition that sees life and living as the principal concerns of philosophical work. As an example of the first approach Dastur gives the Socratic attitude explicated by Cicero and Montaigne: *"The whole life of a Philosopher is the meditation of his death"* (Cicero *Tusculan Disputations,* I, 31; Montaigne *Essays,* book I, ch. 20). And it is Spinoza of course who serves as the paradigmatic example of the second approach: "A free man thinks of nothing less than of death, and his wisdom is a meditation not of death but of life" (Spinoza, *Ethics,* 4th part, prop. LXVII, 183; cf. Lévinas [1982] 1999: 155). But compare this to Montaigne, who also questions the Socratic attitude by writing, "It seems to me, however, that it [death] is indeed the end but not the aim of life; it is its conclusion, its extreme point, yet not its object" (Montaigne *Essays,* III, 12:329).

7. Heidegger writes: "*No one can take the Other's dying away from him.* Of course someone can 'go to his death for another.' But that always means to sacrifice oneself for the Other '*in some definite affair.*' Such dying-for can never signify that the Other has thus had his death taken away in even the slightest degree. Dying is something that every Dasein must take upon itself at the time. By its very essence, death is in every case mine, in so far as it 'is' at all" (Heidegger [1927] 1993: §47 240/284). Lévinas questions the philosophical significance that Heidegger gives to this ontological result about nonreplacement. He argues that we can, and must, override our constitutional solitude by the ethical decision to accompany the dying person. The other's face "commands me not to remain indifferent to this death, to not let the Other die alone, that is, to answer for the life of the other person, at the risk of becoming an accomplice in that person's death" (Lévinas [1982] 1991: 175/109, cf. 1991).

8. Françoise Dastur elaborates on Heidegger's insight by arguing that ultimately death is not a limit to us but a resource: "we are open to the world, related to things and to other beings only because we have a relation to death, because we are mortal

and know this" (Dastur 1998: 34–35). Dastur develops this idea further by claiming that being human is possible only because of the "gift of death": we can become what we are only by the realization and acceptance that we are mortal and will die. Cf. Derrida [1992] 1995.

9. Heidegger's characterization of the other's dead body or, in his own words, of the Dasein of a dying other, was different in his lectures on the history of the concept of time, two years before the publication of *Being and Time*: "When they have died, their being-in-the-world is as such no more. Their being is no longer being 'in' a world, 'involved in' a disclosed world. Their still-being-in-the-world is that of merely being on hand as a corporeal thing. The unique change-over of an entity from the kind of being belonging to Dasein, whose character is being-in-the-world, to a bare something which is still only on hand is especially evident here" (Heidegger [1925] 1979: 427/309–10). We can find similar characterizations of the deceased human being [*Verstorbene*] also in *Being and Time,* but here Heidegger makes clear that the concept of the deceased does not "exhaust the full phenomenological findings" but needs to be corrected with the concept of the dead individual [*Gestorbene*].

10. Hannah Arendt repeats this Heideggerian argument and connects it to Nietzsche's philosophy of life: "The birth and death of human beings are not simply natural occurrences, but are related to a world into which single individuals, unique, unexchangeable, and unrepeatable entities, appear and from which they depart. [...] Without a world into which men are born and from which they die, there would be nothing but changeless eternal recurrence, the deathless everlastingness of the human as of all other animal species. A philosophy of life that does not arrive, as did Nietzsche, at the affirmation of 'eternal recurrence' (*ewige Widerkehr*) as the highest principle of all being, simply does not know what it is talking about" (Arendt 1958: 96–97).

11. Dastur gives the reference to the first book of Aristotle's *Politics* (1252a), but I have not been able to find the relevant passage. Compare to Lévinas's extreme formulation: "There is an ethical significance in this responsibility, this an-archic responsibility, without the present recalling any engagement. It is the significance of a past that concerns me, that 'regards me,' and is 'my businesss' outside of all reminiscence, retention, re-presentation, or reference to a remembered present. The significance of an immemorial past, starting from responsibility for the other person, comes in the heteronomy of an order. Such is my *nonintentional* participation in the history of humanity, in the past of others, who 'regard me'" (Lévinas [1982] 1991: 177/111–12).

12. For historical and anthropological accounts of funerals and burying, see Vovelle 1983, Ariès 1997, Urbain 1998, Thomas 2000, Harrison 2003, Lehtonen 2007.

13. Other phenomenologists, from Husserl to contemporary thinkers, such as Ricoeur and Derrida, have discussed the other's death and its fundamental significance to my life. See, e.g., Husserl Hua15 (e.g., 211–15), Lévinas 1991, Ricoeur 1984, Derrida [1992] 1995; cf. also Derrida 2001.

14. In *A Very Easy Death* (*Une mort très douce* 1964), Simone de Beauvoir describes her experience of the approaching death of her mother: "The transition from my mother to a living corpse had been definitely established. The world had shrunk to the size of her room: when I crossed Paris in a taxi I saw nothing more than a staging in which extras were walking about" (Beauvoir 1964: 103/73; cf. Descartes 1641: 32/21–22), and further: "When someone you love dies [...] her death uncovers for us her unique singularity; she becomes as vast as the world that her absence annihilates

for her and that her presence made exist" (Beauvoir 1964: 134/94). For the ethical implications of Beauvoir's account, see Weiss (1999: 146–63).

Merleau-Ponty argues that a comparable change happens at the event of birth: "In the home in which a child is born, all objects change their signification; they begin to await some as yet indeterminate treatment at his hands; another and different person is there, a new personal history, short or long, has just been initiated, another account has been opened" (Merleau-Ponty [1945] 1993: 467/407).

15. The loss may be so fundamental that it is hard, or even impossible, to describe and discuss the experience. When asked about her relation to Sartre's death, Simone de Beauvoir stated: "'These things cannot be told; they cannot be put into writing; they cannot be formed in one's mind. They are experienced and that is all'" (Beauvoir 1981: 11/3). Cf. Dastur ([1997] 2000: 185–86).

16. David Carr captures the difference: "In one sense we know of it [death] through the death of another, an event within our world. But my own death is not something I could ever experience as an event in the world, for it constitutes the limit of my world. Thus resistant to being thought or experienced, the reality of my own death is more likely to be brought home to me as a 'disposition' such as anxiety. Unlike fear, anxiety has no particular object; what it reveals is the facticity of my being at all, my very being in the world, my engagements in projects in general. My being stands out against the backdrop of my non-being" (Carr [1986] 1991: 81–82).

17. Cf. Lévinas (1947: 92n5/70n43).

18. In his strong emphasis on death as an ontological ground of significance, Heidegger is exceptional among the phenomenologists. Both Husserl and Merleau-Ponty give much more space and emphasis on the facticity of birth. In an essay on Husserl, "The Philosopher and His Shadow" (Le philosophe et son ombre 1959), Merleau-Ponty argues against Heidegger: "The fact that we die alone does not imply that we live alone; and if we consult nothing but suffering and death when we are defining subjectivity, subjective life with others and in the world will become logically impossible" (Merleau-Ponty [1960] 1998: 221/175). We find the same idea in *Phenomenology of Perception* explicated with a reference to Husserl: "Our birth, or, as Husserl has it in his unpublished writings, our 'generativity,' is the basis both of our activity or individuality, and our passivity or generality—that inner weakness which prevents us from ever achieving the density of an absolute individual" (Merleau-Ponty [1945] 1993: 489/428).

19. Thomas Nagel makes the same point about the asymmetry of death and birth by pointing out that the idea of prolonging life is sensible only in respect to the future. He discusses the asymmetry in the framework of objective time, but his formulation is illuminative: "It is true that both the time before a man's birth and the time after his death are times when he does not exist. But the time after his death is time of which his death deprives him. [...] But we cannot say that the time prior to a man's birth is time in which he would have lived had he been born not then but earlier. For [...] he *could* not have been born earlier: anyone born substantially earlier than he was would have been someone else" (Nagel 1970: 79). For a contrary position, see Sorabji (2006: 337–39).

20. The situation is very different in empirical (ontic) life sciences. Heidegger takes the example of botanics, and explains: "I do not think that birth is the other end point of Dasein, which could or should be handled in the same context of problematization

as death. In the investigation of Dasein, one cannot without further ado refer to birth instead of death; in the same way as the botanist in the investigation of a plant, can begin equally well from the root as from the bloom" (Heidegger [1928–29] 1996: 124). Arendt explicates Heidegger's point by arguing that natural movement and change is cyclic and repetitive, whereas human life is linear and proceeds in one direction only. The consequence is that the concepts of *growth* and *decay* have their original sense in the human context (Arendt 1958: 97) and that they function merely metaphorically when applied to plants and animals. Compare Heidegger's and Arendt's explanations to Husserl's argument that the concepts of crisis and renewal belong together with the concepts of choice and freedom and characterize human life, which must be distinguished from animal and vegetative life and its phenomena of growth and decay: "Psychic humanity [*seelisches Menschentum*] has never been complete and never will be, and can never repeat itself" (Husserl Hua6: 320/275, cf. Hua27: 20–43, 97–100).

21. I am thankful to Timo Miettinen for emphasizing the significance of these paragraphs to Heidegger's overall destructive project.

22. The term "the metaphysics of presence" is Derrida's; see, for example, his *Writing and Difference* (*L'écriture et la différence*) (Derrida 1967a: 196–225/134–52, cf. 1976b: 83–86/74–77).

23. To emphasize this, Heidegger uses the term *vorlaufen* for the specific type of anticipation that characterizes being-towards-death and that transcends all possibilities of life ([1927] 1993: §53 262/306).

24. Cf. Dastur ([1997] 2000: 182).

25. This idea can also be found in Husserl's *Kaizo* essays from the early 1920s. In these essays Husserl elaborates on his understanding of human life as a necessarily open whole, and he introduces his notion of human death as a rupture or interruption. He writes, for example, "Only a human being is a person and is not just a subject of action [*Tätigkeiten*] but also sees himself as a subject of an open horizon of life and action [*Wirken*], [only a human being] is permanently threatened by death as a rupture [*Bruch*] of this wakened life and action [*Wirken*] and as a resolution [*Abschluss*] which, in its indefiniteness, is merely an incessantly continuing, never-ending threat" (Husserl Hua27: 98). Cf. Max Scheler: "In der Form dieser Gewissheit steht der Tod nicht am realen Ende des Lebens, oder wäre nur eine auf die Erfahrung gegründete Erwartung dieses Endes, sondern er begleitet das ganze Leben als ein Bestandteil aller seine Momenete" (Scheler [1911–14] 1979: 27).

The conceptual and methodological context of these reflections is in Husserl's genetic phenomenology. In this later phase of his work, Husserl develops detailed analyses of different types of breaks or ruptures that can interrupt the continuous flowing of appearances and the "normal" succession of anticipations and fulfillments in inner time. Husserl makes conceptual distinctions in order to capture the differences between specific types of interruption, such as sleep, unconsciousness by fainting, and change of consciousness by injury. He analyzes these states and processes in terms of anomalousness and normativity. Anthony Steinbock argues that Husserl's concept of death as an interruption presupposes not just his genetic methodology, but also "generative concepts" that are needed for an account of intersubjective temporality (Steinbock 1995: 134–96).

26. Compare to Heidegger [1924–25] 1992: 177–78. With his first explications of the concept of Dasein, Heidegger connects or even fuses existential-phenomenological

concepts with his original and powerful reading of Aristotle. On this fusion of the two philosophical perspectives and on its later development, see van Buren 1992, Backman 2009. For Dilthey's influence on Heidegger, see Carr ([1986] 1991: 80–83).

27. Cf. Backman 2006, 2009.
28. Cf. Schuback 2005.
29. Dastur expresses this as follows: "Death, as an event, is also that which always happens against all expectations, always too early, something impossible that nevertheless happens" ([1997] 2000: 183).

BIBLIOGRAPHY

Note: Date in square brackets is the original publication date; the following date is the edition cited. Where two sets of page numbers are given in citations in text, the first is the cited edition in the original language, and the second is the English edition.

Arendt, Hannah. [1932] 1994. "Søren Kierkegaard." In *Essays in Understanding 1930– 1954: Formation, Exile, and Totalitarianism*, 44–49. New York: Schocken Books.
———. 1958. *The Human Condition*. Chicago: Chicago University Press.
Ariès, Philippe. 1997. *L'homme devant la mort: I. Les temps des gisants, II. La mort ensauvagée*. Paris: Éditions du Seuil.
Backman, Jussi. 2005. "Divine and Mortal Motivation: On the Movement of Life in Aristotle and Heidegger." *Continental Philosophy Review* 38: 241–61.
———. 2009. *Complicated Presence: The Unity of Being in Parmenides and Heidegger*. Doctoral diss. Philosophical Studies from the University of Helsinki 26, Department of Philosophy. Tampere: Juvenes Print.
Beauvoir, Simone. 1964. *Une mort très douce*. Paris: Gallimard. In English *The Very Easy Death*. Trans. Patrick O'Brian. New York: Warner.
———. 1970. *La vieillesse I–II*. Paris: Gallimard. In English *Old Age*. Trans. Patrick O'Brian. London: Weidenfeld and Nicolson, 1972.
———. 1981. "*La cérémonie des adieux*" suivi de "*Entretiens avec Jean-Paul Sartre: août–septembre 1974*." Paris: Gallimard. In English *Adieux: A Farewell to Sartre*. Trans. Patrick O'Brian. New York: Pantheon Books, 1984.
Benhabib, Seyla. 1996. *The Reluctant Modernism of Hannah Arendt*. Thousands Oaks, Calif.: Sage.
Buren, John van. 1992. "The Young Heidegger, Aristotle, Ethics." In *Ethics and Danger: Essays on Heidegger and Continental Thought*, ed. Arleen B. Dallery and Charles E. Scott with P. Holley Roberts. Albany: SUNY.
Carr, David. [1986] 1991. *Time, Narrative, and History*. Bloomington: Indiana University Press.
Cavarero, Adriane 1990. *Nonostante Platone: Figure femminili nella filosofia antica*. Rome: Riuniti. In English *In Spite of Plato: A Feminist Rewriting of Ancient Philosophy*. Trans. Serena Anderlini-D'Onofiro and Áine O'Healy. New York: Routledge, 1995.
Cicero. *Tusculan Disputations*.
Cohen, Richard A. 2006. "Levinas: Thinking Least about Death—contra Heidegger." *International Journal for Philosophy of Religion* 60: 21–39.

Critchley, Simon. 2006. "Being as Inauthentic as Possible." In *The Past's Presence: Essays on the Historicity of Philosophical Thinking*, ed. Marcia Sá Cavalcante Schuback and Hans Ruin, 111–22. Södertörn Philosophical Studies 3. Huddinge, Sweden: Söderntörn University Press: Söderntörn högskola.

Daly, Mary. 1984. *Pure Lust: Elemental Feminist Philosophy*. Boston: Beacon Press.

Dastur, Françoise. 1994. *La mort: essay sur la finitude*. Paris: Hatier. In English *An Essay on Finitude*. Trans. J. Llewelyn. London: Athlone, 1996.

———. [1997] 2000. "Phenomenology of the Event: Waiting and Surprise." *Hypatia* 15, no. 4: 178–89. Original: "Pour une phénoménologie de l'événement: l'attente et la surprise." *Études phénoménologiques* (25): 59–75, 1997.

———. 1998. *Comment vivre avec la mort?* Paris: Peines Feux.

Derrida, Jacques 1967a. *L'écriture et la différence*. Paris: Éditions du Seuil. In English *Writing and Difference*. Trans. Alan Bass. London: Routledge and Kegan Paul, 1985.

———. 1967b. *La voix et le phénomène*. Quadrige: Presses Universitaires de France. In English *Speech and Phenomena and Other Essays on Husserl's Theory of Signs*. Trans. David B. Allison. Evanston, Ill.: Northwestern University Press, 1973.

———. [1992] 1995. *The Gift of Death*. Trans. David Wills. Chicago: University of Chicago Press. Original "Donner la mort," in *L'éthique du don, Jacques Derrida et la pensée du don*.

———. 2001. *The Work of Mourning*. Ed. Pascale-Anne Brault and Michael Naas. Chicago: University of Chicago Press.

Descartes, René. 1641. *Meditationes de Prima Philosophia*. In *Œuvres de Descartes, Band 7*. Ed. Charles Adam and Paul Tannery. Rev. ed. Paris: Vrin/C.N.R.S. In English *Meditations on First Philosophy*. In *The Philosophical Writings of Descartes*. Vol. 2. Trans. John Cottingham, Robert Stoothoff, and Dugald Murdoch. Cambridge: Cambridge University Press, 1991.

Harrison, Robert Pogue. 2003. *The Dominion of the Dead*. Chicago: University of Chicago Press.

Heidegger, Martin. [1924–25] 1992. *Platon: Sophistes (Wintersemester 1924/25), Gesamtsausgabe II. Abteilung: Vorlesungen 1919–1944, Band 19*. Ed. Ingeborg Schüssler. Frankfurt am Main, Vittorio Klosermann.

———. [1925] 1979. *Prolegomena zur Geschichte des Zeitbegriffs, Gesamtausgabe, II. Abteilung: Vorlesungen 1923–1944, Band 20*. Ed. Petra Jaeger. Frankfurt: Vittorio Klostermann. In English *History of the Concept of Time*. Trans. Theodore Kisiel. Bloomington: Indiana University Press, 1992.

———. [1927] 1993. *Sein und Zeit*. Tübingen: Max Niemeyer. In English *Being and Time*. Trans. John Macquarrie and Edward Robinson. Oxford: Blackwell, 1992.

———. [1928–29] 1996. *Einleitung in die Philosophie (Wintersemester 1928/29), Gasamtsausgabe, II. Abteilung: Vorlesungen 1919–1942, Band 27*. Ed. Otto Saame and Ina Saame-Spaidel. Frankfurt am Main: Vittorio Klostermann.

Husserl, Edmund. Hua1. *Cartesianische Meditationen und pariser Vorträge*. Ed. Stephan Strasser. The Hague: Martinus Nijhoff, 1950. In English *Cartesian Meditations*. Trans. Dorion Cairns. Dordrecht: Martinus Nijhoff, 1960.

———. Hua4. *Ideen zu einer reinen Phänomenologie und phänomenologischen Philosophie. Zweites Buch: Phänomenologische Untersuchungen zur Konstitution*. Ed. Marly Bimel. The Hague: Martinus Nijhoff, 1952. In English *Ideas Pertaining to a Pure Phenomenology and to a Phenomenological Philosophy.* 2nd book: *Studies in the Phenomenological Constitution.* Trans. Richard Rojcewicz and André Schuwer. Dordrecht: Kluwer Academic Publishers, 1993.

———. Hua6. *Die Krisis der europäischen Wissenschaften und die transzendentale Phänomenologie: Eine Einleitung in die phänomenologische Philosophie.* Ed. Walter Biemel. The Hague: Martinus Nijhoff, 1954. In English *The Crisis of European Sciences and Transcendental Phenomenology: An Introduction to Phenomenological Philosophy.* Trans. David Carr. Evanston, Ill.: Northwestern University, 1988.

———. Hua15. *Zur Phänomenologie der Intersubjektivität, Texte aus dem Nachlass, Dritter Teil: 1929–1935.* Ed. Iso Kern. The Hague: Martinus Nijhoff, 1973.

———. Hua27. *Aufsätze und Vorträge, 1922–1937.* Ed. T. Nenon and H. R. Sepp. Dordrecht: Kluwer Academic Publishers, 1988.

Jantzen, Grace M. 1998a. *Becoming Divine: Towards a Feminist Philosophy of Religion.* Manchester: Manchester University Press.

———. 1998b. "Necrophilia and Natality: What Does It Mean to Be Religious?" *Scottish Journal of Religious Studies* 19, no. 1: 101–21.

———. 2001. "Before the Rooster Crows: The Betrayal of Knowledge in Modernity." *Litterature and Theology* 15, no. 1: 1–24.

———. 2003. "The Horizon of Natality: Gadamer, Heidegger, and the Limits of Existence." In *Feminist Interpretations of Hans-Georg Gadamer,* ed. Lorraine Code, 285–306. University Park: Pennsylvania University Press.

Lehtonen, Turo-Kimmo. 2007. "Hautaaminen perustana." *Tiede & edistys* 31, no. 4: 306–26.

Lévinas, Emmanuel. 1947: *Le temps et l'autre.* Paris: Quadrige/PUF. In English *Time and the Other.* Trans. Richard A. Cohen. Pittsburgh, Pa.: Duquesne University Press, 1987.

———. [1982] 1991. "Diachronie et représentation." In *Entre nous: essais sur le penser-à-l'autre,* 165–84. Paris: Grasset. In English "Diachrony and Representation." In *Time and the Other,* 97–120. Trans. Richard A. Cohen. Pittsburgh, Pa.: Duquesne University Press, 1987.

———. [1982] 1999. "The Philosopher and Death." In *Alterity and Transcendence* [an interview with Christian Chabanis]. Trans. Michael B. Smith. New York: Columbia University Press. Original "Le philosophe et la mort."

———. 1991. "Mourir pour." In *Entre nous: essai sur le penser-à-l'autre,* 204–14. Paris: Grasset.

Merleau-Ponty, Maurice. [1945] 1993. *Phénoménologie de la perception.* Paris: Gallimard. In English *Phenomenology of Perception.* Trans. Collin Smith. New York: Routledge and Kegan Paul, 1995.

———. [1960] 1998. *Signes.* Paris: Gallimard. In English *Signs.* Trans. Richard C. McCleary. Northwestern University Press, 1964.

Montaigne, Michel de. [1595] 1958. *Essays.* Trans. J. M. Cohen. London: Penguin Books.

Nagel, Thomas. 1970. Death. *Noûs* 4, no. 1: 73–80.

Ricoeur, Paul. 1984. *Temps et récit.* Vols. 1–2. Paris: Seuil. In English *Time and Narrative.* Vol. 1. Trans. Kathelin McLauglin and David Pellauer. Chicago: Chicago University Press.

Scheler, Max. [1911–14] 1979. *Tod und Forleben.* Munich: Francke Verlag.

Schuback, Marcia Sá Cavalcante. 2005. "The Experience of History." In *The Past's Presence*, ed. Marcia Sá Cavalcante Schuback and Hans Ruin, 93–122. Södertörn Philosophical Studies 3. Huddinge, Sweden: Södertörn högskola.

Sorabji, Richard. 2006. *Self: Ancient and Modern Insights about Individuality, Life, and Death*. Oxford: Clarendon Press.

Spinoza. [1677] 1993. *Ethics and Treatise on the Correction of the Intellect*. Trans. Andrew Boyle, rev. G. H. R. Parkinson. London: J. M. Dent.

Steinbock, Anthony. 1995. *Home and Beyond: Generative Phenomenology after Husserl*. Evanston, Ill.: Northwestern University Press.

Suhonen, Marja. 2000. "Toward Biophilic Be-ing: Mary Daly's Feminist Metaethics and the Question of Essentialism." In *Feminist Interpretations of Mary Daly*, ed. Sarah Lucia Hoagland and Marilyn Frye, 112–31. University Park: Pennsylvania University Press.

Thomas, Louis-Vincent. 2000. *Les chairs de la mort*. Paris: Institut d'éditions Sanofi—Synthélabo.

Thomson, Iain. 1999. "Can I Die? Derrida on Heidegger on Death." *Philosophy Today* 43, no. 1: 29–42.

Urbain, Jean-Didier. 1998. *L'archipel des morts*. Paris: Éditions Payot & Rivages.

Vovelle, Michel. 1983. *La mort et l'occident: De 1300 à nos jours*. Paris: Gallimard.

Weiss, Gail. 1999. *Body Images: Embodiment as Intercorporeality*. New York: Routledge.

SIX

Future and Others

SARA HEINÄMAA

Already in the 1940s and 1950s several phenomenologists and existentialists problematized the central role that Heidegger gave to death in his interpretation of human existence. The main idea in these early critiques was that the determining horizon of a person's life is not in his own death but in the relations that bind him to other selves of disparate temporalities. Despite their critical attitude toward Heidegger's discussion on subjectivity, these early critics did not reject his transcendental account of the incompleteness of human life, but problematized this notion and developed it further to articulate the plurality of existence.

The two most well known forms of this critique were presented by Emmanuel Lévinas in *Time and the Other* (Le temps et l'autre 1947) and by Hannah Arendt in *The Human Condition* (1958). But we can find similar intuitions developed in the writings of other phenomenologists and existentialists as well.

For the purposes of unlocking the association between femininity and death, Beauvoir's approach is exceptional, as it links the discussion of mortality with a critical analysis of the asymmetric relation between the sexes. The link is not explicit, but needs to be worked out, and for this aim, it is illuminative to compare Beauvoir's remarks against Heidegger to competing forms of critique. The aim of this chapter is exactly here: to investigate the different ways in which phenomenological and existential thinkers tried to correct or enrich Heidegger's analysis of the temporality of human life.

As said, Heidegger's contemporary critics accepted his explication of death as an interruption and his related account of the essential incompletedness and openness of human life.[1] What they found problematic was the central role that death had in Heidegger's analysis of individuality: they all argued that the uniqueness and singularity of a human life is not established or disclosed by an authentic understanding of death but emerges in expressive relations with others.[2] Merleau-Ponty, for example, pointed out that a simple experience of sense perception already distinguishes and connects us as unique, irreplaceable individuals. According to him, Heidegger's focus on being-towards-death was misleading, because the uniqueness of the subject is inscribed in all experiences and an authentic self-relation can be established in each. Even simple perceptions involve selfhood or ipseity as well as alterity and intersubjectivity (Merleau-Ponty [1945] 1993: 489/428, translation modified, cf. 249–50/215–16, 294/254). The self found in these experiences is not the reflective Kantian "I" that envelops all our objectifying experiences but is a concrete person constituting itself in internal time through sedimentation and habituation of experiences.

Moreover, all Heidegger's early critics emphasized that expressive relations bind us not just to contemporary others or to antecedents, but also to successors. The intersubjective bondage is different in different cases of alterity; all others do not have the same bearing on our own existence. Most importantly, it is the successor, the newcomer, who has a crucial part in the constitution of my life as an open, incomplete whole.

While post-Heideggerians agreed on the basic point that individuality is established or realized not in the experience of mortality but in expressive relations between subjects, they articulated their views very differently and discussed different areas and levels of intersubjectivity. For the purposes of unlocking the association between femininity and mortality, it is important to notice that Beauvoir's account differs from the accounts of the other post-Heideggerians in one crucial respect: while Merleau-Ponty, Arendt, and Lévinas all characterize human intersubjectivity without taking into account the fact that subjectivity and consciousness come in two different types, Beauvoir emphasizes from the start that human becoming is not of one kind only but includes (at least) two variations. Both are spiritual and bodily, and both connect free will to sensibility, but in different ways: "man, like woman, is flesh, and therefore a passivity [. . .] And she, like him, in the midst of her carnal fever, is a consenting, a voluntary gift, an activity; they live in their different ways the strange ambiguity of existence made body" (Beauvoir [1949] 1991: 658/737).[3]

The problem of neglecting the possibility of feminine subjectivity is different in these three post-Heideggerian discussions: Merleau-Ponty does not discuss sexual difference, but as he argues that subjectivity comes in different variations (e.g., Merleau-Ponty [1945] 1993: 144/124), his account provides conceptual resources to distinguish between feminine and masculine subjects.[4] Arendt thematizes sexual difference but only at the level of biological life, which is characterized by repetitive activities and circular temporality; in her explication, the proper discursive level of human activity and futurity bears no traces of sexual difference.[5]

Lévinas's critique of Heidegger is most sensitive to sexual difference, and his alternative account of individuation and futurity is based on the articulation of this difference. He struggles to explicate the radical view that the feminine and the masculine are not two contrary or complementary realities but two ways of constituting reality. He writes: "The difference between the sexes is a formal structure, but one that carves up reality in another sense [than the genus-species division] and conditions the very possibility of reality as multiple, against the unity of being proclaimed by Parmenides" (Lévinas 1947: 77–78/85, cf. [1961] 1971: 301–302/269, 309/276)

But even if Lévinas's discussion of sexual difference questions the principle of unity and challenges traditional unificatory metaphysics, it results in problematic identifications that repeat the commonplaces of ordinary discourse. In *Time and the Other,* Lévinas explains, for example, that the "feminine" movement is modest and withdrawing, and as such opposed to subjectivity and consciousness (Lévinas 1947: 81/88).[6]

Beauvoir's *The Second Sex* challenges all such oppositions and contrasts as androcentric and sets the philosophical task to explain and understand "why woman has been defined as the Other" (Beauvoir [1949] 1993: 32/29). Her critique of Lévinas is direct,[7] but she also questions the neutrality of Merleau-Ponty's account as well as the Kantian and Hegelian intuitions about animality and humanity that inform Arendt's discussion of action and speech. The interpretations developed in this chapter show that even though Arendt, Lévinas, and Beauvoir all argued that one's own futurity is dependent on the temporalities of others, only Beauvoir challenged the dichotomies of our androcentric conceptualization of subjectivity and made ground for a genuinely pluralistic rethinking of human existence.

I will begin by explicating Lévinas's account of human futurity and proceed to study Arendt's alternative conceptualization. The chapter ends in an explication of Beauvoir's discourse, which diverges from those of her contemporaries in thematizing two different variations of subjectivity and two parallel modes of human becoming: the masculine and the feminine.

Eros and Fecundity

Emmanuel Lévinas starts his early lectures on *Time and the Other* by boldly challenging Heidegger's analysis of temporality and subjectivity: "The aim of these lectures is to show that time is not the achievement of an isolated and lone or solitary subject, but that it is the very relationship of the subject with the Other" (1947: 14/39). He continues:

Thus from the start I repudiate the Heideggerian conceptualization that views solitude in the midst of a prior relationship with the other. Though anthropologically incontestable, the conception seems to me ontologically obscure. The relationship with the Other is indeed posed by Heidegger as an ontological structure of *Dasein*, but practically it *plays no role in the drama of being or in the existential analytic.* (1947: 18/40, latter italics mine)

Lévinas's point here is different from most critical remarks that today are issued against Heidegger. He acknowledges that the Heideggerian idea of solitariness may have anthropological or psychological plausibility, but he argues that it is ontologically—that is, philosophically—untenable. This means that Lévinas presents an internal critique of Heidegger's analysis; he does not justify his remarks by any empirical results or by conceptual analyses, but aims at challenging Heidegger's account of the meaning of being on its own criteria of validity (cf. Lévinas [1961] 1971: 310/277).

Three points need to be emphasized here. First, Lévinas attacks the principle that governs the whole of phenomenology from Husserlian beginnings to Heidegger's reinterpretation: he questions the central idea according to which our relationship to ourselves is constitutionally primary to our relationship with others.[8] Second, Lévinas argues that Heidegger's discussion of intersubjectivity or collectivity—*Mitsein* or *Miteinandersein* in Heidegger's terms—is conceptually based on Heidegger's analysis of solitary existence (cf. Lévinas [1961] 1971: 63/67–68, 341/305). According to Lévinas, this leads Heidegger, and his followers, to misconceive our relations with others as relations of homogeneity and simultaneity. Third, Lévinas argues that all such conceptualizations ignore the hierarchical and diachronical structure that is an essential aspect of our relations with others: the other is not an alter ego, not a fellow man or an antagonist, but is irrecoverably foreign, heterogeneous, and asynchronous (Lévinas 1947: 75–76/83–84).

Lévinas takes his starting point from Heidegger's concept of being-towards-death but proceeds to show that in the nearness of death we come to experience or live another form of temporality: the mystery of the newcomer.[9] By introducing the idea of a newcomer, Lévinas argues that one's own death is neither the final limit of life nor the determining perspective of time. Through the realization of mortality, I encounter the future in a completely new way and in a completely new sense:

> The death agony is precisely in this impossibility of ceasing, in the ambiguity of a time that has run out and of a mysterious time that yet remains; death is consequently not reducible to the end of a being. What still remains is totally different from the future that one

welcomes, that one projects forth and in a certain measure draws from oneself […] [the] triumph over death […] is not a new *possibility* offered after the end of every possibility—but a resurrection in the son in whom the rupture of death is embodied. (Lévinas [1961] 1971: 49–50/56, cf. 258/232, 284/253)[10]

We saw above that for Heidegger, the proximity of death meant the articulation of the difference between my possibilities and the possibilities of humans in general. Lévinas argues, however, that in the time that "still remains" the structures of temporality change radically. Heidegger is right in pointing out that time cannot be projected forth from the present toward an open future and that the future is not given as an empty field for my plans and goals. He is wrong, however, in assuming that my death marks the ultimate horizon of my future, my time.

According to Lévinas, mortality is overridden by a new form of temporality: the future of my possibilities is lost, but a different future is regained and received from the other (Lévinas 1947: 64/76–77). My time and the foreign future are separate, separated by an unbridgeable gulf, but this rupture is not an ultimate limit; it allows and constitutes for me an arching into a new dimension of futurity.[11] The future received from a diachronic, asynchronic, and heterogeneous other is not any type of *extension* of or *addition* to my personal existence, as if my identity would be secured and sealed independently of this opening. The break in my time and the arching into a foreign future constitute an inner fissure at the very heart of the subject itself (Lévinas 1947: 20/41, 71–72/81–82, 85/90, cf. [1961] 1971: 281/251, 315/282). Lévinas argues that this opening is provided by the erotic relation. He ends *Time and the Other* by writing: "I have tried to find the temporal transcendence of the present toward the mystery of the future. […] It is the face-to-face without intermediary, and is furnished for us by the eros where, in the other's proximity, distance is integrally maintained" (Lévinas 1947: 89/94).

Thus Lévinas argues that the erotic encounter and the amorous caress between two lovers manifest an alternative form of futurity, which differs from the anticipation of death. His main point is that in erotic love, the subject encounters and opens itself onto a foreign future without being threatened by destruction. Love certainly means vulnerability and suffering; it "invades and wounds us," but "nevertheless the I survives it" (Lévinas 1947: 82/88–89, cf. [1961] 1971: 341/305).[12] This is possible because erotic relations carry traces of our original way of being affected by an alien futurity, prior to all forms of expectation and anticipation.[13] In love, we relate not to any expected or extrapolated *content*, but to the pure *form* of receiving and becoming (Lévinas 1947: 77/84–85, 82/89). So Lévinas describes the erotic relation as an alternative form of futurity, which, in distinction from the anticipation or intensification characteristic of the nearness of death, does not threaten to nihilate or destroy the subject or his world but, on the contrary, opens a new temporal dimension in his life.[14]

The erotic caress exemplifies a specific mode of *moving* that differs from the goal-directed movements of creation and production as well as from the reflexive movements of free action.[15] The caress has no predetermined ends, but neither is it self-regulating. It is a third mode of movement, the finality of which cannot be reduced to *poiesis* or to *praxis*. My hand moves according to the other, according to his gestures, finding its directions in the other's independent movements (cf. Lévinas [1961] 1971: 169–75/158–62). I do not mirror, imitate, or repeat the other's actions, nor do I simply answer to his needs. The movement of the erotic caress lacks the finality of possessing and grasping. It has no pre-established endpoint but proceeds in the mode of experimentation and exploration; its pleasure goes without going to an end (Lévinas [1961] 1971: 290/260, cf. 288–90/257–59, 298–99/266, 1947: 82–83/89). Thus the erotic caress is seeking in its essence (Lévinas 1947: 82/89, cf. 288/258). It requires two separate subjects who are not modifications, duplications, complements, or completions of one another (Lévinas 1947: 78–81/86–88, cf. [1947] 1993: 145/85, 164/96).[16] Their movements are not reciprocal or correlative. Instead of repeating themselves, or each other, they inform and reshape one another. They do not fuse or unite, but preserve themselves as separate in a mutual transformation. Lévinas names this type of experiencing "voluptuous," and views it as a particular kind of intentionality. He writes:

> This intentionality of the voluptuous—the sole intentionality of the future itself, and not an expectation of some future fact—has always been misunderstood by philosophical analysis. [. . .] My thesis, which consists in affirming voluptuousness as the very event of the future, the future purified of all content, the very mystery of the future, seeks to account for its exceptional place. (Lévinas 1947: 82–83/89–90, cf. [1961] 1971: 291–310/259–77)

Paternity and Future

If Lévinas's discussion on futurity in *Time and the Other* ended here, then his alternative to Heidegger's concept of being-towards-death would consist of his concept of the voluptuous. The claim would be that the erotic encounter involves a specific kind of futurity that differs in crucial ways from the futurity of being-towards-death without reintroducing the temporality of das Man or we-in-general. The difference consists of three related aspects: First, the erotic encounter opens a future *between two* separate lives and thus transforms the structure of each life. Second, the new life engendered in an erotic relation exceeds the *possibilities* of each one subject, and the whole framework of possibilities. The subject does not run up against his ultimate limit, nor does he go outside himself in a solitary ex-stasis, but he literally exceeds himself due to the unexpected, marvelous movements of the other. Third, the erotic subject is *receptive*. The future opened in the encounter is not the one that the subject anticipates in his activities, but is a new form of temporality, received from the other. In this sense the subject is passive.

However, Lévinas continues his discussion and subordinates the erotic to the ideas of *fecundity* and *parenthood*. He argues that this step is necessary because the erotic relation is impaired by materiality and sensible corporeality. In erotic sensuous touching, he claims, the self is still "enchained" to its present. It can truly transcend itself and gain a future only through paternity and its discursive freedom (Lévinas 1947: 85/91). In *Totality and Infinity*, Lévinas justifies this linkage of love and parenthood as follows:

> I love fully only if the other loves me, not because I need the rec-
> ognition of the Other, but because my voluptuosity delights in his
> voluptuosity, and because in this unparalleled conjuncture of iden-
> tification, in this *trans-substantiation*, the Same and the Other are
> not united but precisely—beyond every possible projection, beyond
> every meaningful and intelligent power—engender a child. [. . .]
> By a total transcendence, the transcendence of trans-substantiation,
> the I is, in the child, an other. Paternity remains a self-identification,
> but also a distinction within identification. (Lévinas [1961] 1971:
> 298–99/266–67, translation modified)

Two different types of problem strain Lévinas's reasoning here. For a feminist reader, Lévinas's solution is disappointing, and even alarming, because it subordinates the futurity of the erotic encounter to the genealogy of paternity. The feminine beloved is claimed to grant a future to the loving subject, but the son is introduced as the radical newcomer who realizes or accomplishes this opening. Thus the feminine beloved and the erotic relation are presented as mere conditions for paternity and as means to the futurity that the child provides (Lévinas [1961] 1971: 299/267). This is suggestive of the maneuvers of the androcentric tradition of Western philosophizing, in which feminine elements have been handled as mere resources for masculine self-reflections and self-explorations, with no independent function or value of their own.[17]

Several feminist commentators have problematized the way in which Lévinas proceeds from the erotic to the paternal and have asked about its legitimacy.[18] Luce Irigaray, for example, argues harshly: "He [Lévinas's male lover] is forgetful of the fecundity, here and now, of lovemaking: the gift to each of the lovers of sexuate birth and rebirth [. . .] The seduction of the beloved woman serves as a bridge between the Father and the son. Through her, who is only an aspect of himself, the male lover goes beyond love and pleasure toward the ethical" (Irigaray 1984: 187/202, cf. 33/27, 188–90/203–206, 1991: 180–83).[19]

Lévinas's solution is surprising also in the perspective of his own preceding analysis, which proceeds—at least partly—in a phenomenological fashion, clarifying the intentional and temporal structures of the experience of the voluptuous (e.g. Lévinas 1947: 82/89, [1982] 1991: 175/109; cf. Wyschogrod [1974] 2000: 56–57). As there is no necessary, statically, or genetically constitutive connection between the experience of erotic love and that of parenthood, the link that Lévinas makes between the voluptuous and the paternal seems to be motivated by mundane, empirical concerns.[20] At this point Lévinas points out, however, that his approach is not phenomenological but dialectical (Lévinas 1947: 87/92, cf. 36/55, [1961] 1971: 35–39/44–48).[21]

This methodological point is crucial to any understanding of Lévinas's challenge of Heidegger. As pointed out above, *Time and the Other* is developed as an internal critique of Heidegger's existential analysis of the sense of being; Lévinas struggles to radicalize Heidegger's destruction of the unificatory tradition of philosophical ontology, which deduces all sense of being from presence. The idea of the son is introduced for this purpose. Lévinas explains: "I *am* in some way my child. But the words 'I am' here have a significance different from an Eleatic and Platonic significance. There is a multiplicity and a transcendence in this verb 'to exist,' a transcendence that is lacking in even the boldest existential analysis" (Lévinas 1947: 86/91, cf. [1961] 1971: 327–28/294, 332–33/298–99).

What Lévinas is arguing, in other words, is that Heidegger's break with the Greek tradition is not radical enough but is restricted by a certain idea of embodiment. Despite Heidegger's heroic attempt to question the metaphysics of the present and the ontology of the substance, he still assumes that the being of the subject is unitary and manifested only by one living body. But the relation between the father and the son throws this notion into relief and thus forces us to reconsider the semantics of the verb "to exist" when applied to human life. The father *is* his son, Lévinas argues, not by any type of addition or multiplication, but in his very *being*. The father finds himself in the gestures and expressions of the son, and thus realizes himself as other to himself (Lévinas 1947: 86/91, 1961/1971: 299/267; cf. Wyschogrod [1974] 2000: 133–35; Bernet 2002: 97–98).[22]

The son is not a property of the father, nor his product or creation. The activities of *having* and *doing* are inadequate in this case, as the son emerges unexpectedly from the erotic encounter that (re)opens the future (Lévinas 1947: 89/93, cf. [1961] 1971: 310/277; cf. Bernet 2002: 94). This means that the father-son pair is independent of any collectivity established "around something common"; it is a new couple made possible by the love between two different and separate persons.[23] Thus the philosophical significance of paternity is not in its emotional value or in the moral challenges that it raises. It is in the ontological function of introducing "a duality into existence, a duality that concerns the very existing of each subject" (Lévinas 1947: 88/92).

It is worth emphasizing that, despite its terminology, Lévinas's discourse of paternity or parenthood is not biological, psychological, or anthropological and does not refer to natural reproduction or generation. The other person from whom I receive my future is not my son (or daughter) in the biological meaning of offspring but in the philosophical meaning of dual being-there (Lévinas [1961] 1971: 309–10/276–78, 312–13/279–80, 343/306). The example of paternity is given to illuminate the special type of being that is doubly dual: dual in its origin and dual in its thisness (*haecceitas*).[24] But this example is not the only one that we find in Lévinas's argumentation; in the later work *Totality and Infinity* (*Totalité et infini* 1961) he presents and discusses also the prototypical pair of the teacher and the pupil.[25]

To summarize: The main outcome of Lévinas's early critique of Heidegger is the argument for the plurality of the sense of existence.[26] Lévinas claims that the human subject exists in multiple different senses, not just in his own body here and now, but also elsewhere, in the movements and gestures of the descendant. The sense of "being there" or Dasein may sustain or accent the other senses of being, but we should not let ourselves be misled to derive the other sense from any one sense. Especially the sense of being-futural should not be treated as a modification of the sense of being-there.

Despite this ontological rationale of Lévinas's discourse on paternity, philosophers with feminist concerns are left with worries about the role of the feminine in his account. Beauvoir's early problematization of the association of femininity with materiality and passivity is still topical. To be sure, Lévinas explains that femininity is not an attribute of an existent (woman or female) but refers to a special way of moving and relating characteristic of all lovers (Lévinas [1961] 1971: 286/256).[27] Despite this caution, the question remains: What justifies the decision to conceptualize this movement as "feminine"? *Time and the Other* answers by introducing the ideas of withdrawal, hiding, veiling, and passivity; *Totality and Infinity* refers to fragility and muteness (Lévinas 1947: 79–81/88–89, [1961] 1971: 286–87/256–57). These explications are illuminative but also highly problematic, as they repeat the commonplace preconceptions about the sexes that have recurred in Western theoretization since antiquity.

The problem is aggravated by the fact that Lévinas does not use the concept of femininity coherently but also ties it to empirical women. The most well known, and often criticized, paragraphs are to be found in *Totality and Infinity*, in the section on "Habitation and the Feminine" where he reasons, for example, as follows:

> This [feminine] alterity is situated on another plane than language [...] It is comprehensible and exercises its function of interiorization only on the ground of the full human personality, which, however, *in the woman,* can be reserved so as to open the dimension of interiority [...] Those silent comings and goings *of the feminine being* whose footsteps reverberate the secret depths of being are not the turbid mystery of the animal and feline presence. (Lévinas [1971] 1988: 166–67/155–56, my italics, cf. 1984: 55/33)

So as a summary we can state that Lévinas managed to reintroduce the phenomena of birth and generativity into post-Heideggerian philosophy and showed their significance to ontology, but his account still suffers from the androcentric (Kantian-Hegelian) approach, which treats femininity and womanhood as emblems of sensual life and carnality and thus opposes them to human consciousness and subjectivity.

Memory and Natality

Hannah Arendt's discussion of birth and generativity is surprisingly similar to Lévinas's in its basic motivations and goals.[28] Like Lévinas, Arendt struggles to liberate the philosophy of existence from its one-sided focus on death and mortality and from its homogeneous understanding of human life. But whereas Lévinas argues that we receive the future from the newcomer, Arendt aims to show that we carry the basic structure of futurity within ourselves, in our capacity of remembrance. For Lévinas, futurity is based on the erotic encounter *between two* subjects. Arendt argues that our relation to our *own birth* is crucial to all temporality.

The conceptual home of Arendt's discourse of futurity is in Augustine's reflections on man's temporal being.[29] The basic idea that Arendt got from Augustine concerns man's relations to his own origin: man is a remembering being, and as such he can become conscious of his mortal condition by grasping that he has not always been but has once entered the world. The realization of finiteness is based on the realization of natality. This Augustinian teaching includes four points that must be distinguished if we want to see how Arendt's account of the human life diverges from those of Heidegger and Lévinas.

The first point is a quasi-theological or transcendental argument about man's worldly condition. In Augustine's Christian teaching, man is a created being with an otherworldly *origin* (*Ursprung*) as well as an end. In this respect, man is similar to all other created beings, animals as well as inanimate things; all these come to the world at one time and depart from it at another time. Whereas Augustine articulated the idea of origin by stating that man is a "created being" instituted by an eternal and omnipotent God, Arendt struggles to express the same point in nontheological concepts. She coins the concept of *natality* exactly for this purpose: it is introduced to express the transcendental fact that man's being is being-with-an-origin: "[T]he decisive fact determining man as a conscious [. . .] being is birth or 'natality,' that is, the fact that we have entered the world through birth" (Arendt 1996: 51).

The second point that Arendt finds in Augustine's works concerns the self-reflective nature of man's consciousness: as a conscious being man can realize his mortal condition and become aware of the constitutive fact that he has an origin and an end. In this respect, man differs from all other created beings. Man is the only worldly being that can know or understand *that* he has not always been but has entered the world and will eventually depart from it (Arendt 1996: 51, 54).

The third point that Arendt learns from Augustine concerns the content of man's consciousness. Arendt agrees with Augustine in arguing that man can come to know the nature of his origin. So in addition to knowing *that* he has an origin, man can also know *how* he originated. For Augustine, man's origin was otherworldly as man was created by God. For Arendt, human beings originate from other human beings—not in the causal sense of biological reproduction but in a motivational sense of inspiration or imi-tation. This sense is explicated in *The Human Condition* by the concepts of action and speech as follows:

> With word and deed we insert ourselves into the human world, and this insertion is like a second birth, in which we conform and take upon ourselves the naked fact of physical appearance. This insertion is not forced upon us by necessity, like labor, and it is not prompted by utility, like work. It may be stimulated by the presence of others whose company we may wish to join, but it is never conditioned by them; its impulse springs from the beginning which came into the world when we were born and to which we respond by beginning something new on our own initiative. (Arendt 1958: 176–77)

Fourth, and most importantly to our attempt to question the power or supremacy of death in the constitution of subjectivity, Augustine offers an ingenious account of the progression of our consciousness of finite-ness. This account is crucial to Arendt because it allows her to invert the Heideggerian order. Augustine argues that the two poles, death and birth, are not given in consciousness at once, but the realization of the beginning is *primary* and makes possible the anticipation of the end. Arendt applies this idea by arguing that the recollective consciousness of natality is primary, and transformed and projected onto the future. The result of this projection is our anticipatory consciousness of our own death: "Since our expectations and desires are prompted by what we remember and guided by a previous knowledge, it is memory and not expectation (for instance, the anticipa-tion of death as in Heidegger's approach) that gives unity and wholeness to human existence" (Arendt 1996: 56, cf. 47).[30]

In Arendt's explication, Augustine's discussion of our consciousness of finitude and mortality is in direct conflict with Heidegger's description of being-towards-death. Whereas Heidegger suggests that our anticipation of our own death is independent of all references to our original coming to being, Augustine describes anticipatory consciousness as a modification of recollective consciousness. Inspired by Augustine's reflections on remem-brance, Arendt challenges Heidegger's analysis and argues that the anticipa-tion of the end depends on the possibility of remembering the beginning. What is at issue is not our organic emergence but our birth as speaking and acting human persons. The transcendental fact of birth is, in this special sense, deeper than that of death: the constitution of the meaning of death depends on the constitution of the meaning of birth.

Interestingly Arendt's Augustinian argument differs from the contemporary feminist proposal that suggests that a feminine focus on birth can, or must, substitute for the traditional androcentric interest in death. For Arendt, no such substitution is possible because the two types of consciousness—consciousness of one's origin and consciousness of one's possible end—are not on the same footing. So Arendt agrees with Heidegger in arguing that these forms of consciousness cannot substitute one for the other. But the reasons that she gives for this impossibility are different from those of Heidegger. Whereas Heidegger claims that birth and death have very different existential-transcendental functions, Arendt believes that they are interdependent in their constitution: the anticipatory consciousness of death depends on the recollective consciousness of birth, and thus they cannot replace one another.

Arendt's Augustinian line of thinking also diverges from the other contemporary critique of Heidegger. Arendt does not accept the idea that my consciousness of my own mortality would depend on my experience of another person's death. Rather than pointing to painful or terrifying perceptual experiences, she suggests that the crucial type of consciousness that is necessary for the realization of one's own mortality is a remembrance of one's birth as a human—acting and speaking—subject. Such a recollective consciousness differs radically from all possible perceptions and emotions that concern our dying contemporaries. The remembrance or recollection of birth is not about any event given in the human world, or lacking from it, but is about our original passage or entry into this world.[31]

In accordance with Augustine, Arendt argues that we come to the world as strangers, that is, as unique beings, whose arrival cannot be foreseen, expected, or anticipated on the basis of what is or what has been. This holds equally for humankind and for each individual human being. Our arrival and our actions cannot be predicted from the lives of our ancestors; they can only be motivated and prompted by earlier activities. Thus, unexpectedness is a constant possibility in human life. Arendt explains: "It is the nature of beginning that something new is started which cannot be expected from whatever may have happened before. [. . .] The fact that man is capable of action means that the unexpected can be expected from him, that he is able to perform what is infinitely improbable" (Arendt 1958: 178, cf. 144, cf. 257).

Arendt sees natality—unanticipated and spontaneous initiation—as inherent in all human activities and forms of life, but she also argues that natality belongs most properly or most fundamentally to the activities of action and speech (Arendt 1958: 9, 175–77).[32] By these two activities, she claims, we distinguish ourselves from others and insert ourselves into the community as unique individuals. The community that is able to include such individuals is not a collective of natural equals but is an open-ended futural plurality of irreplaceable agents.

In order to understand Arendt's account of human futurity, we need to explicate her three-fold distinction between three types of activity: action, work, and labor. By this distinction, Arendt articulates three different types of permanence and transitoriness.[33]

Action and Narrativity

For Arendt, action is the form of activity that defines us as unique human individuals. As such, action differs fundamentally from the two other forms of activity, labor and work, which define us respectively as similar members of natural collectives and species and as replaceable members of economic communities.[34] For the purpose of understanding Arendt's critique of Heidegger, the most important difference between these three forms of activity is in their temporality: whereas labor ties us to the cyclic time of nature and repetitive generativity, and work chains us to the cumulative tasks of production and manufacturing, only action guarantees the open future of human life. It is worth studying Arendt's analyses of these three types of activity and temporality in detail, as they include three very different senses of futurity.

Arendt defines "labor" as the activity of processing and preparing matter for immediate consumption (Arendt 1958: 99–100, 103). By the "immediacy" of consumption Arendt does not mean just temporal proximity; more importantly, she refers to the relations between producers and consumers. The idea is that labor is an activity in which the very same people who cultivate the matter also consume the outcome; the consumption does not need to happen at the very same place and time as the processing of the material, but it always happens within the immediacy of kinship relations (Arendt 1958: 118). Thus understood, labor includes all activities that are needed for the survival and reproduction of the natural community and the sustenance of individual human bodies as biological organisms.[35] Thus nutrition, clothing, housing, and cleaning, for example, are labor activities in Arendt's terminology (Arendt 1958: 124). But also other activities can be encompassed by labor insofar as they are subjected or subordinated to the needs and necessities of biological life (Arendt 1958: 126–28, cf. 146).

Another, related aspect of labor activity needs to be emphasized. What is crucial is that the end results of labor do not serve any *new types of activities* but are used—immediately—for the ends of maintenance and survival, that is, for the continuation of the laboring itself. In other words, labor serves no other end than the continuation of its own cyclic movement. "Whatever labor produces is meant to be fed into the human life process almost immediately, and this consumption, regenerating the life process, produces—or rather, reproduces—new 'labor power,' needed for the further sustenance of the body" (Arendt 1958: 99).[36]

Two restrictions thus characterize the cycle of laboring: as the products of labor activity are consumed within natural communities, they can function neither as objects of exchange between different communities nor as materials for new types of activities.

Work differs from labor in both respects: its results are transferred from one community to another, and they serve as materials for further activities of production (Arendt 1958: 100).[37] Moreover, such forms of mediation establish traditions of usage, and accustom or habituate us as users. As such, work establishes a world of relatively durable and permanent objects. It leaves behind materials, tools, and artifacts as well as practices and communities of production with ends, means, and models of fabrication (Arendt 1958: 94, cf. 8, 121–22, 139, 144). Thus work activity breaks free from the circular time of labor and establishes a linear time with cumulative results (Arendt 1958: 98, 141–44, 153–54, cf. 96–101).

The temporality of action differs from both these forms of temporality. Action does not reproduce itself in the natural circle of biological life, nor does it aim at establishing material things or sensible tangible objects. It does not "produce" anything in the sense of bringing forth or setting up. Its results are, in Arendt's words, "even less durable and more futile than what we produce for consumption" (Arendt 1958: 95). This should not be taken as a defect or shortcoming, but must be seen as essential to the intentionality of action: instead of bringing forth things, actions manifest or express the spiritual essence of the acting agent, his "unique distinctness" (Arendt 1958: 176, cf. 179–80).

Thus, Arendt argues that the temporality of human action is radically different from the temporalities of work and labor, production and reproduction. Whereas labor connects us as organisms in the cyclic time of nature and work connects us as operators in the cumulative process of production, action binds us together as unique, incomparable subjects who by necessity begin something new, something unforeseen and unpredictable. This means that action is essentially characterized by natality and new beginnings. Arendt claims: "The miracle that saves the world, the realm of human affairs, from its normal, 'natural' ruin is ultimately the fact of natality, in which the faculty of action is ontologically rooted. It is, in other words, the birth of new men and the new beginning, the action they are capable of by virtue of being born" (Arendt 1958: 247, cf. 177, 144).

Despite the lack of all permanent material results—or rather thanks to this—action has a specific type of durability and mediation. The deed vanishes with its performance without leaving any sensible traces, but it can be witnessed by other speaking agents, and the witnesses can testify to the reality, strength, and meaning of the action by their words. Thus action can, as it were, be held alive and continued by narration.[38] Narration establishes a double dependency between the acting subject and the witnesses of the action. The witnesses can convey the action to spatially distant others, persons who did not perceive the action because they were somewhere else. But even more importantly, the witnesses can keep the action alive by narrating it to temporally distant others in successive generations.

This implies that we are dependent on others and especially on diachronic others, successors and newcomers, in the maintenance of our actions in their discursive form. For all its immateriality and spirituality, this mediation is not less real than the world of sensible things that we share in perception (Arendt 1958: 183). On the contrary, it establishes its own links that stand material decay and physical destruction, and thus it secures the stability and continuity of the human world (Arendt 1958: 95–97).

Narrating an action does not mean accounting for it, nor recounting, recording, reproducing, representing, or reduplicating it. Rather, what Arendt has in mind is a mimetic replay or recitation of the action and its setting, which allows the agent to reappear in a new medium and context (Arendt 1958: 187, cf. 181). Thus narration cannot be executed in the third-personal mode but must be presented in first person. Instead of describing the action in declarative language, the narrator takes on the position of the agent and acts as he acted. He becomes the agent by play-acting, by mimetically and imitatively repeating the witnessed or traditionally mediated actions. Thus the activity of the narrator allows the living essence of the original agent to disclose itself again, to shine again in its distinctive uniqueness.

Arendt argues that action always initiates a new process in the human realm, a unique life story (cf. Arendt 1958: 177, 184). But she also insists that action alone is not sufficient to identify and introduce its subject as an agent in the community of unique equals. For this speech is needed, not descriptive language, which is able only to characterize and capture the *what* of the agent, the general qualities that he shares with other agents. "Speech" for Arendt means language in its *indexical* use. Only the indexical "I" is able to address others as possible witnesses of action and draw their attention to the speaker as a unique agent (Arendt 1958: 179).[39]

Together action and speech—action accompanied by speech—start a new process in the community of human agents: action is the source of originality and uniqueness, and speech introduces the process into the publicity and plurality of human lives. The process, Arendt explains, will eventually emerge as a story with an open structure characteristic of human life. In this structure, individual actions and speech acts converge and cohere, and even diversions and larger alterations manifest the unique way that characterizes the particular life as a whole.

Such stories may be recorded in documents and reified in monuments, but they themselves—in their living flowing reality—are of an altogether different nature as such "reifications." The recited life story and the imitative replay of its actions tell us always more about the subject than any record can, not by encompassing a larger set or a larger amount of deeds and words, but by disclosing a unique way of acting and speaking, the living open essence of the agent. The person initiates his story but he does not complete it, as his way of acting and speaking is recited in ever new, unpredictable situations. Arendt explains:

> Although everybody started his life by inserting himself into the human world through action and speech, nobody is the author or producer of his own life story. In other words, the stories, the results of action and speech, reveal their agent, but this agent is not an author or producer. Somebody began it [the story] and is its subject in the twofold sense of the word, namely its actor and sufferer, but nobody is its author. (Arendt 1958: 184; cf. Merleau-Ponty [1945] 1993: 466/407)

The entering into the community, the birth of the subject as a speaking agent, can be remembered, and this memory of the social birth serves as the basis for the anticipatory awareness of death, or the exit from the community of humans. So the ultimate basis of our individuality is not in our being-towards-death but is in our emergence as speaking and acting persons. The ethical and political implications of this view are far-reaching. They concern us not just as contemporaries, but also as members of historical communities.

As a summary, we can state that Arendt comes close to Lévinas in her emphasis on birth as a necessary principle of human life. Moreover, she agrees with Lévinas in arguing that our dependency on others is not just empirical but ontological or transcendental: my life depends on the lives of others not just in the biological sense of survival and reproduction, or in the economic sense of material prospect, but more fundamentally in the existential sense of individual becoming.

In distinction from Lévinas, Arendt does not give sexual difference any role in the establishment of human temporality but positions it at the level of organic life defined by cyclic temporality and replaceable individuals. Thus all discussion about male and female agents would be merely derivative or, worse, senseless in Arendt's conceptual framework. The difference from Lévinas proves smaller, however, when we recall that Lévinas too compromises his radical rethinking of sexual relations by arguing that femine existence only prepares for or assists the establishment of futurity and does not take part in it. In both cases femininity is conceptualized as a nondiscursive phenomenon and as such it falls short of the type of temporality characteristic of genuine human life—ethical or political.

In order to find resources for rethinking intersubjectivity and undoing the associative chains that link femininity to mere sensibility and animality, we need to turn to Beauvoir's feminist reflections. My claim is not that Beauvoir's existentialism is the only resource for theorizing femininity, for certainly there are more recent and more radical contributions. The point is that Beauvoir's philosophical essays include fundamental ontological insights that allow a reasoned affirmation of feminine *subjectivity*, insights that were neglected by her contemporaries and are still often overlooked or misrepresented as merely social-ethical theses.

The Freedom of the Other

Simone de Beauvoir's critical discussion of Heidegger's concept of being-towards-death does not form a systematic argument or an alternative account in the way that Lévinas's and Arendt's discussions do. What we have is just sporadic remarks in her ethical essays *Pyrrhus and Cineas* and *The Ethics of Ambiguity* that address the general nonacademic audience and discuss the concrete problems of oppression, violence, and responsibility in postwar Europe and America (Beauvoir 1944: 61–62/114–15; 1947). However, Beauvoir founds her existential ethics on the view that the self-transcending movement of our lives ties us together in a profound way. Moreover, she argues that the intersubjective connection provides us with a past and a future that surpasses the limits of our birth and death.

Beauvoir explicates her view of intersubjectivity and temporality most clearly in *The Ethics of Ambiguity*. She uses the Sartrean terms of transcendence, freedom, and will to convey her understanding of the fundamental interrelatedness of human subjects, but she explicates these terms by the phenomenological concepts of disclosure and sense-giving. She writes: "For a freedom wills itself authentically only by willing itself as an indefinite movement towards the freedom of others . . . [T]o be free . . . is to be able to surpass the given towards an open future; the existence of others as a freedom defines my situation and is even the condition of my own freedom" (Beauvoir 1947: 127/90–91, translation modified).

Freedom, in Beauvoir's ontological sense, refers to human beings as subjects of world-disclosure and sense bestowal. At the very beginning of her essay, she explains: "To will the disclosure of the world and to will one's own freedom are one and the same movement. Freedom is the source from which all significations and all values spring" (Beauvoir 1947: 34/24, cf. 111/78, 121–22/86–87).[40]

Beauvoir argues that the world is given to us as a network of directions, values, and meanings, and as such it requires our own constitutive involvement (1947: 104–12/74–80). By our intentional acts we give sense to being and can thus relate to multiplicities of different kinds of objects—utensils and tools, artworks and expressions, material things and spiritual entities. However, rather than functioning as open field for unlimited actions or as an object of disinterested observations, the world presents itself as an inheritance or a legacy. Correspondingly, our sense-bestowing activity is not comparable to the act of creation but must be seen as a *re-creation* or *re-enactment* (Beauvoir 1947: 123–24/88).

The idea of the world as an inheritance has two aspects: First, it means that the world is not constructed but received by us, and handed down to us by our predecessors (Beauvoir 1947: 109/77, 129–30/92–93; cf. Husserl Hua15: 37–38, 138–40, 171–73, 218–19, 448–49; Merleau-Ponty [1945] 1993: 498–501/437–39; Beauvoir 1945: 365–66/161–63). Second, the idea of inheritance also implies that our own activities of sense bestowal refer internally to future others who can add new layers of sense to our accomplishments. Thus understood, the activity of sense bestowal is cumulative; it rests on senses already established and adds new layers of meaning to them. Beauvoir argues that we can recognize this trans-generational movement most easily in scientific and artistic practices (1947: 111–13/79–81, cf. 1944: 61/113–14; Merleau-Ponty 1960: 73–75/59–61), but she also emphasizes that it characterizes equally our everyday dealings with utensils and tools.

This means that the activity of intending worldly objects, such as utensils, tools, artworks, or mere material things, presupposes other intending selves, contemporary but also preceding and subsequent. In other words, the movement of transcending ourselves toward the world is, by necessity, communal:

> [F]reedom cannot will itself without aiming at an open future. The ends which it gives itself cannot be transcended by any reflection, but only the freedom of other men can extend them beyond our life. (Beauvoir 1947: 100/71, cf. 40–41/27–28)

> As we have seen, my freedom, in order to realize or fulfill itself, requires that it refers to an open future; it is other men who open the future to me, it is they who constitute the world of tomorrow, define my future. (Beauvoir 1947: 116/82)

The formulations that we find in *The Ethics of Ambiguity* are ambiguous in that they suggest different types of dependency, some of which are weaker and some stronger. The idea of extension implies that the dependency is merely quantitative and that each life is self-sufficient or autonomous in its basic form. In this understanding, the others would, as it were, stretch the temporal dimensions of my life, but they would have nothing to contribute to its form. The prolongation or extension that they provide would be an external addition, and my life would proceed as it proceeds independently of such prospects.

Other paragraphs suggest a more radical line of thought in which the other's freedom is not just conceived as the extension of mine but is understood as the very condition of my self-transcendence. When Beauvoir states that "the existence of others as a freedom defines my situation and is even the condition of my own freedom" (Beauvoir 1947: 127/91), she argues that my life would not have its open futural form without the other selves. This suggests that the other's life does not just prolong my life but is the very condition for the openness and incompleteness of my living. The others do not just prevent the stagnation of my life by their acts of remembrance and reinterpretation, as if in retrospect. The dependency is more intimate: I need to have diachronic others included in my life—as intended and indicated—in order to sustain its openness. This means that I can realize my self-transcendence, my surpassing of myself and the present, only with others; or better, my life opens toward the future due to the coexistence of diachronic others.

Beauvoir's fundamental difference from Heidegger concerns the understanding of subjectivity and its separateness. Beauvoir approves Merleau-Ponty's and Sartre's Cartesian approach, according to which selfhood or ipseity is inscribed in all experiences and can come to the focus in several different ways (Beauvoir 1947: 24–25/17, 222–23/158–59).[41] My social self may be a constituted object, as Sartre contends,[42] but independently of this constitution an absolute, unique ego accompanies my experiences and the continuum of my experiencing. This ego is not the reflective subject but is the temporal form or mode of experiencing characteristic of my intentional personal life. Thus it is not just the possibility of dying that may "awaken" me and make me realize my separation and uniqueness; any experience of radical alterity—threatening or vitalizing—may have the same result. Beauvoir's early novel *She Came to Stay* (*L'invitée* 1943) pictures exactly such an "awakening" experienced by the main character Françoise:

> Face to face with her solitude, beyond space, beyond time, stood this alien presence that had for so long crushed Françoise with her blind shadow: Xavière was there, existing only for herself, entirely self-centered, reducing to nothingness everything for which she had no use; she encompassed the whole world within her own triumphant solitude, boundlessly extending her influence, infinite and unique; everything that she was, she drew from within herself, she barred all dominance over her, she was absolute separateness. (Beauvoir 1941: 440/403–404)[43]

This Cartesian setting connects Beauvoir's existentialism to Lévinas's metaphysical ethics. Both model their accounts of intersubjectivity on Descartes's *Meditations on First Philosophy*, which presents to us not just the *ego cogitatio* but also a subject that unexpectedly comes across an other that exceeds all the measures and standards derived from the subject himself.[44] At the end of the Third Meditation, Descartes describes how the glorious appearance of God interrupts his self-induced meditation and fills him with admiration and joy (Descartes 1641). Lévinas refers explicitly to this paragraph when developing his own account of intersubjectivity: "The last paragraph of the Third Meditation brings us to a relation with infinity in thought which overflows thought and becomes a personal relation" (Lévinas [1961] 1971: 233/212).[45] Beauvoir's references are less direct, but her characterizations of the intersubjectivity of the couple rephrase the Cartesian idea of the encounter with a radically incomparable, measureless other.

The other enters my world by surprise. He appears unexpectedly, overwhelms my life, and interrupts my dealings with environing things and people. He does not simply succumb to or settle in my life but transforms my life by opening a new temporal dimension in it. This means that the self and this other are not just separated in space, as contemporaries are, but also live in temporal disharmony or discord. Insofar as the fundamental gap between the self and the other can be bridged by acts of love and generosity, both lives receive new temporal horizons. Insofar as I can sustain myself in the other's appearance and becoming, I can gain a new future (and past) from him. Insofar as I hear myself in his words and see myself in his movements, gestures, and actions, I find in him my own self enriched with and reformed by another life. In Lévinas's account, such a metamorphosis or transformation can happen between the parent and child, and between the teacher and the pupil, but Beauvoir ventures to suggest that it can also occur between mutually generous members of nonhierarchical couples, such as lovers, coworkers, and writers. What is necessary for such a temporal transformation is generosity and love, not any hierarchy of authority or power.

Insofar as the measureless other is identified with a worldly—or otherworldly—entity, neither Beauvoir nor Lévinas can offer a genuine alternative to Heidegger's transcendental reflection on mortality and death. But neither seems to be satisfied with such a resolution: rather than falling back on empirical accounts of communality or collectivity, both struggle to develop further the existential-phenomenological concept of transcendental intersubjectivity by inquiring into the relations between diachronic subjects,[46] that is, pairs of persons that do not just share time but constitute time together.

Beauvoir's uniqueness in this discussion of human futurity is that she sees our existence as including two different ways of becoming, the feminine and the masculine. No human being is a sexless spirit or a driven animal, but each has a place in the human genealogy that divides into two lines of inheritance, one passing through men and the other passing through women. Both sexes have their own pasts and futures—interrelated but not identical—and both contribute in their own specific ways to the general form of human becoming. Beauvoir argues that the difference between these two ways of being human cannot be defined by the traditional philosophical oppositions between the sensible and the intellectual, the bodily and the spiritual, or the cyclic and the cumulative. Rather than dividing human capacities and functions among them, the two sexes actualize and develop these capacities in their own specific ways.

Finitude, Mortality, and Embodiment

We can now finally return to Beauvoir's thesis about the association of women with finitude and mortality. As we saw in the beginning of the explication, Beauvoir argues that we all, both men and women, tend to associate women with finitude and death, on the one hand, and men with infinitude and pure activity, on the other hand. Her critical thesis is that this association is a relic of a mythical form of thinking that still lumbers and burdens our philosophies of human life despite their conceptual and theoretical sophistication. Women are conceived as messengers or warrantors of death, and death and mortality are pictured by feminine qualities.

The association is repeated throughout our culture; it is inscribed in our artistic and scientific products and engraved even in languages. Beauvoir undertakes the task of analyzing the association in order to undo its hold on our thought and action. She distinguishes two different forms, one that concerns *finitude* and another that concerns *mortality.* Both are grounded on an androcentric interpretation of women's bodily functions. This means that the reconceptualization of finitude and mortality requires that we question our ideas of embodiment and bodily norms.

Beauvoir points out that on the basis of the regular processes of their reproductive lives—menstruation, pregnancies, deliveries, lactation—women are considered to be more intimately bound with their bodies, and more profoundly dominated by them than are men. She argues that we tend to believe or imagine that women are restricted by their bodies more severely than men because men's bodies operate in our discourse as the human norm. When conceptualizing human life, male philosophers and theorists have usually conceived their own adult bodies as the normal case and characterized all other variations of human embodiment as deviations from this standard. Women for their part have accepted this norm and never seriously challenged its validity. As a result, abnormal cases include not just diseased and injured bodies, but also infant bodies and aged bodies; most awkwardly, the female body is understood as a deviation without considering the possibility that it provides an alternative standard and a different basis of normality.

Beauvoir traces this neglect back to a philosophical forgetfulness and lack of self-understanding. She argues that men have failed to realize and acknowledge the subjective character of their own embodiment and have pictured their bodies as universal tools: "He grasps his body as a direct and normal relation with the world, which he believes he apprehends in its objectivity, whereas he regards the body of woman as weighted down by everything specific to it: an obstacle, a prison" (Beauvoir [1949] 1993: 15/15, cf. 242/175).[47]

The tacit, implicit norm of the male body serves as the ground for two associative chains, one that ties women to finitude and the other that ties them to mortality. In both cases women's experiences are considered as divergences from the "human norm" grounded in male experiences.

The first chain of association proceeds from feminine embodiment to animal sensibility and inanimate nature. Women's bodily functions are associated with animals, plants, and earthly elements, and their lived bodies are reduced to the spatial-temporal boundaries of such objects. Woman may appear as rich as the natural world and with all its sensible and perceivable qualities, but by the same token she loses her position and her stand in the process of human becoming, descends into the uniform spatiality of nature, and succumbs to its cyclic time (Beauvoir [1949] 1991: 261–65/187–90).

The other habit of thinking is metonymic. Women are reduced to their generative functions and pictured as birth-givers. When this notion is connected to the idea that birth is the starting point of the process of dying, then women are seen as the messengers of death and the warrantors of mortality. Beauvoir writes:

> The Mother dooms her son to death in giving him life; the loved one lures her lover on to renounce life and abandon himself to the last sleep [. . .]. Born of flesh, the man in love finds fulfillment as flesh, and the flesh is destined to the tomb. Here the alliance between Woman and Death is confirmed; the great harvestress is the inverse figure of the fecundity that makes the grain thrive. But she appears also as the dreadful bride whose skeleton is revealed under her sweet, mendacious flesh. (Beauvoir [1949] 1991 274/197, cf. 282–85/203–205)

Mythical gendered notions about embodiment and sensibility still dominate our discourses on finitude and mortality. These notions cannot be abandoned by simple rejection. What is needed is a reconceptualization of our carnal condition, one that takes into consideration both its variants, the feminine and the masculine, and moreover considers both variants from both viewpoints. We should take seriously what Beauvoir states at the end of *The Second Sex:* woman's relation to the child and to the man will never be the same as man's relation to her and to the child. To learn how these relations are lived, experienced, and symbolized by woman, we have to attend to the descriptions that women issue of their experiences, most importantly those of motherhood and erotic love. These descriptions demonstrate that the mother and her unborn child do not form a simple natural unit, outside of all meaning constitution, but institute a communicative couple. The memory of birth thus involves more than just the recollection of one's entry into public space by spontaneous speech acts; it also includes an archaic memory of being addressed by someone already before being able to form sentences. Similarly we learn that the beloved woman is an active lover; her life does not submerge into pure sensibility but retains its personal expressive form even in the most intimate and sensuous exchanges.

The task is not to construct a theory on the basis of such experiences but to study their content and form in an unprejudiced way. What remains to be articulated is that these experiences are not simply sensuous or merely animal, but are most fundamentally human. This task will challenge and reform our thinking of mortality, death, and life.

NOTES

1. Beauvoir, for example, ends *A Very Easy Death* (*Une mort très douce* 1964) by writing: "All men are mortal: but for each man his own death is an accident, and [...] an undue violence " (1964: 150).

2. Cf. Bernet 2002; Cohen 2006.

3. Prior to Beauvoir's and Merleau-Ponty's conceptualizations, Edith Stein discussed different human *types,* including the sexual types (masculine and feminine), as part of her phenomenology of human life (cf. Stein [1920] 2004: 127–46, 1932–33/2004: 141–44, 2000, 2001). Eugen Fink ([1979] 1995) and José Ortega y Gasset developed later the idea of sexual types, but their discussions are not informed by any equalitarian or feminist insight. Ortega's discussion in *Man and People* (1957) explicitly distances from zoological concepts and characterizes sexual types as similar to artistic genres: "What we call 'woman' is not a product of nature but an invention of history, just as art is [...] Instead of studying woman zoologically, it would be infinitely more fertile to contemplate her as a literary genre or an artistic tradition" (Ortega 1957: 134–35; cf. Merleau-Ponty [1945] 1993: 197–202/169–73; Beauvoir [1949] 1993: 73/66, [1949] 1991: 643/725; Heinämaa 2003). Unfortunately Ortega's descriptions of femininity repeat commonplace preconceptions that associate femininity with ambivalence, ambiguity, and diffuseness (Ortega 1957: 130–37; cf. Rider 1998: 223–29).

4. Judith Butler criticizes Merleau-Ponty for overlooking sexual difference and also for making untenable assumptions about the intentionality of desire. In Butler's reading, Merleau-Ponty's phenomenological account of sexuality is both androcentric and "heteronormative" (Butler 1989). I have argued elsewhere—against Butler and other critics—that Merleau-Ponty's concepts and distinctions can be developed into a fruitful account of sexual difference (Heinämaa 2003, 2005, 2006, 2010a, 2010b, 2010c).

5. The questions of sexuality and sexual difference are excluded from Heidegger's *Being and Time.* Sartre draws attention to this exclusion in *Being and Nothingness* and argues that Heidegger rightly classifies sexuality among *factical* structures (*facticité*) but wrongly concludes from this that sexual difference is an *accidental* and *contingent*—nonnecessary—structure (Sartre [1943] 1998: 423/498–99). For Sartre sexuality, or sexual desire, is an original attitude that is necessarily part of our being-in-the-world ([1943] 1998: 422–47/497–528). Thus fundamental ontology must, in his understanding, include an explication of sexuality (Sartre [1943] 1998: 424/499).

Jacques Derrida defends Heidegger's solution in his *Psyché* essays and argues that the exclusion is not an omission or neglect but required by Heidegger's overall project of reformulating the question about the meaning of being. According to Derrida, Heidegger did not forget or ignore the topics of sexuality and sexual difference; his definition of phenomenology as an inquiry into the meaning of being did not allow for such a study (Derrida 1987a, 1987b). Lévinas attacks exactly this way of thinking and, following Sartre, argues that Heidegger's exclusion of sexual difference was a fundamental philosophical mistake (cf. Wyschogrod [1974] 2000: 131; Sandford 2000: 36). Luce Irigaray's *An Ethics of Sexual Difference* (*Éthique de la différence sexuelle* 1984) develops further the Lévinasian argument against Heidegger but offers also a detailed critique of Lévinas's own assumptions about sexuality (cf. Irigaray 1991).

6. Lévinas states: "While the existent is accomplished [*s'accomplit*] in the 'subjective' and in 'consciousness,' alterity is accomplished in the feminine. This term is on the same level as, but in meaning opposed to, consciousness" (Lévinas 1947: 81/88, translation modified). In the later work *Totality and Infinity,* Lévinas associates femininity with what precedes the ethical constitution of subjectivity, that is, with sensibility, enjoyment, habitation, and dwelling.

7. For Beauvoir's critique of Lévinas's concept of otherness, see Heinämaa (2003: 89–91, 125–27). Cf. Sandford 2000.

8. Lévinas's argument is against the *egological* tradition of modern thinking, which reaches from Kant to Husserl and Heidegger and their existential followers. In "Diachrony and Representation" (Diachronie et représentation 1982), Lévinas sums up his main argument, connecting egological philosophy to oculocentricism: "In *thought* understood as vision, knowledge, and intentionality, intelligibility thus signifies the reduction of the Other [*Autre*] to the Same, synchrony as *being* in its egological gathering. The *known* expresses the unity of the transcendental apperception of the *cogito,* or the Kantian *I think,* the egology of presence affirmed from Descartes to Husserl, and up to Heidegger where, in paragraph 9 of *Being and Time, Dasein's* 'toward-being' [*à-être*] is the source of *Jemeiningkeit* and thus of the Ego" (Lévinas [1982] 1991: 167/99; cf. Bernet 2002; Cohen 2006).

As regards the constitution of the living bodies and worldly objects, Husserl's egology is manifested in his argument about the constitutive primacy of one's own body. In *Crisis,* for example, Husserl explains his view as follows: "Everyone experiences the embodiment of souls in original fashion only in his own case. What properly and essentially makes up the character of a living body I experience only in my own living body, namely, in my constant and immediate holding-sway [over my surroundings] through this physical body alone. Only it is given to me originally and meaningfully as 'organ' and as articulated into particular organs [...] Obviously it is only in this that I have perceptions and, beyond this, other experiences of objects in the world. [...] Only through my own original experienced holding-sway, which is the sole original experience of living-bodiliness as such, can I understand another physical body as a living body in which another 'I' is embodied and holds sway" (Husserl Hua6: 220–21/217–18, cf. Hua1: §44 127–30/96–99, Hua15: Nr. 37 648–57).

9. In *Tod und Fortleben* (1911–14), Max Scheler argues—following Heidegger's remarks in *Being and Time* (§75)—that our consciousness of time develops or changes in the process of aging. Also Beauvoir's discussions with Sartre in *Adieux* (*La cérémonie des adieux* 1981) include an interchange on death and aging that develops further the

philosophical analyses that she outlined in the second volume of her *Old Age* (*La vieillesse* 1970). For Beauvoir's discourse of old age, see Heinämaa 2010c.

10. Lévinas distinguishes his notion of resurrection from the traditional spiritual concept explicated by Spinoza: "Contrary to the Spinozist tradition, this going beyond death is produced not in the universality of thought but in the pluralist relation, in the goodness of being for the Other, in justice" (Lévinas [1961] 1971: 336–37/301–302).

11. In *Totality and Infinity*, Lévinas argues that the idea of limitation is dependent on the idea of totality: "Limitation is produced only within a totality, whereas the relation with the Other breaks the ceiling of the totality" (Lévinas 1961/1971: 187/171).

12. For Lévinas, love is a *personal* relation in the pregnant sense that it preserves the self: "[t]he subject is still a subject through eros" (Lévinas 1947: 82/89). It is, however, not to be understood as a *possibility* of the self (cf. Lévinas [1961] 1971: 50/57).

13. In *Totality and Infinity*, Lévinas explains: "Anticipation grasps possibles; what the caress seeks is not situated in a perspective and in the light of the graspable" (Lévinas [1961] 1971: 288–89/258).

14. Luce Irigaray formulates this idea in an illuminative way: "A future coming not measured by the transcendence of death but by the call to birth of the self and the other. For which each one arranges and rearranges the environment, the body, and the cradle, without closing off any aspect of a room, a house, an identity. The fecundity of a love whose most elementary gesture, or deed, remains the caress" (Irigaray 1984: 174/186).

15. Lévinas makes clear that he is describing a certain level of *intentional movement*: the movement (*movement, marche*) of the caress and its affective intentionality (Lévinas 1947: 81–83/88–89, [1961] 1971: 284/254, 288–92/258–61, 295–96).

16. Here Lévinas develops further the argument that Socrates, paraphrasing Diotima, launches against Aristophanes in Plato's *Symposium*: the goal of love is not fusion, reproduction, or production, but is "engendering and begetting upon beauty" (Plato 1997: 206e, 489–90; cf. Lévinas [1961] 1971: 57–58/63, 285/254–55; Irigaray 1984: 31–33/25–27). On Lévinas's crucial indebtedness to Plato's metaphysics, see Sandford 2000.

17. Cf. Chanter 1995: 199; Sandford 2000.

18. In my mind, the most interesting critique is presented by Stella Sandford in *The Metaphysics of Love* (2000). For other feminist critiques of the dialectical step from the erotic to the paternal, see Chalier 1982, Irigaray 1984, Chanter 1990, Irigaray 1991, Thayse 1998, Chanter 1995: 196–207, Perpich 2001, Chanter 2001, Oliver 2001.

19. A crucial but often ignored part of Irigaray's critical response is her argument that Lévinas conceives of the erotic encounter as a relation between two bodies demarcated by the *visible* contours of *skin*. Thus, Irigaray claims, Lévinas is bound to ignore the tactile dynamics of inner spaces and their mucous membranes, marked by bodily orifices and apertures (Irigaray 1991: 180, cf. 1977: 24–29/24–30, 1984: 24–25/18–19, 107–108/109–11, 176/188–89). Irigaray's critique suggests that Lévinas prioritizes skin as a boundary because it is given, not just tactilely, but also visibly. This is philosophically problematic as it compromises Lévinas's critique of oculocentrism (e.g., Lévinas [1982] 1991). Irigaray contests Lévinas's assumptions about the bodily boundaries by a discussion of Aristotle's concept of place. In Aristotle's *Physics,* she argues, "there is never any idea that the boundary of the containing [feminine] body might be the skin, while passing through the mucous membranes and through the body and the flesh"

(Irigaray 1984: 55/50, cf. 50/44–45). Cf. Rudolf Bernet's discussion of the idea of the living body as "a bag of skin" (*sac de peau*) (Bernet 1998: 92–111).

20. Cf. Sandford (2000: 3–4).

21. Cf. Cohen (2006: 27). Stella Sandford (2000) argues that the crucial tension in Lévinas's thinking is between his phenomenological descriptions and analyses, on the one hand, and his metaphysical arguments, on the other hand. Moreover, Sandford undertakes to show that the feminine has a crucial role in the upholding of this tension: "these analyses also show—against the various attempts to argue otherwise—that the gendered vocabulary of these discussions [. . .] is integral to Levinas' philosophical argument and cannot be rendered innocuous through redescription" (Sandford 2000: 4). Cf. Irigaray 1991: 183.

22. Heidegger offers a more complex analysis of the sense of Da-sein in his later work *Contributions to Philosophy (From Enowning) (Beiträge zur Philosophie [Vom Ereignis]* 1936–38).

23. Cf. Wyschogrod (1974/2000: 133). On this point, Lévinas is influenced by Kierkegaard, who argues that the absolute, immediate relation to God is primary to the social relations between equals mediated by rules and laws (e.g., Lévinas 1961/1971: 282–84/252–53; cf. Arendt 1932/1994: 46). Another source is Husserl's fifth Cartesian Meditation (Hua1), which shows that the sensual-perceptional relation between the self and another living body is constitutionally primary (in the static analysis) to the social and communicative relation between equals. Cf. Römpp 1989; Bernet 1998; Overgaard 2002, 2003.

24. Cf. Aristotle's *Metaphysics* (7.3. 1028b33–1029b13).

25. For a discussion of the mother-daughter pair, see Guenther 2006, Sebbah 2006, Guenther 2007.

26. For an illuminative interpretation, see Sandford 2000.

27. Lévinas opposes the feminine movement to the enlightening (Husserl) and disclosing or unveiling (Heidegger) movements of consciousness and intentional activity: "The movement here is thus reverse. The transcendence of the feminine consists in withdrawing elsewhere, which is a movement opposed to the movement of consciousness," which is a transcendence toward light (Lévinas 1947: 81/88, 1961/1971: 288–92/258–61). For the Nietzschean background of Lévinas's discourse on femininity, see Derrida 1979.

28. Cf. Bernet (2002: 89–90).

29. Arendt wrote her doctoral dissertation on Augustine's concept of love under the supervision of Karl Jaspers in the late 1920s. The title of the work was *Der Liebesbegriff bei Augustin: Versuch einer philosophischen Interpretation* (1929). The work was translated into English by E. B. Ashton in 1963, and published in a revised and edited form with the title *Love and Saint Augustine* (1996). Arendt herself revised Ashton's translation, and two editors, Joanna Vecchiarelli Scott and Judith Chelius Stark, further modified or "Englished" the text (Scott and Stark 1996). It is only the later revised English version that makes explicit Arendt's critical approach to Heidegger's concept of being-towards-death.

30. As said, Arendt explicates her divergence from Heidegger only in the revised English version of her treatise on Augustine. Observe that Arendt speaks about "expectations" and not just anticipation.

31. Cf. Schües 1997, 2000. It must be emphasized that Arendt's concept of natality does not imply that a person would remember the event of his own physical birth. The

memory of one's own physical birth is impossible because the perceiving and recollective self is only born in this event and thus cannot undergo it.

32. In the realm of perceivable activities, action and speech differ from labor and work by being momentary and ephemeral. Action and speech share this characteristic with the nonmaterial and solitary (nonperceivable) activity of thinking (Arendt 1958: 95).

33. Actually Arendt's distinctions are more complex. She introduces and develops two different types of distinction. On the one hand, she distinguishes between three types of activity in relation to the material world: labor, work, and action. On the other hand, she distinguishes also between three types of mental or spiritual life: thinking, willing, and judging. *The Human Condition* is known for the first set of distinctions, whereas the two volumes of her later work, *The Life of the Mind* (1978), clarify the latter set of distinctions. See also her *Between Past and Future: Six Exercises in Political Thought* (1961).

34. To avoid misunderstandings, it must be emphasized that Arendt's distinction between labor, work, and action is a conceptual distinction, not a real distinction. Thus, concrete behavior and conduct can include all three types of activity (see, e.g., Arendt 1958: 138, 143).

35. The paradigmatic and traditional example of labor activity is tilling the soil, which Arendt characterizes as "the most necessary and elementary labor of man" (Arendt 1958: 138–39). However, her concept of labor seems to be modeled primarily on the notion of giving birth: labor is a bodily activity, it is involuntary and painful, and it ties its subject to the private realm divorced from the public world of equal men (Arendt 1958: 47n38, 72–73, 112–15, 119–20, 140). Arendt also uses the term "begetting" for the reproduction of new laboring individuals (Arendt 1958: 117). Cf. Dietz 1991; Benhabib 1996: 134–37.

36. From the point of view of the cyclic life of the species, the individual member is dispensable: "The inexhaustibility of this labor force corresponds to the deathlessness of the species, whose life process as a whole is also not interrupted by the individual births and deaths of its members" (Arendt 1958: 124).

37. Arendt emphasizes that labor can be defined only in the context of and in distinction from work: "The destructive, devouring aspect of laboring activity, to be sure, is visible only from the standpoint of the world and in distinction from work" (Arendt 1958: 100, cf. 94). This means that from its own standpoint, labor cannot be characterized as destructive; in other words, insofar as we experience labor as demanding, devouring, or destructive in its cyclic time and repetitive movements, we have already taken the viewpoint of work (or action) and live in its linear temporality.

38. This involves three types of activity from the part of the witness, the one who continues the activity: first, perceiving an action as a manifestation of thought and a thinking person (seeing and hearing it), not just as an object, but more fundamentally as an expression; second, keeping the perceived action in memory as a manifestation or expression; and third, transforming the action and the manifested thought into tangible and material things that have duration and can be perceived and handed over to others (Arendt 1958: 95).

39. Ludwig Wittgenstein's discussion of the function of the pronoun "I" helps to clarify Arendt's concept of speech. In his late works, *Philosophical Investigations* (1954) and *The Blue Book* (1958), Wittgenstein argues that the *logical* function of the pronoun "I" is not demonstrative but indexical (and performative). When a person uses the

pronoun "I" in a declarative sentences, such as "I have pain," he does not refer to, designate, or pick up any one person among other persons but uses the term to draw attention to himself. So the word "I" does not have the role of the pointing finger; rather it functions in ways similar to a cry (Wittgenstein 1958: 67, cf. [1954] 2003: 190; see also Malcolm 1989: 144–47). Danna Villa argues in *Arendt and Heidegger: The Fate of the Political* (1996) that Arendt's concept of action is fundamentally performative (and aestheticizing); cf. Kharkhordin 2001.

40. Here Beauvoir forges together the Sartrean concept of freedom and the Heideggerian concept of disclosure. Moreover, she connects both to Husserl's idea of sense-bestowing activity that she found explicated in Merleau-Ponty's *Phénoménologie de la perception* (cf. Beauvoir 1945).

41. See especially Merleau-Ponty [1945] 1993: 512–14/448–51.

42. See Sartre 1936–37; cf. Beauvoir 1955.

43. See also Merleau-Ponty 1945; cf. Cutrofello 2005: 358–68; Björk 2009: 157–96.

44. In Cantor's terms, whatever infinity or eternity the ego may find in itself, the other comes with an infinity of a greater cardinality.

45. Lévinas identifies a certain understanding of finiteness as Heidegger's Kantian starting point: "The finite is here no longer conceived by relation to the infinite; quite the contrary, the infinite presupposes the finite, which it amplifies infinitely […] The Kantian finitude is described positively by sensibility, the Heideggerian finitude by being for death. This infinity referring to the finite marks the most anti-Cartesian point of Kantian philosophy as, later, of Heideggerian philosophy" (Lévinas [1961] 1971: 214/196, cf. 231–32/210; cf. Husserl 1997: 442–44; Palmer 1997: 427–29). To this Lévinas opposes his own return to Cartesianism, to the Cartesian understanding of infinity, in which the idea of infinity is "put in" the self by a separate being. For Lévinas the source of infinity is not in God but in the other person (Lévinas [1961] 1971: 215/197).

46. For Husserl's account of the generative intersubjectivity, see Steinbock 1995; Zahavi 1996: ch. IV and ch. V.1.

47. Compare to Hannah Arendt's sympathetic analysis of the philosopher's attitude in *The Life of the Mind:* "To put it quite simply, in the proverbial absentmindedness of the philosopher, everything present is absent because something actually absent is present to his mind, and among the things absent is the philosopher's own body. Both the philosopher's hostility toward politics, 'the petty affairs of men,' and his hostility toward the body have little to do with individual convictions and beliefs; they are inherent in the experience itself. While you are thinking, you are unaware of your own corporality" (1978: 84).

BIBLIOGRAPHY

Note: Date in square brackets is the original publication date; the following date is the edition cited. Where two sets of page numbers are given in citations in text, the first is the cited edition in the original language, and the second is the English edition.

Arendt, Hannah. [1929] 1994. *Der Liebesbegriff bei Augustin: Versuch einer philosophischen Interpretation.* Berlin: Verlag con Julius Springer.

————. [1932] 1994. "Søren Kierkegaard." In *Essays in Understanding 1930–1954: Formation, Exile, and Totalitarianism*. New York: Schocken Books.

————. 1958. *The Human Condition*. Chicago: Chicago University Press.

————. 1961. *Between Past and Future: Six Exercises in Political Thought*. New York: Viking Press.

————. 1978. *The Life of the Mind*. Ed. Mary McCarthy. New York: Harcourt Brace Jovanovich.

————. 1996. *Love and Saint Augustine*. Trans. E. B. Ashton, ed. Joanna Vecchiarelli Scott and Judith Chelius Stark. Chicago: Chicago University Press.

Aristotle. *Metaphysics I–IX*. Trans. Hugh Tredennick. Cambridge, Mass.: Harvard University Press.

Beauvoir, Simone de. 1943. *L'invitée*. Paris: Gallimard. In English *She Came to Stay*. Trans. Yvonne Moyse and Roger Senhouse. New York: Norton, 1990.

————. 1944. *Pyrrhus et Cinéas*. Paris: Gallimard. In English *Pyrrhus and Cineas*. Trans. Marybeth Timmermann. In *The Beauvoir Series*, volume 1: *Philosophical Writings by Simone de Beauvoir*. Ed. M. A. Simons and S. Le Bon de Beauvoir, 92–149. Urbana: University of Illinois Press.

————. 1945. "La phénoménologie de la perception de Maurice Merleau-Ponty." *Les temps modernes* 1, no. 2: 363–67. In English "A review of *Phenomenology of Perception* by Maurice Merleau-Ponty." Trans. Marybeth Timmermann. In *The Beauvoir Series*, vol. 1: *Philosophical Writings by Simone de Beauvoir*. Ed. M. A. Simons and S. Le Bon de Beauvoir, 159–64. Urbana: University of Illinois Press.

————. 1947. *Pour une morale de l'ambiguïté*. Paris: Gallimard. In English *The Ethics of Ambiguity*. Trans. Bernard Frechtman. New York: Carol Publishing Group Editions, 1994.

————. [1949] 1993. *Le deuxième sexe I: les faits et les mythes*. Paris: Gallimard. In English *The Second Sex*. Ed. and trans. H. M. Parshley. Harmondsworth: Penguin, 1987.

————. [1949] 1991: *Le deuxième sexe II: l'expérience vécue*. Paris: Gallimard. In English *The Second Sex*. Ed. and trans. H. M. Parshley. Harmondsworth: Penguin, 1987.

————. 1955. "Merleau-Ponty et le pseudo-sartreanism." In *Privilèges*. Paris: Gallimard. Originally in *Les temps modernes* 10 (114–15): 2072–122. In English "Merleau-Ponty and pseudo-sartreanism." Trans. Veronique Zaytzeff. In *International Studies in Philosophy* 21 (1989): 3–48. Reprinted in *The Debate between Sartre and Merleau-Ponty*, ed. Jon Stewart. Evanston, Ill.: Northwestern University Press, 1998.

————. 1964. *Une mort très douce*. Paris: Gallimard. *A Very Easy Death*, trans. Patrick O'Brian. New York: Warner.

————. 1970. *La vieillesse I–II*. Paris: Gallimard. In English *Old Age*. Trans. Patrick O'Brian. London: Penguin, 1972.

————. 1981. *La cérémonie des adieux suivi de Entretiens avec Jean-Paul Sartre: août–septembre 1974*. Paris: Gallimard. In English *Adieux: A Farewell to Sartre*. Trans. Patrick O'Brian. New York: Pantheon Books, 1984.

Benhabib, Seyla. 1996. *The Reluctant Modernism of Hannah Arendt*. Thousands Oaks, Calif.: Sage.

Bernet, Rudolf. 1998. "Encounter with the Stranger: Two Interpretations of the Vulnerability of the Skin." In *Phenomenology of Interculturality and Life-World*, ed. Ernest Wolfgang Orth and Chan-Fai Cheung, 89–111. Freiburg: Verlag Karl Alber.

————. 2002. "Levinas' Critique of Husserl." In *The Cambridge Companion to Levinas,*
ed. Simon Critchley and Robert Bernasconi, 82–99. Cambridge: Cambridge
University Press.

Björk, Ulrika. 2009. *Poetics of Subjectivity: Existence and Expressivity in Simone de
Beauvoir's Philosophy.* Doctoral diss. Philosophical Studies from the University of
Helsinki 21. Helsinki: Helsinki University Press.

Butler, Judith. 1989. "Sexual Ideology and Phenomenological Description: A Feminist
Critique of Merleau-Ponty's Phenomenology of Perception." In *Thinking Muse:
Feminism and Modern French Philosophy,* ed. Jeffner Allen and Iris Marion Young,
85–100. Bloomington: Indiana University Press.

Chalier, Catherine. 1982. *Figures du féminin: lecture d'Emmanuel Lévinas.* Paris: La nuit
surveillée.

Chanter, Tina. 1990. "The Alterity and Immodesty of Time: Death as Future and
Eros as Feminine in Levinas." In *Writing the Future,* ed. David Wood, 137–154.
London: Routledge.

————. 1995. *Ethics of Eros: Irigaray's Rewriting of the Philosophers.* New York:
Routledge.

————. 2001. *Time, Death, and the Feminine: Lévinas with Heidegger.* Stanford, Calif.:
Stanford University Press.

Cohen, Richard A. 2006. "Levinas: Thinking Least about Death—contra Heidegger."
International Journal for Philosophy of Religion 60: 21–39.

Cutrofello, Andrew. 2005. *Continental Philosophy: A Contemporary Interpretation.* New
York: Routledge.

Derrida, Jacques. 1979. *Spurs: Nietzsche's Styles / Éperons: Les Styles de Nietzsche.*
Chicago: University of Chicago Press.

————. 1987a. "*Geschlect I:* Différence sexuelle, différence ontologique." In *Psyché:
Inventions de l'autre,* Tome 2, 15–34. Paris: Galilée.

————. 1987b. "Le main de Heidegger (Geschlecht II)." In *Psyché: Inventions de l'autre,*
Tome 2, 35–68. Paris: Galilée.

Descartes, René. 1641. *Meditationes de Prima Philosophia.* In *Œuvres de Descartes, Band
7.* Ed. Charles Adam and Paul Tannery. Rev. ed. Paris: Vrin/C.N.R.S. In English
Meditations on First Philosophy. In *The Philosophical Writings of Descartes.* Vol. 2.
Trans. John Cottingham, Robert Stoothoff, and Dugald Murdoch. Cambridge:
Cambridge University Press, 1991.

Dietz, Mary G. 1991. "Hannah Arendt and Feminist Politics." In *Feminist
Interpretations and Political Theory,* ed. Mary Lyndon Shanley and Carole
Pateman, 232–52. Oxford: Polity.

Guenther, Lisa. 2006. "'Like a Maternal Body': Emmanuel Levinas and the Motherhood
of Moses." *Hypatia* 21, no. 1: 119–136.

————. 2007. *The Gift of the Other: Levinas and the Poetics of Reproduction.* New York:
SUNY.

Fink, Eugen. [1979] 1995. *Grundphänomene des menschlichen Daseins.* Freiburg: Karl
Alber.

Heidegger, Martin. [1927] 1993. *Sein und Zeit.* Tübingen: Max Niemeyer. In English
Being and Time. Trans. John Macquarrie and Edward Robinson. Oxford:
Blackwell, 1992.

————. [1936–38] 1994. *Beiträge zur Philosophie (Vom Ereignis), Gesamtausgabe, Band
65.* Ed. F.-W. von Herrmann, 2nd ed. Frankfurt am Main: Vittorio Klostermann.

In English *Contributions to Philosophy (From Enowning)*, trans. Parvis Enad and Kenneth Maly. Bloomington: Indiana University Press, 1999.

Heinämaa, Sara. 2003. *Toward a Phenomenology of Sexual Difference: Husserl, Merleau-Ponty, Beauvoir.* Lanham, Md.: Rowman and Littlefield.

———. 2005. "The Soul-Body Union and Its Sexuality: From Descartes to Merleau-Ponty and Beauvoir." In *Feminist Reflections on the History of Philosophy,* ed. Lilli Alanen and Charlotte Witt, 137–51. Dordrecht: Kluwer, 2004.

———. 2006. "Feminism." In *A Companion to Phenomenology and Existentialism,* ed. Hubert Dreyfus and Mark Wrathall, 500–513. Malden, U.K.: Blackwell.

———. 2010a. "A Phenomenology of Sexual Difference: Types, Styles, and Persons." In *Feminist Metaphysics: Explorations in the Ontology of Sex, Gender and Identity,* ed. Charlotte Witt. Dordrecht: Springer. Forthcoming.

———. 2010b. "Personality, Anonymity and Sexual Difference: The Temporal Formation of the Transcendental Ego." In *Time in Feminist Philosophy,* ed. Christina Schües, Dorothea Olkowski, and Helen Fielding. Bloomington: Indiana University Press. Forthcoming.

———. 2010c. "Transformations of Old Age: Selfhood, Normativity, and Time." In *Age Aging: On Simone de Beauvoir's* The Coming of Age, ed. Silvia Stoller. Forthcoming.

Husserl, Edmund. Hua1. *Cartesianische Meditationen und pariser Vorträge.* Ed. Stephan Strasser. The Hague: Martinus Nijhoff, 1950. In English *Cartesian Meditations.* Trans. Dorion Cairns. Dordrecht: Martinus Nijhoff, 1960.

———. Hua6. *Die Krisis der europäischen Wissenschaften und die transzendentale Phänomenologie: Eine Einleitung in die phänomenologische Philosophie.* Ed. Walter Biemel. The Hague: Martinus Nijhoff, 1954. In English *The Crisis of European Sciences and Transcendental Phenomenology: An Introduction to Phenomenological Philosophy.* Trans. David Carr. Evanston, Ill.: Northwestern University, 1988.

———. 1997. *Psychological and Transcendental Phenomenology and the Confrontation with Heidegger (1927–1931).* Ed. and trans. Thomas Sheehan and Richard E. Palmer, 434–71. Dordrecht: Kluwer Academic Publishers.

Irigaray, Luce. 1977. *Ce sexe qui n'en est pas une.* Paris: Minuit. In English *This Sex Which Is Not One.* Trans. Catherine Porter with Carolyn Burke. Ithaca, N.Y.: Cornell University Press, 1985.

———. 1984. *Éthique de la différence sexuelle.* Paris: Minuit. In English *An Ethics of Sexual Difference.* Trans. Carolyn Burke and Gillian C. Gill. Ithaca, N.Y.: Cornell University Press, 1993.

———. 1991. "Questions to Emmanuel Levinas." In *The Irigaray Reader,* ed. Margaret Whitford. Oxford: Basil Blackwell.

Kharkhordin, Oleg. 2001. "Nation, Nature and Natality: New Dimensions of Political Action." *European Journal of Social Theory* 4, no. 4: 459–78.

Lévinas, Emmanuel. 1947. *Le temps et l'autre.* Paris: Quadrige/PUF. In English *Time and the Other.* Trans. Richard A. Cohen. Pittsburgh, Pa.: Duquesne University Press, 1987.

———. [1947] 1993. *De l'existence à l'existants.* Paris: Vrin. In English *Existence and Existents.* Trans. Alphonso Lingis. Dordrecht: Kluwer Academic Publishers.

———. [1961] 1971. *Totalité et infini: Essai sur l'extériorité.* Paris: Kluwer Academic. In English *Totality and Infinity.* Trans. Alphonso Lingis. Pittsburgh, Pa.: Duquesne University Press.

————. [1982] 1991. "Diachronie et représentation." In *Entre nous: essais sur le penser-à-l'autre*, 165–84. Paris: Grasset. In English "Diachrony and Representation." In *Time and the Other*, 97–120. Trans. Richard A. Cohen. Pittsburgh, Pa.: Duquesne University Press, 1987.

————. 1984: *Difficile liberté*. 3rd ed. Paris: Albin Michel. In English *Difficult Freedom*. Trans. Seán Hand. Baltimore, Md.: Johns Hopkins University Press, 1990.

Malcolm, Norman. 1989. *Wittgenstein: Nothing Is Hidden*. Oxford: Basil Blackwell.

Merleau-Ponty, Maurice. 1945. "Le roman et la métaphysique." *Cahiers du Sud 22*, no. 270. Reprinted in *Sen et non-sens*, 34–52. Paris: Gallimard, 1966. In English: "Metaphysics and the Novel." In *Sense and Non-Sense*, 26–40. Trans. Hubert L. Dreyfus and Patricia Allen Dreyfus. Evanston, Ill.: Northwestern University Press, 1964.

————. [1945] 1993. *Phénoménologie de la perception*. Paris: Gallimard. In English *Phenomenology of Perception*. Trans. Collin Smith. New York: Routledge and Kegan Paul, 1995.

————. 1960. "La langage indirect et les voix du silence (a Jean-Paul Sartre)." In *Signes*. Paris: Gallimard. In English "Indirect Language and the Voices of Silence (to Jean-Paul Sartre)." In *Signs*. Trans. Richard C. McCleary. Evanston, Ill.: Northwestern University Press, 1964.

Oliver, Kelly. 2001. "Parental Election and the Absent Father." In *Feminist Interpretations of Emmanuel Levinas*, ed. Tina Chanter. University Park: Pennsylvania State University Press.

Ortega y Gasset, José. 1957. *Man and People*. Trans. Willard R. Task. New York: Norton. Original *El hombre y la gente*.

Overgaard, Søren. 2002. "Epoche and Solipsistic Reduction." *Husserl Studies* 18, no. 3: 209–22.

————. 2003. "On Levinas' Critique of Husserl." In *Metaphysics, Facticity, Interpretation: Phenomenology in the Nordic Countries*, ed. Dan Zahavi, Sara Heinämaa, and Hans Ruin, 115–38. The Hague: Kluwer.

Palmer, Richard E. 1997. "An Introduction to Husserl's Marginal Remarks in *Kant and the Problem of Metaphysics*." In Edmund Husserl, *Psychological and Transcendental Phenomenology and the Confrontation with Heidegger (1927–1931)*, ed. and trans. Thomas Sheehan and Richard E. Palmer, 425–33. Dordrecht: Kluwer Academic Publishers.

Perpich, Diane. 2001. "From the Caress to the World: Transcendence and the Feminine in the Philosophy of Emmanuel Levinas." In *Feminist Interpretations of Emmanuel Levinas*, ed. Tina Chanter. University Park: Pennsylvania State University Press.

Plato. 1997. *Symposium*. Trans. Alexander Nehamas and Paul Woodruff. In *Completed Works*. Indianapolis: Hackett.

Rider, Sharon P. 1998. *Avoiding the Subject: A Critical Inquiry into Contemporary Theories of Subjectivity*. Stockholm: Thales.

Römpp, G. 1989. "Der Andere als Zukunft und Gegenwart: Zur Interpretation der Erfahrung fremder Personalität in temporalen Begriffen bei Lévinas und Husserl." *Husserl Studies* 6, no. 2: 129–54.

Sandford, Stella. 2000. *The Metaphysics of Love*. London: Athlone Press.

Sartre, Jean-Paul. 1936–37. *La transcendance de l'ego: esquisse d'une decription phéno-ménologique*. *Recherches Philosophiques*. Vol. 6. In English *The Transcendence of the*

Ego: An Existentialist Theory of Consciousness. Trans. Forrest Williams and Robert Kirkpatrick. New York: Hill and Wang, 1960.

———. [1943] 1998. *L'être et le néant: essai d'ontologie phénoménologique*. Paris: Gallimard. In English *Being and Nothingness: A Phenomenological Essay on Ontology*. Trans. Hazel E. Barnes. New York: Washington Square Press.

Scheler, Max. [1911–14] 1979. *Tod und Fortleben*. Munich: Francke Verlag.

Schües, Christina. 1997. "The Birth of Difference." *Human Studies* 20: 243–52.

———. 2000. "Empirical and Transcendental Subjectivity: An Enigmatic Relation?" In *The Empirical and the Transcendental: A Fusion of Horizons*, ed. B. Gupta. Lanham, Md.: Rowman and Littlefield.

Scott, Joanna Vecchiarelli, and Judith Chelius Stark. 1996. Preface. In Hannah Arendt, *Love and Saint Augustine*. Ed. Joanna Vecchiarelli Scott and Judith Chelius Stark. Chicago: University of Chicago Press.

Sebbah, François-David. 2006. "Levinas: Father / Son / Mother / Daughter." *Studia Phenomenologica* 6: 261–73.

Stein, Edith. [1920] 2004. *Einführung in die Philosophie, Edith Stein Gesamtausgabe 8*. Ed. Claudia Mariéle Wulf. Freiburg: Herder.

———. [1932–33] 2004. *Der Aufbau der menschlichen Person: Vorlesung zur philosophischen Anthropologie, Edith Stein Gesamtausgabe 14*. Ed. Beate Beckmann-Zöller. Freiburg: Herder.

———. 2000. *Die Frau: Fragestellungen und Reflexionen, Edith Stein Gesamtausgabe 13*. Ed. Maria Amata Neyer. Freiburg: Herder. In English *Essays on Woman, The Collected Works of Edith Stein II*. Trans. Freda Mary Oben. 2nd rev. ed. Washington: ICS Publications, 1996.

———. 2001. *Bildung und Entfaltung der Individualität: Beiträge zum christlichen Erziehungsauftrag, Edith Stein Gesamtausgabe 16*. Ed. Maria Amata Neyer and Beate Beckmann. Freiburg: Herder.

Taminieux, Jacques. 1992. *La fille de Thrace et le penseur professionel: Arendt et Heidegger*. Paris: Éditions Payot.

Thayse, Jean-Luc. 1998. *Eros et fécondité chez le jeune Levinas*. Paris: L'Harmattan.

Villa, Dana R. 1996. *Arendt and Heidegger: The Fate of the Political*. Princeton, N.J.: Princeton University Press.

Wittgenstein, Ludwig. [1954] 2003. *Philosophische Untersuchungen*. Frankfurt am Main: Suhrkamp Verlag.

———. 1958. *Blue and Brown Books*. Ed. Rush Rhees. New York: Harper and Row.

Wyschogrod, Edith. [1974] 2000. *Emmanuel Levinas: The Problem of Ethical Metaphysics*. New York: Fordham University Press.

Zahavi, Dan. 1996. *Husserl und die transzendentale Intersubjektivität: Eine Antwort auf die sprachpragmatische Kritik*. Dordrecht: Kluwer.

PART 3
Nietzsche's Philosophy of Life

SEVEN

Nietzsche's Philosophy of Birth
SIGRIDUR THORGEIRSDOTTIR

Friedrich Nietzsche is a philosopher of birth and the body. The metaphor of birth is at the center of his philosophy of embodied life. In his philosophy Nietzsche introduces the conception of birth to convey an understanding of Dionysian philosophy as a form of thinking that is in tune with embodied life as both natal and mortal. By incorporating features that have in the history of Western philosophy been associated with the feminine into his idea of the Dionysian philosopher, Nietzsche transcends a traditional one-sided masculine philosophical conception of the self (Thorgeirsdottir 2004). As a result a fuller understanding of human life as embodied life emerges. With this "natal turn" Nietzsche opposes a denial of the body and a focus on mortality that he views as paradigmatic for our philosophical tradition ever since the days of Socrates (Shchyttsova 2008: 155).

Ever since the beginning of the reception of Nietzsche's philosophy women and feminist philosophers have discussed his philosophical notions of birth and the body both critically and affirmatively. These interpretations give an insight into how a growing philosophy of birth contributes to a more diversified understanding of the human subject as both natal and mortal, individual and relational, masculine and feminine, natural and cultural. At the same time, it becomes more apparent how a philosophical tradition that focuses on the "mortal subject" emphasizes a solitary and disembodied notion of the self. The goal of the following is to examine how Nietzsche's philosophy of birth can be seen as a resource for developing a richer notion of the subject. This idea of the subject will in the following be termed as the *natal* subject because it is examined in light of the philosophy of birth. The first part of this interpretation will thus consist in an examination of Nietzsche's philosophy of birth and death as a backdrop to his conception of the natal subject. Special emphasis will be given to how Nietzsche in his reflections on the feminine and birth pluralizes sexual difference to arrive at a more integrated conception of the natal subject. The conception of birth is necessarily an important metaphor for intersubjective relations, as Julia Kristeva has argued (Kristeva 1986). The metaphor of birth in Nietzsche's philosophy primarily represents the ability of the creative philosopher to explore and harness plurality within himself, and recreate or give birth to himself. The relational implications of this conception of birth are secondary, and it requires thinkers who are especially interested in relational dimensions of the self to shed light on the natal subject in Nietzsche's philosophy from the point of view of relations to the other. The second part will thus in the first place give special attention to psychoanalytically inspired interpretations of Nietzsche's philosophy of birth that draw attention to the relational features of it and discuss how the interpersonal constitutes the personal (Kelly Oliver, Julia Kristeva, Sabina Spielrein, Lou Andreas-Salomé). Secondly, Hannah Arendt's anti-solipsistic and political philosophy of natality will be discussed, but it is influenced by Nietzsche's philosophy of birth and very critical of it at the same time. Exploring Nietzsche's philosophy of birth in light of these thinkers thus allows us to shed critical light on it, and to uncover resources within it to go beyond an arelational tendency and the problematic political implications of that tendency.

Nietzsche is interested in birth as an experience that is characterized by a combination of pain and joy. Birth is for him a paradigmatic example of a phenomenon in which great pain and lust come together, in which something ends and something new begins. He wants birth to trump death and mortality, which have been seen as a definitive basis for a philosophical outlook on human existence. What is at stake for him is not to deny or repress the thought of death and mortality, but rather to affirm the continuity of life with death. By abstracting from real, physical birth he turns birth into a metaphor for the creative disposition of the Dionysian philosopher, who thinks in tune with life and the body. Such philosophers of the future are a counterproposal to the disembodied rationality of the Enlightenment-project that Nietzsche attacks. The creativity of the philosophers of the future is not restricted to production of works of art. It is rather creativity in the much wider sense of the ability for a creative form of embodied thinking, a thinking that Nietzsche thinks is more in tune with life itself.

Because Nietzsche describes the Dionysian philosopher as being pregnant with and giving birth to his thoughts and actions, Derrida claims that Nietzsche is the thinker of pregnancy, which is no less praiseworthy in a man than in a woman (Derrida 1979: 65). In describing Dionysian creativity as pregnancy and birth Nietzsche has, however, been criticized in feminist scholarship for appropriating a feminine experience for a masculine ideal. The elevation of procreation in Nietzsche's statements about the philosophical disposition is reminiscent of the ancient dream of the superfluity of women that Vigdis Songe-Møller finds in the philosophies of ancient Greek thinkers in her book *Philosophy without Women: The Birth of Sexism in Western Thought* (Songe-Møller 2002). Despite opening philosophy up to its forgotten other, birth and the body, Nietzsche is criticized by Luce Irigaray for disregarding and repressing the maternal, forgetting the one who gives life, and thus for committing matricide (Irigaray 1991: 26–27). Nietzsche's apparent disregard of the maternal and the other as constitutive aspects of the self furthermore seems to be based on a misogynistic out-look.[1] Nietzsche is thus charged with appropriating elements traditionally associated with the feminine, such as birth and the body, in his attempts to portray the sovereign, self-creating individual that results in an image of a male endowed with elements of the feminine (Singer 1998; Schutte 1998).

Quite apart from questions about Nietzsche's appropriation of the feminine, feminist interpretations are characterized by attempts to mine Nietzsche's philosophy for resources to think sexual difference, and differ-ence in general, in a manner that can be of importance for feminist philoso-phy and philosophy of difference. Thus I shall argue that with his philosophy of birth Nietzsche deconstructs sexual difference, undermines essentialist ideas about the sexes, and thus opens up possibilities of change. He over-throws the idea of sexual dichotomy in favor of a plurality of sexual dif-ferences.[2] Nietzsche connects the Dionysian and birth, and that reinforces the ambiguous nature of this deity as both masculine and feminine. That allows the Dionysian to represent a possibility of a plurality of sexual iden-tities. Given that there are numerous descriptions of women in Nietzsche's philosophy that echo traditional, essentialist, sexist clichés, one has to ask whether he envisions that women remain the same, and only men should strive for a more pluralistic sexual identity. That is possibly the case, even though such a state of affairs would not be advantageous to the pluraliza-tion of sexual differences. The general thrust of his thought on the matter of sexual difference is, namely, that difference is of vital importance. He is opposed to equality of the sexes, for he assumes that its goal is to render the sexes the same. That in his view undermines plurality and a necessary vital tension that differences bring about.

As compared with Nietzsche's ideas on sexual difference, the topic of birth has been much less examined. In Nietzsche's late philosophy the Dionysian is at one point represented by a feminine figure, Baubo, who plays a role in the ancient Greek myth about Demeter. This myth, which Nietzsche alludes to at the end of the preface to the second edition of *The Gay Science* (1886), concerns birth. The myth illustrates for Nietzsche the thought of life as eternal return, affirming time and the natural world. The eternal return is becoming-of-life as will to power. Life as a battle of wills is characterized by growth and decay, becoming and perishing. The conception of birth fore-closes a simplistic interpretation of will to power as mere domination. One of the features of birth is that it entails submitting to a process, opening oneself up to something that overtakes one. With his conception of birth, Nietzsche suggests a complex understanding of the interplay of passivity and activity, submission and domination, control and spontaneity. The conception of the natal self that emerges in these reflections shows another Nietzsche, a Nietzsche who presents a dynamic understanding of the self in terms of strength and vulnerability. It is not the Nietzsche who pushes a traditional, masculine ideal of the autonomous and self-sufficient individual to its extreme, culminating in a self-defeating notion of strength as Theodor Adorno has argued.[3] One can find both types of ideals in his writings, a "wise" and a "strong" type, but each in its own way represents different pos-sibilities that Nietzsche experiments with in his philosophy (Müller-Lauter 1999: 84–90). Before discussion of this other Nietzsche of the natal self the main lines of the interpretation need to be introduced.

The Relational, Natal Self

The strengths and vulnerabilities of the natal self become apparent in the relation to itself as well as in exposure to others. Therefore special attention has to be given to the question of intersubjectivity with regard to Nietzsche's conception of birth. For that purpose one has to go beyond the subjectivist aspects of Nietzsche's multifaceted conception of birth, which reads "at times like an escape from others" as Rosalyn Diprose writes. Yet, as Diprose claims, even creative self-formation "incurs a debt to the other" (Diprose 1993: 3). One of the first interpreters of Nietzsche's philosophy, Lou Andreas-Salomé, so much emphasized that one does not create oneself that she had it as a motto for her own biography (Andreas-Salomé 1991). Reflections on preg-nancy and birth in Nietzsche's philosophy do contain a challenge to the masculine ideal of a disengaged, autonomous self. Nietzsche's conception of birth displays the manner in which wills interact with each other both on the intrapersonal level and on the intersubjective level. The individual is for Nietzsche a divided self, as he writes in *Human, All Too Human* (1876–78) a "plurality of lived beings" (Nietzsche 1996: 53, I [57]), and as will to power the individual can measure him- or herself only against other wills. The individual can therefore, as Werner Stegmaier argues, understand him- or herself only in relation to other individuals (Stegmaier 1997: 319). With one aspect of his conception of birth Nietzsche describes the transformative processes that take place in relation to oneself and to others. Birth is a prime example of an encounter with otherness that is a precondition for seeing oneself and the other in a new and different light.

The idea of the self-creation of the Dionysian philosopher who gives birth to himself and to his works entails some reflections on the paternal and the maternal dimensions of relations. Kelly Oliver does not accept Irigaray's interpretation as to matricide in Nietzsche's philosophy, but argues instead that the maternal becomes a "masculine mother" (Oliver 1995: xvi). In her view, such a model of the mother lacks the real, physical features of the relations of the maternal body to the fetus and the placenta that prefigure, for Oliver, an "inter-subjective theory of subjectivity as a process of exchanges" (Oliver 1995: xvii). Even though Nietzsche does appropriate and abject the physical dimensions of the maternal for his conception of Dionysian creativity, the relational implications of his conception of birth do in my view offer some resources for such an idea of intersubjective exchange (Oliver 1994: 53–67). I argue that there are aspects to Nietzsche's model of birth that do have intersubjective features that go beyond the model of domination and submission that Oliver claims Nietzsche exclusively adheres to. Based on a distinction of the feminine and the maternal, Oliver argues that Nietzsche equates the maternal with nature, which has to be controlled and conquered (Oliver 1994: xvi). Despite his appropriation of the maternal, Nietzsche does also in my view account for relations to the maternal that are social relations and not only relations to nature in this above-mentioned sense. This becomes evident in a passage in *The Gay Science* where he distinguishes between female mothers and artists as "male mothers":

> The females find in their children satisfaction for their desire to dominate, a possession, an occupation, something that is wholly intelligible to them and can be chattered with. The sum of all this is what mother love is; it is to be compared with an artist's love for his work. Pregnancy has made women kinder, more patient, more timid, more pleased to submit, and just so does spiritual pregnancy produce the character of the contemplative type, which is closely related to the feminine character: it consists of male mothers. (Nietzsche 1974: 129 [72])

This description of philosopher-artists as male mothers displays how Nietzsche abstracts from real physical birth as a female experience. Arendt, for whom natality was a central conception of her philosophy, has also been criticized for not taking the bodily basis of natality into account (Honig 1995: 1–16). In her book on Arendt, Kristeva has shown how Nietzsche's thought of life as eternal return is a major point of departure for Arendt's philosophy of natality (Kristeva 2001: 44).[4] Kristeva interprets Arendt's conception of natality as implicitly based on the relation between the mother and the child she gives birth to. This relation prefigures for her—as also for Oliver, who explicitly acknowledges her debt to Kristeva in this matter—the relation to the other.

Natality is arguably one of the central motives of Arendt's thought; the eternal return of life as will to power is likewise Nietzsche's central doctrine. There are great differences between Nietzsche's philosophy of birth and Arendt's philosophy of natality, in terms of both philosophical context and intention, as Arendt acknowledges in her reflections on Nietzsche (Arendt 1978: 158–71). Whereas Arendt discusses natality primarily with reference to active (political) life, the notion of birth in Nietzsche's philosophy is tied to questions concerning an embodied existential, creative disposition of the individual. Nietzsche's idea of the eternal return as eternal repetition has a dimension of negativity that Arendt's in many ways more sympathetic notion of natality does not have. Common to both authors is, however, an idea of creativity as disposition of openness to newness, otherness, and plurality. In viewing Nietzsche's notion of birth in light of Arendt's anti-solipsistic understanding of the natal self, the political implications of Nietzsche's idea of the natal self become apparent. Both authors share the idea of the importance of creative renewal in the areas of culture and politics, for which birth/natality is the metaphor.

In examination of Nietzsche's philosophy as a background for important aspects of Arendt's conception of natality, special attention will be given to how Nietzsche's idea of natal, creative existence is one point of departure for Arendt's conception of natality. The purpose of the comparison of Arendt and Nietzsche is twofold. It establishes in the first place a connection between the Nietzschean philosophy of birth and Arendt's philosophy of natality that has not been worked out in research on philosophies of birth. In the second place, it serves to show the importance of the body and intersubjective relations in philosophical reflections on issues pertaining to birth and natality. Despite some underrepresented feminine features of birth in Nietzsche's philosophy, his physiology of embodiment is not restricted only to the male body, but opens a way to address lived, feminine experiences of embodiment, as Kristen Brown has argued (Brown 2007: 7, 27–44). Compared to Arendt's conception of natality as a hopeful beginning of something new, Nietzsche's conception of birth displays features of ambivalence because the experience of the eternal return entails dimensions of dread and horror. This ambivalence of creation and destruction was of interest to early psychoanalytical interpreters of Nietzsche's philosophy. The dimension of ambivalence is rooted in Nietzsche's understanding of the continuity of life with death. A discussion of the notion of ambivalence in Nietzsche's conception of birth can offer a possibility of discussing difficult features of birth that have to do with embodiment and relations to one self and others in a way Arendt's conception of natality does not.

Meanings of "Birth"

Before proceeding to work out bodily and relational aspects of the conception of birth, it is necessary to list the major meanings given to birth in Nietzsche's philosophy. Birth is a metaphor for metaphysics of life as a vital force, which constitutes as such a continuous process of becoming and dying (Thorgeirsdottir 2000). It has both an aesthetic and an epistemological meaning, which have to do with the creative production of knowledge and values by the Dionysian philosopher. Birth has existential meaning, since it demonstrates the interdependence of joy and suffering in life that one has to learn to accept in accord with Nietzsche's idea of *amor fati*, or learning to love one's destiny. Furthermore, life seen as birth implies the wonder of Dionysian self-renewal. As opposed to the ancient understanding of philosophical wonder, which Plato regarded as the origin of philosophy, and as an insight of the intellect, the birth metaphor illustrates for Nietzsche an experience of wonder and newness in which body and mind come together.[5] Such an experience of wonder is an encounter with otherness, and it entails a spiritual dimension because it locates the spiritual in the physical. It is an event that generates unpredictability and difference. This idea of birth corresponds to Gilles Deleuze's interpretation of the eternal return, as an eternal rebirth of difference, as reproduction of diversity (Deleuze 1983). A thinking that confronts otherness is a precondition for plurality and creative thinking that can question and go beyond given morals.

The concept of birth is a common denominator in all encounters with the other, be it in oneself, others, or life itself. In the first place, the other is the other of the embodied self, its prediscursive reality as well as its hidden or less-known aspects, in opposition to the rational and autonomous self. Secondly, it is the otherness in the encounter between two that marks the difference between self and other; and thirdly, it is the otherness in life when one experiences something as unexpected, different, wondrous, or new. Self as understood in light of these aspects of otherness is a natal self. It is a self that is embodied and in a continuous process of being born. It is a self in the process of becoming through encounters that transfigure both the self and the other. A dialogue is creative when two different partners create something new that they cannot generate alone. The concept of birth in Nietzsche's philosophy is here primarily interpreted from this perspective of giving birth as a metaphor for a creative, transforming, mutually empowering experience. Less emphasis is put on other aspects of birth, such as parturition, the succession of generations, and genealogies.

Philosophy of Natal Life beyond Submission and Dominance

Life, body, and nature, understood in light of birth, are things to which one has to open oneself and submit. This is a precondition for the experience that Nietzsche views as the basic philosophical experience of wonder as an experience of the other. As something that man has limited control over, the notion of birth sheds light on aspects of the will to power that have to do with vulnerability, dependence, passivity, devotion, and spontaneity, as opposed to aspects that have to do with self-assertion and dominance.

Understood as a natal phenomenon, life acquires a dimension of enigma and elicits respect. This conception of life goes beyond a notion according to which life is mainly seen as making and production. Natal life is in important respects excluded from fabrication. As such, natal life symbolizes the creative, spontaneous powers that Nietzsche juxtaposes to technical, instrumental, disembodied rationality. Nietzsche's idea of natal life as spontaneity can be seen as offering a basis for setting limits and restrictions to a dehumanizing view of life as an object of manipulation, control, and violence. This aspect of his philosophy needs to be thought alongside the more robust dimensions of the will to power.

Nietzsche opposes binary thinking about mind and body, birth and death, self and other, that has been gender coded. By linking the Dionysian and the concept of birth Nietzsche thus undermines the predominantly male-oriented idea of man so common in Western philosophy. At the same time his idea of Dionysian creativity as ecstatic, eruptive, unrestrained, and aggressive accords with customary notions and clichés about virility and masculinity. If one wants to be ironic, Nietzsche's appropriation of the feminine can be seen as comparable to wearing drag, and Nietzsche, the philosopher of birth, as a kind of a drag queen in philosophy.[6] On a less-ironic note, the attempt undertaken here consists in directing attention to aspects of

Nietzsche's philosophy that yield a philosophy of embodied, relational, and pluralistic sexual identity. For in his philosophy Nietzsche was struggling with issues of sexual identity, experimenting with homosexual and bisexual elements, "feminine" and "masculine" parts of himself, thus raising issues regarding the self as the same [sex] and as other [sex]. He also described his creative need as a longing for children, who become something different than himself. This complicates matters, making Irigaray's interpretation of annihilation of the mother—insofar as it entails reproduction of the same rather than opening up to the feminine other—too simplistic an explanation for his philosophy of birth (Irigaray 1991: 187).

The early psychoanalytical thinkers Sabina Spielrein and Lou Andreas-Salomé were fascinated by Nietzsche's struggle with sexual identity in his philosophy of natal and mortal life. They were among the first to discuss how Nietzsche dissolves a strict division between the feminine and the masculine in his reflections about his own identity. This led them to uncover complex patterns in his reflections on birth and creation and on death and destruction. Their psychoanalytic interpretations point to the varied dynamics in the relation to the other in Nietzsche's texts. These are presumably the first interpretations of Nietzsche's philosophy in which the category of gender is applied to draw out the "unthought" in the texts by analyzing images and metaphors, omissions and paradoxes.[7]

These interpretations also make evident Nietzsche's nonidealized view of relationality and "motherhood." Love and aggression, care and violence, often coexist in a relation to the other. Nietzsche does not replace a traditional, philosophical notion of death with birth, in the way that Grace Jantzen does, who proposes natality and flourishing as an alternative to the fixation on death that she associates with violence (Jantzen 2004). Birth and death are rather to be seen as complementary concepts of Nietzsche's philosophy of life. They are intertwined with his idea of life as struggle of wills to power. Life entails giving and taking, receiving and loosing, greeting and parting.[8] Sexual difference is central to Nietzsche's conception of birth insofar as it represents the opposite forces that bring life into being. As a metaphor for relations, birth entails opening up toward the other, and that necessarily disarms one and makes one vulnerable. Can the aggressive, self-centered Dionysian pathos really allow for such a disposition? It can insofar as it is understood as merely one aspect of the many sides of the Dionysian self that Nietzsche articulates with his idea of the plurality of sexual differences. Life understood as birth is the very phenomenon in which the plurality of forces, as expression of different wills, comes to play.

Philosophy of Life

The tradition of *Lebensphilosophie,* or philosophy of life, from the latter part of the nineteenth century to the beginning of the twentieth century, had life as the central category. The proponents of this tradition, among them Arthur Schopenhauer, Henri Bergson, and Friedrich Nietzsche, held different views on what life is, whether "will to life," "élan vital," or "will to power." Common to them all, however, is the idea that a philosophical inquiry into what it means to be must start out from the question of what life is. In its most basic form, life is generative power, a dynamic, natural phenomenon. Birth and death are forces that interact in life as circulatory processes of becoming and decay. In terms of human beings, life is also a lived experience of the embodied mind. Although this coincides with the ancient Greek distinction between *zōē,* the simple condition of being alive common to all living beings, and *bios,* the way of living proper to a human individual or group, Nietzsche does not uphold the distinction.[9] It is one that was determinative of the traditional mind/body dualism of Western philosophy, something that Nietzsche seeks to undermine. His goal is to show how life is the generative power inherent in everything that lives and that the life that has been associated with man and social existence is part of life as will to power. His belief in the creative power of human beings to transform themselves is based on his belief in the creative powers of life itself. To be in tune with such powers does require effort on behalf of the creative philosopher, who, for Nietzsche, is basically the person who creates his or her own life. That often causes pain and suffering because the creative person is frequently at odds with dominant morals, values, and outlooks. Giving birth to oneself by emancipating oneself from repressive morals is often painful and involves sacrifices.

With its emphasis on life as generative power, exemplified by the metaphor of birth, Nietzsche's critical stance toward a philosophical tradition that has seen human mortality as of major importance for a philosophical view of life becomes apparent. The Socratic model of mortality and immortality is for Nietzsche central to this tradition. Common to this both ancient and modern philosophy of death (for example, Martin Heidegger's philosophy of death) is the idea that finiteness gives human existence its ultimate meaning. If life were endless it would not have meaning or purpose. Human life would be endless, like circular nature.

The idea that human life is distinct and separate from nature in this regard goes together with the ancient idea of the immortality of the soul, according to which the soul survives the mortal fate of the body. In death men were able to escape the mortal fate they were thrown into through the fact of their birth. Birth marked the entrance into mortality, bodily nature, and impermanence. Death on the other hand marked the liberation from mortal nature and elevation to immortality and purity of thought.

Philosophy of Death

Nietzsche seriously questioned this duality of human life and nature that has prevailed in our philosophical tradition. The goal of his philosophical anthropology was to put man back into nature that he might regain an understanding of human life as a natural phenomenon. He was opposed to an understanding of human nature as something that transcends its natural confinement for the sole reason that he believed that the duality of body and soul devalued human and earthly life. He believed that this denaturalizing tradition laid the groundwork for subsequent European philosophy. His interpretation of the condemnation of the body in this tradition is at times one-sided, but he represents it in this way in order to oppose his own philosophy of the natal and mortal body to it. The criticism of the Socratic model of mortality and immortality is directed at death insofar as it represents disembodied rationality as a theoretical ideal for pure knowledge and as a regulative principle as to what it is to lead an authentic life in face of one's mortality.

For Nietzsche, "birth" and "death" are concepts that need to be explained both in a naturalistic fashion, as central to an understanding of life as a natural process of becoming and deterioration, and in terms of their existential meaning for the way one lives one's life. Different philosophical conceptions of birth and death thus reveal, in his view, how we *value* life. Birth is for him a metaphor for a creative life and for an accepting and life-affirming disposition. Life is a continuous creation; man is a creative being, and insofar as it unites great pain and ecstatic joy, birth is the metaphor that illustrates an intensity of creative living. Birth thus symbolizes life as it is experienced at its fullest. Such an intense sensing of life should in Nietzsche's view be a basis for a strong outlook on life, as well as enabling a creative mastering of one's existence. Nietzsche regards philosophers as having been overly preoccupied with death; in his view this is counterfactual to how people really think. He writes in *The Gay Science* that "men do not want at all to think the thought of death! I should like very much to do something that would make the thought of life even a hundred times more appealing to them" (Nietzsche 1974: 225 [278]).

For Socrates, as Nietzsche portrays him, death is either a long sleep or an afterlife where one can be united with other great souls in a realm of pure spiritual being. This sense of death is the basis of metaphysical conceptions of death and is intimately linked to Christian notions of death. Due to its deep-seated reluctance to accept human mortality, Nietzsche views European philosophy as having been preoccupied ever since the time of Socrates with the idea of the immortality of the human soul, a belief that became a cornerstone of Platonist and Christian doctrines. As a critic of this tradition, Nietzsche argues in *Antichrist* (1888) that the notion of the immortality of the human soul is nothing less than an attack on humanity (Nietzsche 1976: 619 [43]). It is an attack on humanity because it denies and disrespects embodiment. A sense of eternity and infinitude is something one acquires through bodily states. Despite insistence on the finiteness of the individual human life, Nietzsche nevertheless develops a notion of an experience of eternity and also an idea of immortality through his conception of life as ever-renewing birth. Getting closer to the body through physically intense experiences can open up a possibility of metaphysical experiences of otherness traditionally associated with the soul. In the sense of locating the "meta" as the basic principle in the "physical," he dissolves the traditional opposition between finitude and infinity, natural and supernatural, mortality and immortality. This interpretation of Nietzsche's philosophy of birth therefore has the body as its grounding and is to be distinguished from philosophies of natality in which birth or the fact of being born are given meanings that are detached from our bodily being. Even though Nietzsche's conception of birth is incomplete and in many ways detached from actual birth, it is always rooted in embodied life.

Given that the Nietzschean rethinking of death and birth takes the Socratic tradition as its point of departure, it must be kept in mind that the concept of birth also plays an important role in the Socratic idea of philosophizing. Socrates presented the workings of the philosopher as those of a midwife who helps in the birth of thoughts. As midwife, the philosopher helps bring thoughts into the light, to see if they can withstand argumentative scrutiny when illuminated by wisdom. The philosopher-midwife aids the dialogue partner to gain new insights and thus to transform himself. Nietzsche holds on to this idea with his notion of encounter as birth. This Socratic idea of birth is, however, of little consequence compared to the kind of rebirth the soul undergoes in death, when it returns to a pure state in which it can theorize without any bodily distractions. In this sense absolute abstract thinking is possible only in such an unpolluted, disembodied condition. Theoretical reflection is a divine state, associated with an immortal condition beyond a bodily state. Birth here involves no reference to the experience of actual physical birth and sexual difference.

Birth, Death, and Sexual Difference

In Nietzsche's philosophy, reflections on death and birth are closely linked to his philosophy of women. Since in the philosophical tradition women have been associated with man's other in terms of their corporeal and emotional aspects, Nietzsche's use of womanly metaphors serves to draw attention to the bodily aspect of man's nature, which has been undervalued and despised in the tradition he seeks to overcome. Nietzsche works in his texts with symbols of women who represent traditional views on mortality and immortality. Such symbols illuminate prevailing attitudes toward death in Western thought insofar as they are, in his view, indebted to a Platonic-Christian outlook on life.[10] In several aphorisms in *The Gay Science,* for example, Nietzsche draws attention to the traditional association of woman with nature and death. Immortality and eternal life on the other hand are traditionally linked to the idea of the male, to whom an immortal soul is attributed. In light of this opposition of life and death marked by sexual difference, Nietzsche criticizes and ridicules the yearning for immortality in Western philosophical thought as based on contempt for life as a natural phenomenon, something that womanly nature has been made to represent. He subsequently uncovers and analyzes attempts to elevate our earthly nature as reflected in attitudes toward women. Since the time of Plato and Aristotle, philosophers have interpreted the fact that women give birth in a way that represents them as bringing mortality into life, for it is through woman that man is born into earthly existence and mortal fate. Thus for ancient philosophers, woman is a reminder of what has in our tradition been viewed as the greatest banality in life: death and the mere physicality of human life. Nietzsche describes how repugnance toward physical nature is still evident in attitudes toward women and the womanly. In *The Gay Science* he writes:

> When we love a woman, we easily conceive a hatred for nature on account of all the repulsive natural functions to which every woman is subject. We prefer not to think of all this; but when our soul touches on these matters for once, it shrugs as it were and looks

contemptuously at nature: we feel insulted; nature seems to encroach on our possessions, and with the most profane hands at that. Then we refuse to pay any heed to physiology and decree secretly: "I want to hear nothing about the fact that a human being is something more than *soul and form.*" (Nietzsche 1974: 122 [59])

In *Beyond Good and Evil* (1886), Nietzsche writes that the reason for this repulsion is a mixture of fascination and fear: "That about woman which fascinates and often makes us fearful is her nature, which is more natural than a man's nature" (Nietzsche 1966: 169 [239]). Since this attitude is based on an outlook that denigrates the earthly and bodily nature of man, Nietzsche rejects it. The need to overlook that nature, the need to see the human being exclusively in terms of soul and form, is for him a stepping stone into fantasy and idealization of the immortality of human life. The fear of the natural and bodily nature of women is in effect terror of the finiteness of human life. This fear results in an ambivalent view of women, who are seen either as earthly and akin to animals, or as pure, ethereal, unearthly beings, often in the guise of angels or fairies. Images of women as sublime beings disconnected from nature serve as a denial of the natural and bodily aspects of human life. Nature is thus denied a place in accounts of what makes human life noble. It is eternal, rational soul that gives man his god-like dignity, while the animal nature supposedly represented by woman casts a shadow over this picture and must thus be eliminated from it.

Since philosophers of the tradition do not want to face the earthly nature that women remind them of, they project onto the image of the woman a state that transcends nature. It is an escapist gesture that allows them not to have to confront their mortal nature. This elevated image of woman associates her with death, as the well-known passage about "Women and their action at a distance" from the *Gay Science* illustrates.[11] In the image of the elevated woman Nietzsche uncovers a yearning for immortality based on a denial of the finitude of human life. He interprets this yearning as an escapist disposition and sees it as driven by a longing for permanence, immutability, that is, for death. The yearning for immortality is in his view a latent longing for death as a state of total immobility.[12]

Lack of trust in life and fear of losing control are for Nietzsche the motives for the Socratic idealization of disembodied reason and the immortal soul. The rationalistic disposition toward life for which Socrates, in Nietzsche's view, laid the groundwork resulted from an attempt to gain control. The cultural, political, and moral situation in the Athenian republic was, during Socrates' lifetime, in a state of dissolution. "Everywhere the instincts were in anarchy; everywhere one was within five paces of excess," as he writes in *Twilight of the Idols* (Nietzsche 1976: 477, "The Problem of Socrates" [9]). The only stable thing that gave a sense of being in command was the reality of reason. By means of reason Socrates and his successors created a world of ideas that Nietzsche claims were nothing but "concept mummies" (Nietzsche 1976: 479, "'Reason' in Philosophy" [1]). Philosophers in this tradition have opted for being and discarded becoming: "Death, change, old age, as well as procreation and growth, are to their minds objections—even refutations" (Nietzsche 1976: 479). This in turn resulted in the creation of an idea of a supernatural world, which Nietzsche wants to bring down to earth, back to where it originated.

Naturalization of Life and Death

There are basically two approaches in Nietzsche's attempt to overcome the metaphysical duality of life and death. The first approach is derived from his biological conception of life, a conception he developed from his readings in the natural sciences of his time (especially physiology, which was considered to be a fundamental discipline by the end of the nineteenth century). This approach can be characterized as a naturalization of life and consists in a fusion of life and death. It is imperative to face the reality of life as an earthly phenomenon. The second approach is based on his Dionysian conception of life as birth, according to which self-creation consists in becoming other in giving birth to oneself.

The Gay Science has sections on Nietzsche's vitalistic understanding of life. Life is not a living being that can expand, since the totality of force in the universe is constant and can thus neither be created nor destroyed. Nietzsche refutes the mechanical conception of life and the universe. Life is not an ordered whole the regularity of which can be analyzed and defined in accordance with eternally valid laws of nature. He shuns the conception of life that seeks to understand it as an "organism." He writes:

> Let us beware of thinking that the world is a living being. Where should it expand? On what should it feed? How could it grow and multiply? We have some notion of the nature of the organic, and we should not reinterpret the exceedingly derivative, later, rare, accidental, that we perceive only on the crust of the earth and make of

it something essential, universal, and eternal, which is what those
people do who call the universe an organism. (Nietzsche 1974:
167 [109])

In place of such an organic conception of life, Nietzsche develops his
theory of the will to power to explicate the dynamic workings of life as a
battle between separate wills to power. Instead of using the word "organism,"
he talks about the will to power as an "organization" of either organic or
inorganic matter (Thorgeirsdottir 1996: chs. 3 and 4). An individual is, as
such, an organization, a "system of life" (*KSA* 9, 443).[13] But what is important about this understanding of life is the fact that Nietzsche employs it
to undermine the notion that life and death are opposites. He claims that
this duality is a product of a metaphysical and theological understanding of
nature. He writes: "Let us beware of saying that death is opposed to life. The
living is merely a type of what is dead, and a very rare type" (Nietzsche 1974:
168 [109]). The dead and the living are both aspects of the same organic and
inorganic processes we usually call "life."

"Life" and "the living" are not necessarily the best categories to help
us understand how will works in nature. In contemporary philosophy of
biology one finds similar proposals, such as that "biologists do not need a
definition of *life* to help them recognize what they are talking about."[14] A
definition of life as something that exists in and of itself is not possible. Life
is here rather understood as the upshot of the fact that living beings come
into existence, evolve, and die. Having a category of "life" would amount to
having a universal principle that would explain life's real essence. Nietzsche
strives for a "de-deification of nature" and a "naturalize[d]" humanity
(Nietzsche 1974: 169 [109]). At the same time, life, as eternal force of life,
can have spiritual dimensions. His conception of life undermines the opposition of man and nature, matter and spirit, and thus also diminishes the
traditional gap between the human and the animal (Lemm 2009).

Life as Dionysian Procreation

The concept of birth figures prominently in the first book that Nietzsche
published, *The Birth of Tragedy* (1872). There are pessimistic aspects to this
book, as for example when Nietzsche refers to the ancient Greek idea that it is
better not to be born than to be born. Being thrown into the world through
birth is a brute facticity. Despite this bleak view of birth that Nietzsche later
regretted, vitality and celebration of life are seen as central to the tragic view
of life.

The concept of "birth" in this book refers to the origin of ancient Greek tragedy as it is born out of life as suffering on the one hand and life as celebration and joy on the other hand. The source of Greek tragedy is the forces in Greek mythical culture, the Dionysian and the Apollonian, which give rise to tragic situations when they come in conflict. The notion of fecundity is important since it symbolizes the everlasting power of life to recreate itself despite its tragic character of suffering and mortality.

The mother is present in the background of this text, but in an unpublished fragment that belongs to a collection of notes for *The Birth of Tragedy*, Nietzsche talks of Demeter, mother earth, as the mother of Dionysus, and thus replaces Persephone with Dionysus. Demeter, who is in grief because Dionysus had been slain, rejoices as she learns that she will be able to give birth to Dionysus again.[15] Nietzsche allows himself to bring Dionysus into the story of Demeter by alluding to the story of Baubo, a maid, who, laughing and using obscene gestures, showed Demeter that she could give birth again. She did this by lifting her skirt, and there one could see the baby Iakchos, coming out of her, laughing and waving his hand. In some ancient sources Dionysus is identified with Iakchos, which gives Nietzsche the opportunity to tell the story of the birth and rebirth of Dionysus.[16]

There is a dimension of sexual difference in the duality of the Dionysian and Apollonian in the book on tragedy. Dionysus represents some elements traditionally associated with the feminine other, such as nature, embodiment, and feeling. The power and insight of the Dionysian needs to be contained and channeled with the organizing power of the Apollonian, which represents other elements associated with the masculine. Nietzsche's theory about the birth of tragedy has therefore been interpreted as the offspring of two fathers, insofar as the feminine elements are given to a masculine deity (Baracchi 2005). In line with such a reading, the story of the birth of Dionysus amounts to a destruction of the maternal/feminine genealogy that Demeter and Persephone represent, and thus a usurping of the feminine. Sarah Kofman counters such a reading with her essay on Baubo, whom she interprets as Nietzsche's "affirmative woman" (Kofman 1998). Oppel interprets the Dionysian in a vein similar to Nietzsche's restoration of an archaic feminine (Oppel 2005: 77). For Oppel the Apollonian also represents feminine traits, and thus this pair of gods serves to disrupt the heterosexual binary division of the feminine and the masculine (Oppel 2005: 79). Nietzsche replaces the mother-daughter dyad of Demeter and Persephone with the dyad of Demeter and Dionysus. From Oppel's point of view this replacement cannot be seen simply as a masculine appropriation of the feminine because Dionysus is both feminine and masculine. The fact that the Dionysian was primarily a woman's cult also lends support to this claim. Such a reading is, however, too reverent of Nietzsche in its effort to make his thinking of the Dionysian in this context compatible with feminist philosophy. Persephone is erased out of the picture, and hence the possibility of discussing the Dionysian philosophy of birth in light of a mother-daughter relationship is undermined.

In his late philosophical writings, Nietzsche returns to the relation between artistic creation and birth. In connection with the significance of art in Nietzsche's understanding of the role of philosophy, these reflections focus on birth as a metaphor and motivation for a philosophical outlook. These reflections tie in directly with the early philosophy, insofar as they take up the Dionysian view of life. In one of his last works, *Twilight of the Idols* (1888), Nietzsche uses the phenomenon of birth as a metaphor for Dionysian creativity and spontaneity, which he takes as the basis for a philosophical disposition:

> For the Greeks . . . every single element in the act of procreation, of pregnancy, and of birth, aroused the highest and most solemn feelings. In the doctrines of the mysteries, *pain* is pronounced as holy: the pangs of the woman giving birth hallow all pain; all becoming and growing—all that guarantees a future—involves pain. That there may be the eternal joy of creating, that the will to life may eternally affirm itself, the agony of the woman giving birth *must* also be there eternally. (Nietzsche 1976: 561–62, "What I owe to the Ancients" [4])

In this phase of his philosophy, Nietzsche was preoccupied with sketching a life-affirming outlook of the philosophers of the future, whom he describes as Dionysian, artistic philosophers. These philosophers have overcome the need to find any religious justification for suffering in life, and have learned to accept life with its extremes of both suffering and joy. In his view, this gives them a chance to outgrow values that devalue life. Socrates, on the other hand, is portrayed by Nietzsche as despising life and yearning for death. This one-sided view of Socrates serves to make him responsible for the repression of the body in the philosophical tradition Nietzsche attacks. The role of the philosophers of the future is to strive for a reevaluation of values, and the starting point for this is an affirming view of life and an acceptance of suffering, as illustrated by the metaphor of birth.

Iris Murdoch writes that "romanticism tended to transform the idea of death into the idea of suffering," and indeed Nietzsche is far more interested in suffering than in death as a philosophical motive (Murdoch 2002: 80). Death is for Nietzsche merely an integral part of finite human life. He is critical of the religious idea that suffering will be rewarded in the afterlife. In this respect he is responding to the way suffering in life has been interpreted and dealt with in the Christian tradition. Nietzsche wants to understand suffering not just as an unavoidable part of life, but also as intricately linked to lust for life. Birth is for him the quintessential example of understanding suffering as the flip side of joy and ecstasy. Employing the metaphor of birth, he aims to modify a fixation on suffering, which he regards as characteristic of a life-condemning religious outlook. He also believes that his notion of birth enables him to retrieve a lost sense of and passion for life that he thinks was characteristic of a pre-Socratic, mythical worldview. The story of Baubo giving Demeter a glimpse into the monstrous source of life, accompanied with Baubo's laughter, illustrates this lust for life that Nietzsche admires in ancient Greek mythical thinking. The Socratic turn in philosophy, which brought about the ancient Greek enlightenment, entailed a break with mythical thinking and the victory of a logical mindset. In Nietzsche's reading it led to an alienation from life as a natural phenomenon also insofar as it introduced an elevated sense of death as immortality at the expense of life.

Does Nietzsche leave us with a reduced notion of death in terms of its existential meaning? Not necessarily, if death and the loss of a beloved one is viewed as one major cause of the pain and suffering present in life. The concept of death is, however, marginal to his philosophy when we consider the orientation toward death characteristic of the tradition he criticizes. If one would like to apply basic motifs of the philosophical occupation with mortality to Nietzsche's philosophy of the creative self, one can argue that the awareness of the proximity of death can be a very creative impulse that Nietzsche failed to acknowledge. The uncertainties that the possibility of death entails can make philosophical thinking more subtle. The fact that death is uncertain—we do not know when it will happen—makes everything uncertain. Philosophical thinking that deals with uncertainties is more in line with the experimental thinking of Nietzsche than the rationalistic mode of securing grounds and arriving at conclusions that he attacks. Seen in this way death means that one has to live with uncertainties and cannot be fully in control, just as in birth nature has to take its course. The very nature of the Dionysian means such submitting to life as a process of becoming and dying. It takes a lot of effort, as becomes most apparent in Nietzsche's account of accepting the thought of the eternal return. This thought is for him a challenge similar to the thought of death insofar as it requires an acceptance of the "natural" facts that make life hard.

Birth, Death, and Others

Pregnancy and birth are typically relational experiences, but their inter-relational features are missing in Nietzsche's above-mentioned description of artistic creativity as giving birth. When we are born we are born into different kinds of dependencies, not only to our parents and family, but also to our culture, society, and nation. Birth entails a relation between mother and child, mother and father, father and child, and so on. The fetus is an example of a being that is neither self nor other, but something that is in between and becoming. Birth as a philosophical concept has become a para-digmatic phenomenon for understanding relations of self to other, as well as relationships in general, insofar as they have dimensions of asymmetry and elements of foreignness, as we see, for example, in Kristeva's reflections on pregnancy and birth. The first thought of most parents when seeing their newborn child is how wonderful the baby is as a completely new configu-ration. There is a sense of otherness as well as a sense of interdependence in that encounter. Kristeva, in her analysis of the relation of the mother to the fetus and to the newborn child, also accounts for the narcissism of the mother, who is dependent on the child for her sense of self.

Metaphors of conception, pregnancy, and birth that acknowledge the relational and dependency characteristics of these phenomena do more than just dissolve the sharp distinction between self and other. They also under-mine one-sided notions of a self-contained self and independent subjec-tivity. Nietzsche often emphasizes human relations in terms of a battle of individual wills. For Oliver, Nietzsche's model of intersubjective relations is therefore a Hegelian model stuck at the level of the master-slave fight to the death. More subtle notions of interrelationality based on recogni-tion between self and other are paradigmatic for experiences of natality and mortality. Are Nietzsche's views on the meaning of birth and death thus bound to be limited insofar as he mainly focuses on the creative self who affirms him- or herself against others? Does such an understanding of the creative self imply a solipsistic view of death? Death is surely an individual matter insofar as each human being faces his or her own finitude and death, but death also has intersubjective dimensions. We have to live with the death of others, and this also reminds us of our own finitude. Nietzsche did indeed reflect on parting and grieving, as becomes evident in this passage from *Thus Spoke Zarathustra:* "Verily, through a hundred souls I have already passed on my way, and through a hundred cradles and birth pangs. Many a farewell have I taken; I know the heartrending last hours" (Nietzsche 1976: 199, "Upon the blessed isles").

One way of dealing with personal grief and parting is to look at death within the larger perspective of life. For that purpose Nietzsche advocates a depersonalized view of death, as Rosi Braidotti argues (Braidotti 2006: 217). If individual life is viewed as part of a repetitious cycle of becoming and degeneration, individual existence is embedded in a continuous flow of life. Personal death is less a final point than a process in which life is transformed into something else. The my-ness of death emphasized in the philosophical tradition is challenged by such a "non-anthropocentric" view of human life (Braidotti 2006: 217). The "I" of the individual life that is transformed is dissolved as the self is seen merely as a temporary condition of life. Life is thus characterized by a structural difference between the self and the (living) non-self, which one becomes in death.[17]

Finiteness and Eternal Life

Although human death and birth are seen primarily as facts of the biological life-cycle, they maintain a dimension of immortality in Nietzsche's philosophy. The eternal circularity of natural processes endows human life with the immortality that the ancient Greeks, according to Hannah Arendt, reserved for nature (Arendt 1958: 18). By putting man back into the context of the circularity of nature, Nietzsche bestows upon him the immortality of life as a natural phenomenon. Man becomes immortal again in this earthly sense, a part of the never-ending cycle of nature. From this perspective, birth and death are transformational events. Birth does not mean a transition from non-being to being, and death does not mean a transition from being to non-being. Rather do birth and death mean that one goes from one stage of life into another. Life goes on, with the individual existence that comes between birth and death merely being one stage thereof. Once it is over, that existence is transformed into other forms of life. From the perspective of the metaphysical tradition Nietzsche aims to overcome, this means accepting the finitude of individual existence. In order not to halt at the bleak perspective of the brute facticity of human finitude, Nietzsche develops his idea of the existential dimensions of the thought of eternal recurrence. Experiences that offer insight into the eternal return of all things echo metaphysical ideas of a transcendent eternity. The sense of eternity experienced when confronted with the idea of eternal recurrence is supposed to fill the metaphysical void left by the death of God and the deconstruction of any transcendent reality. It is conceived as an immanent sense of eternity derived from a Dionysian understanding of life. So the glorious illusion of an eternal soul is to be replaced by a more realistic illusion of the eternity of life as a natural phenomenon. Nietzsche envisioned an experience in which one is in awe and speechless before the infinite. So he retains a notion, at least in his late philosophy, of spiritual experience. It is a spiritual life that is dependent on matter, body, and nature.

Birth, Death, and Eternity

In describing the experience of eternity, Nietzsche ties it to the idea of birth and having a child.

> Five, six seconds and no more: then you suddenly feel the presence of eternal harmony. Man in his mortal frame cannot bear it; he must either physically transform himself or die. . . . In these five seconds I would live the whole of human existence, I would give my whole life for it. . . . In order to endure this any longer one would have to transform oneself physically. I believe man would cease to beget. *Why have children when the goal is reached?* (*KSA* 13, 146)[18]

With his theory of the eternal return, Nietzsche strives to cater to a metaphysical need that cannot be met by a scientific worldview. Arthur Schopenhauer, his predecessor in naturalized metaphysics, had taken mortality as the basis of the metaphysical need to seek fundamental principles about being and life. By merely looking at death as part of the life-cycle, however, Nietzsche wants to emphasize life itself. More importantly, he sees Schopenhauer's focus on death as one reason for that philosopher's pessimism, a disposition that Nietzsche sought to overcome. Moreover, when viewed from the Nietzschean perspective, this focus on personal mortality, which is so defining of existential earnestness for philosophers from Socrates to Schopenhauer, is tied to a narcissistic fixation on the personal, individual self, which one transcends in the experience of eternity as he describes it.

Thus the notion of eternity that Nietzsche wants to "rescue" stands in opposition both to the idea of a personal kind of immortality and to the substantial notion of eternal, other-worldly life in the Platonic-Christian tradition. Parallel to the overcoming of the duality of death and birth in Nietzsche's philosophy runs the attempt to overcome traditional, Platonic-Christian ideas of eternity and finitude, timeless eternity, and finite time. His counterproposal does not, however, consist in a reduction of the eternal to the finite, but rather in an attempt to imagine an experience of the eternal within the confines of inner-worldly time. We cannot go beyond time, and therefore have to think eternity immanently within the horizon of time. Life as such is eternal, and each person is part of it. Life as generative energy lives on through a circulation of becoming and dying. So even for Nietzsche death is not the end. On the contrary, personal death is a transfiguration of life, and not a transition to inert, lifeless matter. Life and death are together one vital energy, not two opposing forces. For this reason, the experience of eternity entails both pain and lust as birth does. It is an experience of otherness that combines the erotic, the sublime, and the numinous, all at once (List 1993: 182–83). In this sense Nietzsche's description of the ecstatic experience of eternity has affinities with descriptions of religious, or more precisely mystic, experiences of *nunc stans*. Even though he would not agree to the fascination with the idea of God, his idea of an ecstatic experience resonates in many respects with Theresa of Avila's description of religious ecstasy. For her it evokes a sense of great pain, yet the sweetness of that pain is so great that she wishes it would never end.[19] Pain is important in this context, for it is something that overwhelms one. The body is not an agent but is, rather, overtaken by pain. This coincides with the idea that the embodied self is to a degree depersonalized, to the extent that it can be overtaken by sentiments that require surrender to them. At the same time it is through physical experiences such as pain that self-discovery is possible, because the self is a bodily self. Beyond this, Nietzsche's idea of ecstasy conveys a sense of oceanic spirituality and of wholeness that runs counter to the fragmented world of a nihilistic and materialistic outlook.

Andreas-Salomé claimed that Nietzsche suffered a great deal over the death of God, and claimed that he was feminine in his spiritual nature (Andreas-Salomé 1911: 38–39). From her point of view, the idea of life as eternal comes across as a substitute for a religious disposition, although it does not amount to a new religion, for that would be contrary to Nietzsche's attack on the institution of religion. This is a controversial claim. Interpreters who stress the atheistic nature of Nietzsche's philosophy find those aspects of the eternal return that are emphasized here rather uncomfortable. For Ulrich Irion, the idea of the eternal power of life to regenerate itself, insofar as it amounts to a worshiping of life, is a diffuse and overblown "geotheism" (Irion 1992: 98). For other interpreters, Nietzsche's attempt is therefore bound to be nihilistic when measured against revelatory (Christian) religion.[20] In the eyes of more recent interpreters, Nietzsche's criticism of Christianity can serve as a basis for a reconstruction of religious beliefs (Biser 2002), thus laying the ground for a post-theistic religiosity/spirituality.[21] It means not fearing death (becoming "deathless") and having faith in life, trusting that life will carry on. Nietzsche is critical of religious institutions and obviously attacks the religious basis of morality, but he leaves open the possibility of a form of religiosity that is immanent, subjective, and private, and makes man responsible, not a god. For that purpose he claims that strong people may create for themselves a strong god if necessary to perpetuate their strength, as he argues in *Antichrist* (Nietzsche 1976: 582 [16]). Such a god is beyond good and evil. It is not a god of morals, but rather a god of a way of thinking that confronts itself with otherness in order to question given morals (Stegmaier 2003: 174). It is Dionysus; and for that reason Habermas claims that Nietzsche promotes a kind of Dionysian Messianism (Habermas 1990: 83–105). The "strong" Dionysus is an unsympathetic figure for such purposes, and that may be the reason that Nietzsche in his last works gives softer and even loving attributes to this deity, yielding a notion of a "wise" Dionysus.

For Irion, ideas of this kind constitute a regression compared to the more realistic materialism of the cycle of life and death in Nietzsche's earlier philosophy (Irion 1992: 97). Nietzsche, however, thought that realism (based on a materialistic and scientific outlook) could not replace the Platonic-Christian worldview and thus overcome nihilism. Something other than materialism and mechanism and thus something more than down-to-earth realism (which he knew could also be dogmatic) is needed to reconcile human beings with their finite fate. He believed it necessary for their self-empowerment to sense themselves as part of a larger scheme of life itself. It is also necessary to counteract the pessimism that accompanies the so-called realistic outlook, and the rationalization of society that accompanies modernization, to use a Weberian term. Modernization results in disenchantment. In a psychological sense the notion of the eternal Dionysian life is needed to liberate modern man from the discontents of civilization and teach joy in life.

If one takes a Dionysian Messianism literally, the Dionysian ecstasy as a paradigmatic example of the experience of eternal life is a regressive move into irrationality and an ancient mythical worldview, as Habermas interprets it (Habermas 1990). If, however, one interprets Dionysus, as I suggest, as a way of connecting with otherness, understood as a suppressed precondition of culture or as a disclosure of a new possibility, this figure makes more sense. Nietzsche considers it essential that the artistic, creative imagination should be kept alive through ecstatic experience so as not to succumb to a clichéd rationalistic understanding of the world. The driving force behind creative thinking is the sensuality and embodiment represented by the feminine, which needs to be appropriated by the Dionysian philosopher.

The Body, Nature, and the Other

In his ideas about birth, Nietzsche ties together metaphysical and spiritual experience with bodily experience, and knowledge of nature with knowledge of the body. His philosophy contains both naturalistic and constructivist ideas about the embodied subject because there has never been such a thing as natural humankind (*KSA* 12, 417). His philosophy of the bodily self succumbs to neither reductionist biology nor superficial constructivism, but ties together the external and internal forces that shape the body.

The naturalistic and constructivist approaches each relate to the distinction that can be made between two different words for the body in German, *Leib* and *Körper*. *Leib* is the body we sense, experience, or live. Bodily sentiments can transcend what is visible and graspable, as when an amputee senses a "phantom limb."[22] *Körper* on the other hand can be understood as the body as defined in scientific discourse and other discourses that form our understanding of the body, and influence how we experience our bodily selves. Schopenhauer and Nietzsche turned the body into a philosophical topic par excellence, and thus expressed the need to see man as a whole, in opposition to the prevailing Cartesian understanding of the duality of body and soul. Their conception of the *Leib* is a precursor to later phenomenologies of embodiment, such as those of Hermann Schmitz and Maurice Merleau-Ponty. It reflects the lived experience of the body and articulates the way in which the body has an orientation of its own.

The metaphor of birth as creative activity illustrates a condition that disrupts pre-given notions and representations, and allows one to retrieve a "wild being" (*être sauvage*), to use a phrase of Merleau-Ponty, a wild being that underlies our representations of nature (Merleau-Ponty 1968). Ecstasy as exemplified by the metaphor of birth is for Nietzsche a condition that facilitates a transfiguration of idealizations and representations, since it brings one closer to nature. In the language of phenomenology one would say that such experiences allow us to experience the "phenomenal body" that has been forgotten. In *Human, All Too Human* Nietzsche describes this experience as a forgetting of the scientific rationalization of nature that facilitates access to the illogical parts of our being. The "illogical," he writes, is also necessary for the human being.

In the light of the metaphor of birth the encounter with the other can be one of wonder, both in the sense of seeing the familiar in a new light and as acknowledging the unfamiliar as something that sheds new light on oneself. Nietzsche writes that all encounters are "only about pregnancy" (*KSA* 10,

32), which means that encounters are between two that are different, and something new is produced through their encounter.[23] In that sense this aspect of his conception of birth resembles the dimensions of newness and plurality that are central to Arendt's idea of natality.

NOTES

1. Feminist interpretations of Nietzsche's philosophy of women have very much centered around the question whether his philosophy is totally, partly, or even hardly misogynistic. There are undeniable explicit misogynistic dimensions to many of his reflections on women. A number of the apparently misogynistic statements can, however, be seen to be far more ambiguous at a closer look. See, for example, Oliver and Pearsall 1998 and Deutscher 2002.

2. For a similar conclusion see Oppel 2005.

3. For "in reality" the strong, "lone individual" is "impotent" simply to "set up new norms and new commandments based on his own subjective whim" (Adorno 2001: 174).

4. With this interpretation Kristeva orders Nietzsche in a series of philosophers succeeding him who have discussed and given birth a prominent place in their philosophies, such as Simone de Beauvoir, Luce Irigaray, and Grace Jantzen, as well as Arendt and Kristeva herself.

5. Plato, *Theaetetus,* 155d (Hamilton and Cairns 1980: 860).

6. I thank Elizabeth Grosz and Nicole Fermon for this characterization of Nietzsche's appropriation of the feminine in his philosophy.

7. For a further discussion of such a type of feminist reading of philosophy see Deutscher 1997.

8. Schrift and Diprose have argued that Nietzsche's reflections on intersubjective relations such as generosity and giving go beyond a model of contractual relations between sovereign individuals, battle, or revenge. See Diprose 2002 and Schrift 1997.

9. For a discussion of this distinction see Agamben 1998. Nietzsche's conception of life is different from Agamben's idea of $z\bar{o}\bar{e}$ as "bare life" subject to a sovereignty that controls and dehumanizes it. Nietzsche wrote about repressing morals that control and weaken life, but his main understanding of life centers on the creative, dynamic power of life to grow as will to power.

10. The traditional dualities of birth/death, body/soul, being/appearance, and truth/lie have been gender-denoted in Western thought, with women representing the negative side of each duality, men the positive. In his deconstruction of these dualistic schemes, Nietzsche takes as point of departure the gender opposition. See my article "Nietzsche's Feminization of Metaphysics and Its Significance for Theories of Gender Difference" (2004).

11. "Women and their action at a distance"; "a large sailboat, gliding along as silently as a ghost. Oh, what ghostly beauty! How magically it touches me! Has all the calm and taciturnity of the world embarked on it? Does my happiness itself sit in this quiet place—my happier ego, my second, departed self? Not to be dead and yet no longer alive?" (Nietzsche 1974, 123 [60]).

12. The image of the elevated woman was in fact a familiar topos in the art and literature of the romantic period, so Nietzsche was addressing that kind of imagery while at the same time attempting to overcome its implications, i.e., the longing for transcendent eternity.

13. Nietzsche, *Sämtliche Werke: Kritische Studienausgabe (KSA)*, vol. 11, 282. When referring to unpublished notes in the German edition of Nietzsche's works, I shall use the system: *KSA* volume number, page.

14. See Sterelny and Griffiths 1999: 357.

15. The myth, writes Nietzsche, tells us that Demeter grieves over Dionysus, "who has been torn apart, and rejoices when she is told that she will be able to give birth to Dionysus *once again.*" *KSA* 7, 178.

16. Clemens Alexandrinus, Protreptikos, 2, 20–21. Quoted in Devereux 1985: 27.

17. Helmut Plessner, who was influenced by Nietzsche's philosophy of life, defined the structural difference between self and non-self that defines life. See Plessner 1975.

18. English translation in Critchley 1997: 70.

19. See Teresa of Avila 2007.

20. See Schlechta 1959.

21. See, for example, Richard Rorty and Gianni Vattimo, 2005, in which Rorty and Vattimo ponder on how religiosity survives without the foundations of objective truth and god.

22. See Schmitz 1995: 115.

23. Such encounters are not necessarily symmetrical, as they may be more productive for one than the other. See *KSA* 10, 55.

BIBLIOGRAPHY

Adorno, Theodor W. 2001. *Problems of Moral Philosophy.* Stanford, Calif.: Stanford University Press.

Agamben, Giorgio. 1998. *Homo Sacer: Sovereign Power and Bare Life.* Stanford, Calif.: Stanford University Press.

Andreas-Salomé, Lou. 1911. *Friedrich Nietzsche in seinen Werken.* Vienna: Verlagsbuchhandlung Carl Konegen.

———. 1991. *Looking Back: Memoirs.* St. Paul: Paragon House.

Arendt, Hannah. 1958. *The Human Condition.* Chicago: University of Chicago Press.

———. 1978. *The Life of the Mind.* New York: Harcourt Brace Jovanovich.

Baracchi, Claudia. 2005. "Elemental Translations: From Friedrich Nietzsche and Luce Irigaray." *Research in Phenomenology* 35: 219–48.

Biser, Eugen. 2002. *Nietzsche. Zerstörer oder Erneuerer des Christentums?* Darmstadt: Wissenschaftliche Buchgesellschaft.

Braidotti, Rosi. 2006. *Transpositions. On Nomadic Ethics.* London: Polity Press.

Brown, Kristen. 2007. *Nietzsche and Embodiment: Discerning Bodies and Non-dualism.* Albany: SUNY Press.

Critchley, Simon. 1997. *Very Little . . . Almost Nothing: Death, Philosophy, Literature.* London: Routledge.

Deleuze, Gilles. 1983. *Nietzsche and Philosophy.* New York: Columbia University Press.

Derrida, Jacques. 1979. *Spurs/Eperons: Nietzsche's Styles/Les Styles de Nietzsche.* Chicago: University of Chicago Press.

Deutscher, Penelope. 1997. *Yielding Gender: Feminism, Deconstruction and the History of Philosophy.* London: Routledge.

———. 2002. "'Is it not remarkable that Nietzsche . . . should have hated Rousseau?' Woman, Femininity: Distancing Nietzsche from Rousseau." In *Feminism and History of Philosophy,* ed. Genevieve Lloyd, 322–47. Oxford: Oxford University Press.

Devereux, Georges. 1985. *Die mythische Vulva.* Frankfurt: Europäische Verlagsanstalt.

Diprose, Rosalyn. 1993. "Nietzsche and the Pathos of Distance." In *Nietzsche, Feminism and Political Theory,* ed. Paul Patton, 1–26. London: Routledge.

———. 2002. *Corporeal Generosity: On Giving with Nietzsche, Merleau-Ponty, and Levinas.* New York: SUNY Press.

Habermas, Jürgen. 1990. "The Entry into Postmodernity: Nietzsche as a Turning Point." In *The Philosophical Discourse of Modernity,* 83–105. Cambridge: Cambridge University Press.

Hamilton, E., and H. Cairns, eds. 1980. *Plato: The Collected Works.* Princeton, N.J.: Princeton University Press.

Honig, Bonnie. 1995. "Introduction: The Arendt Question in Feminism." In *Feminist Interpretations of Hannah Arendt,* ed. Bonnie Honig, 1–16. University Park: Pennsylvania State University Press.

Irigaray, Luce. 1991. *Marine Lover of Friedrich Nietzsche.* New York: Columbia University Press.

Irion, Ulrich. 1992. *Eros und Thanatos in der Moderne.* Würzburg: Königshausen & Neumann.

Jantzen, Grace. 2004. *The Foundations of Violence: Death and the Displacement of Beauty.* London: Routledge.

Kofman, Sarah. 1998. "Baubô: Theological Perversion and Fetishism." In Oliver and Pearsall 1998, 21–49.

Kristeva, Julia. 1986. "Stabat Mater." In *The Kristeva Reader,* ed. Toril Moi, 160–86. New York: Columbia University Press.

———. 2001. *Hannah Arendt.* New York: Columbia University Press.

Lemm, Vanessa. 2009. *Nietzsche's Animal Philosophy: Culture, Politics, and the Animality of the Human Being.* New York: Fordham University Press.

List, Elisabeth. 1993. *Die Präsenz des Anderen.* Frankfurt: Suhrkamp.

Merleau-Ponty, Maurice. 1968. *The Visible and the Invisible.* Evanston, Ill.: Northwestern University Press.

Müller-Lauter, Wolfgang. 1999. *Nietzsche: His Philosophy of Contradictions and the Contradictions of his Philosophy.* Champaign, Ill.: University of Chicago Press.

Murdoch, Iris. 2002. *The Sovereignty of Good.* London: Routledge.

Nietzsche, Friedrich. 1966. *Beyond Good and Evil.* New York: Vintage.

———. 1974. *The Gay Science.* New York: Vintage Books.

———. 1976. *Antichrist.* In *The Portable Nietzsche.* Ed. Walter Kaufmann. New York: Penguin.

———. 1976. *Thus Spoke Zarathustra.* In *The Portable Nietzsche.* Ed. Walter Kaufmann. New York: Penguin.

———. 1976. *Twilight of the Idols.* In *The Portable Nietzsche.* Ed. Walter Kaufmann. New York: Penguin.

———. 1980. *Sämtliche Werke: Kritische Studienausgabe (KSA).* 15 vols. Ed. Giorgio Colli and Mazzino Montinari. Berlin: de Gruyter.

————. 1996. *Human, All Too Human*. Lincoln: University of Nebraska Press.

Oliver, Kelly. 1994. "Nietzsche's Abject." In *Nietzsche and the Feminine*, ed. Peter J. Burgard, 53–67. Charlottesville: University of Virginia Press.

————. 1995. *Womanizing Nietzsche*. New York/London: Routledge.

Oliver, Kelly, and Marilyn Pearsall, eds. 1998. *Feminist Interpretations of Friedrich Nietzsche*. University Park: Pennsylvania State University Press.

Oppel, Francis Nesbitt. 2005. *Nietzsche on Gender: Beyond Man and Woman*. Charlottesville: University of Virginia Press.

Plessner, Helmut. 1975. *Die Stufen des Organischen und der Mensch. Einleitung in die philosophische Anthropologie*. Berlin: de Gruyter.

Rorty, Richard, and Gianni Vattimo. 2005. *The Future of Religion*, ed. Santiago Zabala. New York: Columbia University Press.

Schlechta, Karl. 1959. *Der Fall Nietzsche*. Hamburg: Hanser.

Schmitz, Hermann. 1995. *Der unerschöpfliche Gegenstand*. Bonn: Bouvier.

Schrift, Alan D., ed. 1997. *The Logic of the Gift: Toward an Ethic of Generosity*. New York: Routledge.

Schutte, Ofelia. 1998. "Nietzsche's Politics." In Oliver and Pearsall 1998, 282–305.

Shchyttsova, Tatiana. 2008. "Natality and Community: Overcoming Deathcenteredness of the Classical Metaphysical Thinking." *Topos* 2, no. 19: 155–68.

Singer, Linda. 1998. "Nietzschean Mythologies: The Inversion of Value and the War against Women." In Oliver and Pearsall 1998, 173–86.

Songe-Møller, Vigdis. 2002. *Philosophy without Women: The Birth of Sexism in Western Thought*. London: Continuum.

Stegmaier, Werner. 1997. "Levinas' Humanismus des anderen Menschen—ein Anti-Nietzscheanismus oder ein Nietzscheanismus?" In *Jüdischer Nietzscheanismus*, ed. Werner Stegmaier and Daniel Krochmalnik, 303–323. Berlin: de Gruyter.

————. 2003. "Advokat Gottes und des Teufels: Nietzsches Theologie." In *Theodizee im Zeichen des Dionysus: Nietzsches Fragen jenseits Moral und Religion*, ed. Ulrich Willers, 163–77. Hamburg: LIT Verlag.

Sterelny, Kim, and Paul E. Griffiths. 1999. *Sex and Death: An Introduction to Philosophy of Biology*. Chicago: University of Chicago Press.

Teresa of Avila. 2007. *The Book of my Life*. Boston: New Seeds.

Thorgeirsdottir, Sigridur. 1996. *Vis creativa. Kunst und Wahrheit in der Philosophie Nietzsches*. Würzburg: Königshausen & Neumann.

————. 2000. "Metaphysik." In *Nietzsche Handbuch*, ed. Henning Ottmann, 281–83. Stuttgart: Metzler Verlag.

————. 2004. "Nietzsche's Feminization of Metaphysics and Its Significance for Theories of Gender Difference." In *Feminist Reflections on the History of Philosophy*, ed. L. Alanen and C. Witt, 51–68. Netherlands: Kluwer Academic Publishers.

EIGHT

The Natal Self

The Natal Self and the Other

Nietzsche's depiction of human encounters as birth and his discussion of the natal self are the basis for an idea of an embodied self that is in a continuous process of emerging. Nietzsche reflects on what it means to be a natal being, which we can achieve primarily through our creative capacities in a way that he suggests is in tune with the emergent character of life itself. His philosophy of birth is meant to underscore how life offers itself to us as a source of possibilities rather than promoting denial of earthly life, as he thinks has been the case in philosophies of mortality in our tradition.

Nietzsche's famous saying that one is always an other accounts for otherness within the embodied subject.[1] He yearned for "an ever new widening of distances within the soul itself, the development of ever higher, rarer, more remote, further-stretching, more comprehensive states," as he wrote in *Beyond Good and Evil* (Nietzsche 1966: 201 [257]). Being two is the minimal and irreducible difference within the same (Zupancic 2003). The individual is a composite of different wills that mutually interpret and modify each other (*KSA* 12, 104).[2] He thus showed how the subject is a constant process of becoming by trying out different possibilities.

Nietzsche's writings on how relationality is constitutive of the subject yield a dynamic idea of the self in terms of giving and taking, proximity and distance, recognition and disrespect, friendship and animosity, forgiveness and revenge. Such an idea of the relational self opposes a strict division between self and other, subject and object, mind and body. These reflections stand in contrast to the solipsistic idea of the self and a one-sided model of dominance in Nietzsche's philosophy. The struggles with relationality and with the solipsistic individual that these reflections display are the point of departure for the interpretations of Nietzsche's conception of birth by both early and more recent women psychoanalytical thinkers. For Hannah Arendt natality exemplifies the very plurality and difference that makes life and political culture thrive. This is in accord with Nietzsche's view that difference is a precondition for transfiguring encounters. If partners or adversaries were "equal" in every respect they would be unable to challenge each other in a significant way. There has to be a struggle of forces that can change and alter the other. That is a precondition for growth and the avoidance of stagnation. Some kind of asymmetry is necessary if a relation is to be fruitful and transforming. Esteem for the other must therefore be based on respect for the alterity of the other (but Nietzsche also advocates being selective about opponents). The teacher-student relationship is of great interest to Nietzsche. He focuses on the ability of the teacher to help the student to recognize his or her unique strength.[3] In his texts he at times also enters into dialogue with his readers, pondering different aspects of the relationship between reader and writer. He describes the relationship between the partners in a good dialogue as a maieutic relationship, such that one of them looks for a midwife for his thoughts, the other for someone who can be assisted (Nietzsche 1966: 88 [136]).

Encounter and Birth

The emphasis on otherness in Nietzsche's conception of birth coincides with his notion of justice, at least in one sense. "'Men are *not equal!*'—So speaks—justice," he writes (*KSA* 10, 58).[4] Here he warns against a notion of equality that he fears consists in an undermining of differences. For there to be justice differences must be accounted for as people are not identical. So Nietzsche rejects the moral-political ideal of equality, not the least with regard to the sexes, insofar as it consists in an "increase in similarity," as he writes in *Twilight of the Idols* (Nietzsche 1976b: 540, "Skirmishes of an Untimely Man" [37]). In opposition to this he calls for a morality of "actions of many colors," and a celebration of a multiplicity of types (Nietzsche 1966: 146 [215]). The encounter with otherness is for him fruitful if it yields a productive tension or antagonism that leads to a mutual interpretation of wills, in which wills, as representatives of meanings and opinions, transfigure each other. The encounter thus produces new and unique meanings and contributes to plurality. It is this idea of encounter as birth and the idea of self and the relationality it entails that concern us here.

The self, interpreted from this point of view of birth as encounter, is individualistic yet relational, and narcissistic yet open and generous toward the other. Such a self is searching in terms of gender identity, as Nietzsche himself exemplifies, with his experiments with feminine and masculine attributes (Thorgeirsdottir 2009). The self is embedded in relations and social contexts, but the strong individual is also able to counteract inhibiting social and interpersonal structures. Being a self therefore amounts to being contradictory in some respects, and such a conception allows us to grasp how a self is also in conflict with itself. Features associated with natality (relationality, creation) and features associated with mortality (separation, destruction) are basic to Nietzsche's understanding of the self. His understanding of the self shows how conceptions of the self-contained and autonomous self are insufficient for grasping many of the relational and corporeal aspects of the self.

The very encounter with otherness is the essence of the creative powers of Dionysian philosophy that Nietzsche illustrates with his idea of birth. He emphasizes the longing to give birth and become a mother, and transfers this desire onto his own work, seeing his philosophical work as his offspring. There is a tendency toward reproduction of the same in his depiction of this longing, but at the same time it also offers a way to conceptualize the reproduction of oneself in an other, as an other and not the same. Thus Nietzsche portrays both a narcissistic conception of birth and a receptive idea of birth as encounter with otherness. These are two aspects of the phenomenon of birth, as Kristeva has illustrated in her discussion of the narcissistic longing of the mother and her openness to the child as the other (Kristeva 1986). In accordance with this latter aspect Nietzsche writes in *Thus Spoke Zarathustra*, "I want children, I do not want *myself*" (Nietzsche 1976a: 434, "The Drunken Song" [9]). He also claims that one must create a being that does not suffer as much as oneself (*KSA* 10, 522). The self-centered idea of reproduction of the same and self-determination is thus juxtaposed to Nietzsche's idea of yielding to the other and to life. How does this move from active to receptive mode furthermore offer grounds for conceiving of the subject as interdependent with others?

We have seen that the concept of birth as encounter with the other involves the transformative threshold through which new configurations will occur. Involvement with others is what makes us single, unique human beings, as Arendt argues (Arendt 1990: 86). Yet the other as a concrete other person is missing in Nietzsche's accounts of artistic creativity as birth. Two of the pioneers among women in psychoanalysis, Sabina Spielrein and Lou Andreas-Salomé, were the first to point to the complicated dynamics of the interrelationality associated with the conception of birth and motherhood in Nietzsche's philosophy. They showed that Nietzsche reflects on intersubjective relations both in light of antagonism and in ways that acknowledge the role that other human beings and otherness play in them, and that thereby obviate a mere choice between either dominance or submission. For a relationship to be in accord with a relational notion of birth entails that the partners in a relationship transform each other through the encounter. They have to give in to each other, and they both need the other to "give birth" to them.

Sexual Difference and the Plural Self

Both in theory and in practice, psychoanalysis is largely concerned with relationships, how one relates to oneself and to others. At the same time, psychoanalytic theories are grounded in a philosophy of life according to which all becoming presupposes destruction, which is somewhat similar to Nietzsche's idea of the unity of life and death. It is therefore illuminating to study how Spielrein and Andreas-Salomé interpret birth and death in Nietzsche's philosophy, both as a metaphor for metaphysics of life and as a metaphor for the self in relation to itself and others.

Spielrein views the idea of the interdependence of birth and death in the light of destructive drives, but her general approach is drive-oriented. In 1912 she published a paper entitled "Destruction as the Origin of Becoming," in which she takes Nietzsche's philosophy of birth as a case in point for her theory as to how birth and rebirth presuppose death (Spielrein 1912: 465–503). She draws attention to Nietzsche's use of symbols of creation and destruction when describing how he gives birth to thoughts (which replace children). Spielrein's idea of birth is more encompassing than Grace Jantzen's rather one-sided and idealized view of birth. Conception is for Spielrein inherently tied to some basic form of anguish. For that reason it provides a basis for addressing ambivalent, difficult, or sad features of birth, such as miscarriage, unwanted or violently induced pregnancy, unsuccessful attempts to become pregnant using technical reproductive means, or totalitarian politics of reproduction.

In Spielrein's view a form of negativity is built into processes of reproduction. Processes in nature show us that to be fertile entails annihilation or destruction of the self. Destruction is the "origin" of becoming.[5] In conceiving, the man wishes (subconsciously) to annihilate himself and to achieve the annihilation of woman. In this sense reproduction is a form of self-sacrifice. This echoes Nietzsche's idea about the creative philosopher, who is ready to go under in advancing his pursuit of knowledge.[6] Spielrein also points to lack as a motive for creation. She detects in Nietzsche's words about giving birth to works as his imaginary children the need of a lonely person to compensate for his loneliness. Whether or not it is accurate, her analysis is interesting in the context of this interpretation of the relational self, because it sheds light on Nietzsche's struggle to overcome isolation. Because of his loneliness, Spielrein asserts, his love drive was directed toward himself (Spielrein 1912: 481). As a response to the loneliness he suffered, he invented an ideal friend, Zarathustra, with whom he identified. Spielrein goes on to examine how this creation revealed Nietzsche's struggle with feminine and masculine elements in his own person. The Zarathustra figure allowed him to become both man and woman, and to give birth to his creation like a mother. Nietzsche, as he himself writes, becomes his own mother. He unites with the maternal, and gives birth to his thoughts (Nietzsche 1976a: 232–36, "Immaculate Perception"). What Spielrein in fact diagnoses in her analysis of the creation of Zarathustra is a similar elevation of the maternal powers that was discussed in the previous chapter in relation to the usurping of the maternal in the construction of the Dionysian philosopher. At the same time she accentuates the way in which the desire to be a mother is the motivation for Nietzsche's philosophizing. Spielrein shows how Nietzsche describes the quest for knowledge as an act of love, as a desire for creation. In such descriptions philosophy becomes an expression of life as a continuous procreation with ambivalent features of creation and destruction. If this metaphor of birth is to be understood as yielding more than a kind of late romantic pathos of philosophy, it must be put into the context of Nietzsche's identity as a creative philosopher, as Spielrein does. In his appropriation of the maternal she sees an "autoerotic isolation" and a homosexual component. Homosexuality manifests itself here in the form of a disposition toward oneself in terms of the inner dynamics of autoeroticism. In the identification with the maternal, Nietzsche is the passive one, and the mother is the man. This coincides with two directions of love that Spielrein distinguishes. On the one hand, there is the subject that loves the object. On the other, there is the one who changes into a lover and loves her or himself as object. Women more commonly occupy the latter position, according to Spielrein, giving them a stronger disposition toward autoerotic and homosexual tendencies, which she believes are manifest in the common cuddling and kissing of adolescent girls.

Spielrein's reflections are representative of her outlook on the different situations of men and women at the beginning of the last century. It does not really matter whether such psychoanalytic diagnoses of male and female roles and sexual orientations are true or not as factual renderings of sexual psychology. The significance of Spielrein's discussion of autoeroticism and homosexuality lies in the insight it yields into a predicament of a subjectivity that is struggling to realize sexual difference and otherness within itself. Her analysis of Nietzsche illustrates her point that most people are "bisexual" insofar as women have subjectivizing ideas about themselves while men also have objectivizing ideas about themselves. Lou Andreas-Salomé, Nietzsche's onetime friend, also diagnosed his sexuality as bisexuality.[7] And Joachim Köhler in his biography of Nietzsche sees homosexuality as a key to understanding Nietzsche's worship of Dionysus (Köhler 2002). He claims that this god was for Nietzsche a mysterious, ambivalent symbol of sexuality, ambivalent because it does not distinguish between love of the same sex and love of the other. Dionysus is therefore depicted by the Greeks as hermaphrodite, "appearing to women as a desirable man and to men as being possessed of seductive feminine eyes" (Köhler 2002: 52).

It is beside the point to link Nietzsche's philosophy of Dionysian creativity directly to homosexuality or bisexuality. As Oppel argues, it is conceptually limiting to say that Nietzsche with his late idea of Dionysus means bisexual individuals, because the concept is too prescriptive and dualistic in light of his philosophy of a pluralistic identity (Oppel 2005: 5). It would, moreover, lead to an essentialist position to base different forms of creativity on actual sexual orientations. Nietzsche envisions beings who are able to transcend the dualistic ideologies that restrict sexual identities. His philosophy of Dionysian creativity can therefore be interpreted as linking psychological bisexuality or pluralized sexuality to creative genius. Kristeva links the two, seeing bisexuality as "a fact that applies to both sexes, with the dominant factor varying between sexes and between individuals."[8] So the psychoanalytic reading of Nietzsche highlights the struggle within oneself and between selves in terms of sameness and alterity. Pluralistic forms of identity confront us with far more extreme forms of other, challenging us to be receptive to otherness without identifying, or by only partially identifying, with it. This requires an effort, a very considerable effort, experiential or ontological, to understand ourselves, others, those who are close to us, and those who are not so close. For Kristeva, individuals who push deviation from standardized norms to its furthest limit are most unique and genial. That requires calling into question one's own age and challenging the socio-historical conditions of one's identity.

Kristeva claims that Hannah Arendt, with her philosophy of natality, which she believes has one source in Nietzsche's philosophy of the eternal return, represents such uniqueness. Arendt, Kristeva writes, "took the initiative in reopening the question of birth by breathing new meaning into the freedom of being." She adds that "therein lays the brilliance of her genius, whose very core touches on the crisis of modern culture along with its ultimate fate of life or death" (Kristeva 2001: 48). What Kristeva in effect claims is that with her conception of birth Arendt challenges a one-sidedly masculine emphasis on death in our philosophical tradition. By bringing birth and natality to the fore Nietzsche and Arendt thus add a feature to the philosophical vocabulary that extends it, and also pluralizes it in terms of sexual difference.

Arendt's Philosophy of Natality and Nietzsche's Philosophy of Birth

In her book on Arendt, Kristeva mentions two authors who have influenced Arendt's conception of natality. In the first place Arendt was inspired by her early reading of the philosophy of Augustine, according to which men are *initium*, or beginning, and beginners by virtue of birth (Arendt 1958: 177–78). In the second place the basis of natality is in life itself, and not only the fact of being born. Nietzsche's philosophy of life as eternal return is a resource for Arendt in that respect. Arendt, so Kristeva contends, looked to Nietzsche's "eternal return" "for a way of thinking about joy, admiration, and amor fati, 'the highest possible formula of affirmation'" (Kristeva 2001: 152).

The fact that Arendt spoke about "natality" rather than "birth" implies, to begin with, at least two things. For one, she, like Nietzsche, juxtaposed natality and mortality, and opposed the emphasis on mortality in Western philosophy, which has led to a forgetfulness of natality. She writes that ever since the time of Plato it is as if people have not taken the fact of being born seriously, but only dying (Arendt 2002: 463). Secondly, the term "natality" is a broader and more abstract notion than is birth as a natural process. "Natality" is a term that designates new beginnings, the human ability to begin something new, and to create a new world (but Arendt elaborated the concept in a world shaken to the core by the destruction of totalitarian terror in the Second World War). As a philosophical concept, natality, she claims, is the precondition of a life of action (*vita activa*). Natality is broadly speaking a political concept, but Arendt conveys a broad understanding of politics as the art of creating something new, as a form of action invigorated by new impulses and a plurality of voices. Natality designates an ethos of a political culture that celebrates freedom, thrives on and nurtures plurality.

The Nietzschean point of departure for Arendt's conception of natality remains in many ways unexplored. Dana Villa, who has written extensively on the relation between Nietzsche's and Arendt's conceptions of politics, claims that Arendt's uniqueness "can only be measured through a sustained investigation of the Nietzschean dimension, pro and contra, of her work."[9] Reading Arendt's works shows that Nietzsche's philosophy was for her a resource that she mined considerably.[10] Reflections on embodied life as a natural phenomenon, the will, and power are worked out in a critical reading of Nietzsche's texts.[11] The facticity of birth and the possibilities of new beginnings are expressed in Nietzsche's idea of eternal recurrence as being simultaneously necessity and possibility. For Arendt the emphasis is not on the eternal return as eternal return of the same, or mere accepting of life as it is, but rather the return of the same as a new effort. Arendt thus writes: "What makes [Nietzsche's 'thought of the Eternal Return'] modern is the pathetic tone in which it is expressed, indicating the amount of willful intensity needed by modern man to regain the simple admiring and affirming wonder, *thaumazein*, which once, for Plato, was the beginning of philosophy" (Arendt 1978b: 21). With her conception of natality, new beginnings and the joy over newcomers are therefore celebrated, but Arendt does not share with Nietzsche the "pathetic" dimension of his view of birth. Facing the challenge of the eternal return is, according to Nietzsche, a painful birth that gives one a new outlook. The chapter on the eternal return in *Thus Spoke Zarathustra* has the title "Die Genesung" (recovery), but one of the old meanings of the word *Genesung* is recovery after childbirth. The fact that life returns eternally undermines any hope of some kind of culminating point in history or final redemption as postulated in the Christian eschatological history of mankind. The thought of the eternal return is associated with an abysmal and nauseating fear. Facing this fear precedes the ecstatic joy in affirming life as an eternal return according to Nietzsche's description of the experience of the thought of the eternal return in *Thus Spoke Zarathustra*. In Arendt's appropriation of this idea the sense of horror and void is modified, resulting in a milder and gentler idea of rebirth, and taking initiative as a kind of leap of faith. Kristeva underscores the biblical, evangelical, and Augustinian traditions that color Arendt's idea that "each birth is the 'miracle' of this reviving, threatening, and promising 'Eternal Return'" (Kristeva 2001: 44). Stegmaier points to the celebration of birth and newcomers in the Jewish tradition, but that can also be seen as one background for Arendt's life-rejoicing idea of natality (Stegmaier 2000).

There are, however, other reasons than a different kind of *pathos* that make it seem contradictory to emphasize the Nietzschean philosophy of life as one aspect of a philosophical point of departure for Arendt's philosophy of natality. Arendt is highly ambivalent as to her view of Nietzsche's philosophy of life. She condemns the emphasis on life for contributing to loss of interest in a common public world of politics, and she condemns Nietzsche's focus on the individual and failure to take the other into account. For that reason Nietzsche's philosophy of the will to power, as Arendt portrays it in *The Life of the Mind*, is according to Elizabeth Young-Bruehl "the most absurd chapter in the long history of philosophical hostility toward action and the desire to be freed from its unpredictability by the assertion of a solitary mental life divorced from the world" (Young-Bruehl 2006: 194).

Arendt is critical of Nietzsche's idea of life as overabundance (*Überfülle*) because she considers it to be preemptive of a totalitarian view of certain groups of men as being in excess and unneeded. She also thinks that his conception of life has contributed to the fabrication of life (Arendt 1958: 313). The upshot of this is that she mainly thinks of the human body with reference to how it is dominated and dehumanized. One of Arendt's greatest concerns is that technological control of life is leading to increased automatism and robotization of human life. In her dystopian vision of the jobholder society we are progressing toward men who are cogs in a machine and who have become incapable of acquiring the freedom and power that the public sphere of politics offers. The last chapter of *The Human Condition* is titled the "Victory of the *Animal Laborans*," or the labor animal. The *animal laborans* is not creative in the natal sense of the word, but only works in the service of production. By associating Nietzsche's conception of life with this development, Arendt blocks out his criticism of a mass culture, but he was of the opinion that it turns people into a controllable mass, foreclosing plurality and creativity. Nietzsche's notion of life and fecundity has to do with diversity and freedom, although he is not conscious like Arendt of how democratic politics and institutions are needed to guarantee freedom and plurality in the biopolitical sphere.

The critical tone in which Arendt speaks about philosophy of life overshadows how she is indebted to certain aspects of the notion of life in Nietzsche's philosophy. Arendt, just as Nietzsche, has to embed her ideal of natality in a conception of life as interplay of freedom and necessity. Otherwise she would not be able to give a convincing account of natality as creativity, spontaneity, and unpredictability. To that effect she writes that "trust in the reality of life" depends on the "intensity with which life is felt" (Arendt 1958: 120). She states that the "recurrent rhythm" of the biological life-cycle and "pain and effort" condition natural pleasures and guarantee "liveliness and vitality" (Arendt 1958: 120). In a similar vein to Nietzsche, Arendt views embodied life as a vital source for the uniqueness that is a condition for plurality. The body is thus, as Zerilli writes, necessarily for Arendt "a drive force that animates the plural subject of action" (Zerilli 1995: 184).

With her conception of natality Arendt abstracts from physical birth and articulates this bond with life primarily in terms of intersubjective relations. Natality exhibits itself when people come together in the political sphere. When the individual speaks and acts, he or she experiences a "second birth" insofar as interaction and new constellations reveal and disclose the person and others in a new way (Arendt 1958: 182). I argue, in the first place, that it is this notion of natality as a creative and transfiguring power that Arendt has in common with Nietzsche's idea of Dionysian creativity as giving birth. Secondly, I argue that her conception of natality as freedom is based on an idea of the self as other that has some affinity with Nietzsche's notion of the natal self. This affinity does not turn Nietzsche into a thinker of the kind of political action Arendt has in mind, but it shows that Nietzsche's idea of the self does have a relational dimension that Arendt fails to acknowledge. This dimension will be discussed in response to Arendt's criticism of the solipsistic individual in Nietzsche's philosophy. Thirdly, embedding Arendt's notion of natality in life as a natural process opens a possibility for a richer understanding of natality than found in interpretations of this concept as a principle for Arendt's ideal of politics. The body is a mediating factor between life and creative existence. As such a mediating factor, the body in Arendt's philosophy cannot be purely biological, strictly private and mute, in the way that Bonnie Honig has argued that it is (Honig 1995: 7). The body has to be included in authentic human interaction, as appearance, voice, gestures, and the like (Betz Hull 2002: 169). Differences in bodily givens thus contribute to the plurality of the political, and sexual difference is a prime distinction according to Arendt (Arendt 1990: 103). The body of the mother is, however, absent in Arendt's conception of natality. Strangely enough, she like Nietzsche replaces the mother-daughter genealogy of Demeter and Persephone with a paternal one when referring to the Dionysian mysteries (Arendt 1958: 63). Why is that? The comparison with Nietzsche's idea of maternal creativity is an occasion for inquiring about dimensions of natality in Arendt's thought that can be associated with the maternal, as is found in Kristeva's interpretation. This can be only a preliminary investigation into aspects of the connection between Arendt's and Nietzsche's conceptions of birth that have to do with questions of the relational and embodied self. It still holds what Honig wrote several years ago, that "much remains to be done on this front" (Honig 1993, 529).

Birth, Plurality, and Politics

Arendt contrasts her thinking about natality as the action of a plurality of actors with Nietzsche, who thinks of birth in terms of creative individual existence. Action, she writes, is "ontologically rooted" in the fact of natality (Arendt 1958: 247). Action is "the only activity that goes on directly between men . . . [and it] . . . corresponds to the human condition of plurality, to the fact that men, not Man, live on the earth and inhabit the world" (Arendt 1958: 7). The sphere of the political should thus be characterized by a "paradoxical plurality of unique beings" (Arendt 1958: 176). Newcomers sustain the continuous re-creation of plurality. Even though Nietzsche was skeptical of democratic politics, his reflections on justice and difference can nevertheless be interpreted as a defense for uniqueness and the political necessity of plurality that Arendt argues for with her idea of natality.[12] This becomes evident, for example, in the hope that Nietzsche places in the power of people of marginal groups to revaluate values. The Jews in Europe, women, and outsiders, in his view, have the necessary distance to go against the norms of outdated morals. Groups that have been powerless and dependent have had to adapt themselves to new circumstances all the time, as Nietzsche writes in *The Gay Science* (Nietzsche 1974: 316 [361]). They are therefore better able to discern new solutions and introduce them from the margins to the center.[13] In a similar manner Arendt herself, based on her own experience of exile and immigration, held the political perspective of the pariah as an outsider and newcomer invaluable (Arendt 1978a).

Every birth carries with it simultaneously hope and risk. The contribution of the newcomers results in new and unpredictable constellations. The fact of natality is therefore also the reason for the frailty of human affairs, the risk inherent in new beginnings and the unpredictability as to outcome (Arendt 1958: 191). At the same time natality is the miracle that Arendt believes can save and heal the world, and guarantee the human condition. She comes to this conclusion not the least by way of her analysis of totalitarian regimes, in which taking initiative and spontaneous actions are made impossible in the public sphere. It cannot be a topic of concern here how Arendt envisions a sphere in which her idea of politics can be realized. What is of concern here is merely that the conception of natality is a means of articulating "the human passions" that set action in the political sphere in motion (Arendt 1978b: 191). These passions as the spontaneous, unpredictable force in human action and the drive for freedom are descriptively vague unless embedded in a notion of embodied life.

Birth, the Body, and the Maternal

Feminist interpreters of Arendt's notion of natality have criticized Arendt for a conception of natality that takes neither the body nor sexual difference into account, and that is furthermore based on a sharp distinction between public life and the privacy of the household (Honig 1995). Together with Betz Hull and Kristeva I argue that the body in Arendt's philosophy is not as "apolitical" and "generic" as it seems to be (Betz Hull 2002: 169; Kristeva 2001: 178). With the blurring of the distinction between the private and the public in modern times, the body is, as Arendt writes, not restricted to the private sphere as in ancient times (Arendt 1958: 73). The fact that "the modern age emancipated the working classes and the women at nearly the same historical moment," she writes, shows that this age "no longer believes that bodily functions" should be hidden (Arendt 1958: 73). With her conception of natality, Arendt did not take the maternal body out of hiding. She, however, writes that the difference between male and female is essential to the "plurality of man," out of which the "whole realm of human affairs" arises (Arendt 1990: 103). She therefore admits that sexual difference is part of the uniqueness of the person, but she does not acknowledge the political implications of this difference. One reason for this is that she is skeptical of any group or collective identities that can be derived from so-called givens, such as being born a woman or a Jew. Arendt thinks that any generalizing definition of such identities can restrict the possibilities of uniqueness of one's individual identity.[14] Insofar as generalizing definitions of identity curb the growth of plurality, it can be assumed that she ideally defends pluralized, becoming identities. Arendt is well aware of the fact that given identities are often an incentive for becoming politically active, but she does not want to endorse identity-based politics that are in her view necessarily excluding. On this basis the maternal dimensions Kristeva detects in Arendt's notion of natality are not exclusive of others than mothers and women. The relational implications of the maternal body are precisely what lead Kristeva to her interpretation of Arendt's notion of natality. She comes to the conclusion that Arendt's philosophy of natality expresses "maternal love for the ordinary life" that can guarantee our human condition (Kristeva 2001: 48). Kristeva claims that maternal love is derived from the bond between the mother and the child to whom she gives birth.[15] In her recent version of the model of maternal love in her book on Arendt, Kristeva extends the model beyond the body of the mother. She turns this into a model that is primarily about certain forms of relationality, and she underscores the central importance of the relation to the other by capitalizing the "Other." Maternal love is for her "a bond that results not from a desire for an object (or a subject) but from a love for the Other. Maternal love could be seen as the dawning of the bond with the Other" (Kristeva 2001: 46). Kristeva claims that maternal love for ordinary life is not a concern only of women, although she does grant women a special capability, responsibility, and dignity in this respect and is aware of the power and of the vulnerability that accompanies actual motherhood. Together with Spielrein, she claims that psychic bisexuality, which psychoanalysis sees in everyone, allows the assumption that men can also assume maternal love of ordinary life (Kristeva 2001: 48). Spielrein's psychoanalytical interpretation of Nietzsche's conception of birth can also be interpreted as such an opening up the maternal, as well as entailing dissolution of strict binary schemes of sexual difference.

For Arendt the decisive difference between her and Nietzsche is, as I have already pointed out, that his conception of birth is limited to the individual. Arendt bases her view on passages from *Thus Spoke Zarathustra* in which Nietzsche writes that to be creative in one's own life means being both the child that is born and the mother who in pain gives birth to the child: "The creator must also want to be the mother who gives birth and the pangs of the birth-giver" (Nietzsche 1976a: 199). Despite the solitary nature of this kind of birth as self-creation, Nietzsche, contrary to Arendt's verdict, does in other passages reflect on how the child is an other to oneself, from which one learns to see oneself and the world in a different way. That does add an intersubjective dimension to this idea of the "motherless child," as I discussed in the previous chapter (Oliver 1995: 144).

Nietzsche's reflections on love for the other encompass different types of relations that cannot be distinguished and delineated here. Love for an other can take many forms, but Nietzsche's description of the love of Dionysus for the other is a case in point for the type of love for the other that Kristeva could assume "results not from a desire for an object (or a subject) but from a love for the Other" (Kristeva 2001: 46). Nietzsche depicts Dionysus as a generous god, the one who approaches the other. In the chapter titled "The Genius of the Heart" in *Beyond Good and Evil*, he claims that Dionysus is a philosophizing god who has the ability to reach to the depths of people's souls. He has the ability to sense other minds and hearts, which allows him to get the best out of those he reaches. Everything loud and self-indulgent is silenced, so that "rough souls" become smooth (Nietzsche 1966: 233 [295]). These souls touched by the Dionysian sense a yearning to "lie still as a mirror, that the deep sky may mirror itself in them." In order to reach the other, Dionysus displays an artistic, tactile way of approaching and speaking to the other. Indeed the listener in this description becomes a mirror that reflects the deity, while at the same time everything crude about him vanishes, rendering visible the sweetest aspects and activating his best features. Such encounters give rise to newness in the manner of birth. This encounter makes the other feel new and different from how he was previously. It is an encounter that transfigures. At the same time it is an encounter in which there is a sense of touching, listening, and speaking, implying the bodily dimensions of the encounter.

Nietzsche's reflections on Dionysian generosity and the child do show that his conception of the individual is not as hopelessly solipsistic as Arendt sees it, although he does not discuss the dynamics of men acting together in the way Arendt does. Self-empowerment would be empty without any reference to intersubjective features of it. Nietzsche does reflect on the dynamics of intersubjective relations (such as friendship, relation to the reader, the teacher-disciple relation, parent-child relation). His writings on the difficult aspects of his relation to his mother have given many interpreters the impression that all his reflections on the parent-child relation are exclusively focused on problematic and tense aspects of it. His writings on his mother are often seen as symptomatic of both his rejection of the maternal and his solipsistic stand (Oliver 1995: 144). Arendt works out her notion of power in opposition to Nietzsche, whom she criticizes for seeing "the source of all power in the will power of the isolated individual" (Arendt 1958: 245). For her it makes no sense to talk about power in terms of the solitary individual. Power springs up between men when they act together, and it vanishes when they disperse. One can claim that the dynamics of different types of human relations that Nietzsche discusses are pre-political insofar as they are preemptive of certain dynamics of people acting together in larger groups. Nietzsche is aware of the fact that humans mutually empower or disempower each other, and the description of the generosity of Dionysus is a case in point of a gesture to empower the other. Nietzsche does not only reflect on the transfiguring power of love from the perspective of the creative, giving Dionysian self. He also talks about how one's self is affected and transformed by the other, although he has in general more to say about giving and generosity than about receiving.[16] The child, for example, often stands in his writings for the other who opens one's eyes. In one of his unpublished fragments he writes that the child is supposed to hold the mirror in front of me on which "the world is written."[17] In another fragment he asks if men's greatest beneficiaries are the ones who despise them the most, and he adds, "take the child away—its gaze kills!"[18] Despite the forceful tone of this second fragment, the idea behind the confrontation with the child is similar to Arendt's idea as to the role of newcomers. They can show us ourselves and the world in a fresh light, also because each generation has to impose itself on the world, change it in accord with its presence in it. Such an encounter of generations can give birth to something new, but that requires of the older ones that they are willing to accept that the newcomers do not cherish and hold dear the same things. On the contrary, Nietzsche writes, "the child cannot live if it does not demolish anything" (*KSA* 13, 560). Arendt herself, in her writings about children, also emphasizes that children should be allowed to be children, and should not be instrumentalized for any political purposes, in order to be able to begin something new in due time when they are ready.[19] And when they as grown-ups enter the scene, they will put their own mark on the world, often in opposition to the preceding generation.

This kind of dynamics of transfiguring encounters epitomizes both Arendt's and Nietzsche's conceptions about the self as other. Arendt speaks of the "*duality* of myself with myself that makes thinking a true activity, in which I am both the one who asks and the one who answers."[20] Her description of thinking "as though there were two wills present in the same man, fighting with each other for power over his mind" resonates with Nietzsche's conception of man as a plurality of wills rather than a will (Arendt 2000: 452).

Birth, Life, and Freedom

Miguel Vatter claims that Kristeva abstracts Arendt's conception of natality from her complex theory of life (Vatter 2006: 138). This is not wholly correct, for Kristeva does relate natality to life, but as the comparison of Arendt and Nietzsche shows, the connection between life and natality in Arendt's work is more multifaceted than Kristeva assumes. In her interpretation Kristeva mainly discusses how Arendt's conception of natality is embedded in her philosophy of life as a transition from animal life (*zōē*) to human life (*bios*). On the surface there is a clear distinction in *The Human Condition* between life as natural processes or animal life on the one hand and human life on the other hand (Arendt 1958: 97). Arendt's conception of politics is thus often interpreted as being based on the distinction between *bios* and *zōē* derived from Aristotle (Kristeva 2001: 41). In accord with this distinction human life of action and freedom seems to stand in opposition to the ever-recurring cycle of becoming. A closer look at Arendt's conception of natality shows, however, that this distinction between animal life and human life is not so clear-cut. In line with her understanding of the maternal as located between nature and culture, Kristeva interprets the maternal as a "passageway" between animal life and human life (Kristeva 2001: 47). Vatter interprets natality in a fashion similar to Kristeva as the "ceasura" that makes possible the transition "from life as object of power to life as subject of freedom" (Vatter 2006: 147). Arendt brings both together in her idea of birth: "Because he *is* a beginning, man can begin; to be human and to be free are one and the same" (Arendt 2000: 457). For her even birth and death are, properly speaking, not "natural occurrences" since they can have the meaning of growth or decay only within a human world (Arendt 1958: 97).

This idea of the becoming or decaying of life is in line with Nietzsche's understanding of the eternal return, which is based on his idea of nature as a creative force, and which undermines the distinction between *zōē* and *bios*. Nietzsche does distinguish between nature as a process of creation and human creativity, but he mediates between the two by basing some of the vital sources of human creativity in the body. Being creative entails, for him, to be able to express and articulate sentiments, emotions, and dispositions that are prereflective and prediscursive. He describes the artistic creative process as something that overcomes one and that one has no choice but to open up to. In *Ecce Homo* he describes how the phenomenon of creative inspiration brings together freedom and necessity, and entails an experience of power and growth: "Everything is in the highest degree involuntary but takes place in a tempest of a feeling of freedom" (Nietzsche 1992: 73).

Arendt might object to this affiliation with Nietzsche because she claimed in her late work on *The Life of the Mind* that the capacity for beginning something does not have to do with creativity or talent, but with the fact that human beings are being born (Arendt 1978b: 217). This statement presents a narrowing of her former idea that participation in the political sphere is a kind of a second birth of the person. Insofar as her statement could be taken as a criticism of Nietzsche's view of birth as creativity, it is one-sided. Nietzsche's philosophy cannot be reduced to the "desire for unbounded self-invention" (Komprimidis 2006: 191). He is concerned both with life as becoming through newcomers and with the enhancement of culture. Nietzsche set his hopes on creative individuals who can revalue values, envision alternative possibilities, and thus give new meaning to culture. In that sense Honig has described Nietzsche's aesthetics of self-creation as "pre-political," as a precondition for the political type of activity Arendt envisions, if not political as a disposition that challenges power (Honig 1993: 533). Arendt claims in a similar vein that freedom has to be understood as breaking free of something oppressive and calling something new into being.

In addition to that, Arendt does in fact have a highly aesthetic notion of how people become active on the political stage. One discloses one's self "without ever either knowing himself or being able to calculate beforehand whom he reveals" (Arendt 1958: 192). For Arendt it was precisely this kind of disclosure, which both she and Nietzsche describe as birth, that can reclaim the dignity of the political realm. Komprimidis interprets Nietzsche and Arendt as theorists of disclosure, that is, of creative and emancipatory politics in the broad sense that go against ways of thinking that primarily serve the status quo. He defends their theories against Habermas's charges of aestheticism, and argues for the importance of aesthetically inspired politics for theories of democracy (Komprimidis 2006: 191–99). As opposed to Nietzsche, Arendt was aware of how anti-democratic political creativity could never benefit from the plurality that is the privilege of the kind of political freedom that only democracy can guarantee.[21]

The Strength and Vulnerability of the Natal Body

Nietzsche's reflections on the child as a break with the old and as a new beginning are in line with his notion of birth as demanding, painful, and ecstatic. He compares it with the workings of nature when he writes that birth is "the death of innumerable other beings" (*KSA* 1, 768).[22] In his notes on birth as a self-transformative process he also underscores the accompanying discomforting physical features. The one who gives birth "is sick" and the one who has given birth is "unclean," as he writes in *Thus Spoke Zarathustra* (Nietzsche 1976a: 403). By mentioning impurity Nietzsche seems to echo religious and biblical ideas about the impurity of the bleeding and birth-giving female body. In light of his criticism of "immaculate perception" in *Thus Spoke Zarathustra,* these depictions of the impurity of the birth-giving body have to be understood as a rejection of the moral condemnation of what has been considered to be the impure (Nietzsche 1976a: 232–36). Perhaps for this reason he is fond of using the metaphor of writing with blood (Nietzsche 1976a: 152). What he aims at is turning the tables to give the bodily dimension of man the dignity of which it has been robbed in the Christian tradition. It was out of resentment, he writes in *Twilight of the Idols,* that Christian morals condemned the body and sex as something impure: "It was Christianity, with its *ressentiment* against life ... which first made something unclean of sexuality ... the presupposition of our life" (Nietzsche 1976b: 562).

In these statements the physical features of birth-giving as a natural process are accentuated, while at the same time the conception and the birth of a human being are seen as a miracle of nature itself. Birth is a coming into being against extreme odds in nature. As a form of creativity birth is not a product of calculation in accord with deterministic laws of nature. Arendt also understands natality as the spontaneous creativity of life itself. Natality, she writes, is, in the language of natural science, "the infinite improbability which occurs regularly." Birth seen in this way is like a "peculiar deviation from the common natural rule of cyclical movement" (Arendt 1958: 246). Birth, therefore, is both part of law like nature *and* unpredictable.

The unpredictability of birth stands in contrast to efforts to control and manipulate natal processes in life. For Arendt and Nietzsche morals, science, and technology are all means to direct, manipulate, and control human, embodied life. These are measures in the service of what Michel Foucault terms biopolitical governance, be it in the form of external regulation or self-imposed control (Foucault 1990). The very forces within the human being that are the source of spontaneity and unpredictability can oppose and break up the disciplinary patterns that structure our ways of thinking and modes of practice. With their idea of natality as spontaneity and freedom Nietzsche and Arendt are, however, not contrasting some kind of an original nature with nature that has been manipulated. Both of them are interested in the interplay of the natural and the cultural whereby there can be no clear distinction between the two. The measure for the interplay can be only some kind of an idea of balance or imbalance.

Nietzsche has a somewhat different take on the control and the taming of the human animal than does Arendt. For him the body has been discredited due to repressive morals, and the affective dimensions of thinking have not been acknowledged, resulting in a disembodied ideal of rationality. He opposes the ideals of rationality that have prevailed ever since the beginning of Platonic philosophy and that have hindered thinking from attuning to life, writing: "We philosophers . . . are not thinking frogs, nor objectifying and registering mechanisms with their innards removed: constantly, we have to give birth to our thoughts out of our pain and, like mothers, endow them with all we have of blood, heart, fire, pleasure, passion, agony, conscience, fate, and catastrophe" (Nietzsche 1974: 35–36 [3]).

In light of this passage from *The Gay Science*, it may seem at first sight that Arendt and Nietzsche stand opposed to one another in regard to the animality of man. Whereas Arendt criticizes the way in which men are turned into working animals, Nietzsche calls for the animal within to be given its dignity. The animal within, in the context of Nietzsche's philosophy, is neither good nor bad, but merely denotes drives, impulses, sentiments, and inner conditions.[23] Arendt criticizes a human type that cannot be creative in terms of political action, and Nietzsche criticizes a human type that cannot be creative in terms of thinking and acting. So, despite the difference in emphasis, both Arendt and Nietzsche criticize the way in which corporeal human beings are controlled and directed. Arendt does this by pointing at the iron cage of technological production and consumer society that depoliticizes men. Nietzsche does it by showing how morals have tamed man in a way that represses the sources of creativity in the body. Both Arendt and Nietzsche therefore set their hopes on the spontaneous forces that can resist domination, which both of them associate with birth or natality. Natality seen in this way yields a conception of politics as driven by reactive and proactive motives. Actions are initiated, but resistance that precedes new beginnings often has its origin in a reaction to domination. This is in accord with Nietzsche's statement from *The Gay Science* that it is either "hunger" or "superabundance" that is the drive behind becoming creative and doing something (Nietzsche 1974: 329 [370]).

Arendt accused Nietzsche of postulating a conception of the will to power that is "unearthly" (*unirdisch*) because it fails to acknowledge the empowering presence of the other(s) (Arendt 2002: 454). Her own conception of natality is, through the lens of Nietzsche's philosophy, a bit "unearthly" due to its inadequate acknowledgment of some relevant implications of embodied life. The comparison with Nietzsche unearths some resources in Arendt's writings for thinking natality with reference to life as a natural process. Natality as a philosophical conception can thus be better attuned to the positive and negative realities associated with it in life. That yields a conception of natality that better accounts for understanding natality both as free and spontaneous and as the "ontological root" it is supposed to be, and that has to be embodied life itself. A more complex conception of natality can better serve the Arendtian intention of *amor mundi* that Kristeva describes as love of ordinary life. Arendt considered the solipsistic idea of man that has permeated Western philosophy, culminating in Nietzsche's idea of the Dionysian self-creator. For Arendt the solipsistic idea of man has contributed to a dehumanizing twentieth century. By uncovering relational and dialogical dimensions of this idea of natal man in Nietzsche's philosophy, one finds resources to counter the solipsistic tendency in his thought. By shedding light on Arendt's philosophy of natality from the perspective of a Nietzschean philosophy of embodied, natal life one finds resources for thinking natality with reference to the body. That opens the body in Arendt's philosophy to further reflection on differences, such as sexual differences, that have to do with embodiment. Her philosophy of natality remains incomplete without relating it to the embodied basis of natality and the differences it entails. The comparison with Nietzsche's idea of birth as both creation and destruction, and as entailing both empowerment and disempowerment, also yields a richer notion of natality. The conception of natality in *The Human Condition* is idealistic to the extent that it lacks the tension that Arendt acknowledges as being inherent to the political. Arendt's idea of natality can even be said to be "light-minded" on the topic of domination in the public sphere.[24] The tension inherent to the political derives from lived experiences of lack of power or as a sense of empowerment. Life as human embodied life is a condition under which both domination and freedom are played out. Natality as reproduction has always had political implications that affect and determine the life of the sexes differently, traditionally yielding a subordinate political position for women and a lack of responsibility for men. Natality has also political implications that can be a source of freedom and empowerment in the way that Kristeva argues. Arendt largely thought of human embodiment in terms of how it is controlled or dehumanized with political use of technologies. Embodied and relational experiences of natality display it as a blend of vulnerability and strength. In juxtaposing and comparing Nietzsche's and Arendt's philosophies of birth, some of the dynamics inherent in the conception of birth become apparent.

Birth and Transfiguration

This interpretation of Nietzsche's philosophy of birth is, in important respects, inspired by several interpretations of it by several women thinkers. The works of Andreas-Salomé, Spielrein, Arendt, Oliver, and Kristeva span more or less the history of the reception of Nietzsche's philosophy from its very beginning until today. Women interpreters have been much more interested in Nietzsche's philosophy of birth and sexual difference than male interpreters, and many feminist philosophers have been interested in Nietzsche's philosophy.[25] The widespread German reception of Nietzsche by women at the beginning of the twentieth century, in which Andreas-Salomé and Spielrein took part, was the first massive participation of women in philosophical discourse and a major intervention against misogyny in Germany. In Nietzsche's thought women found philosophical resources to reflect on sexual difference and emancipation and social transformation. The position of early feminist interpreters was also characterized by ambivalence due to the misogynistic side of Nietzsche's philosophy. Such aspects were less questioned by conservative women such as Elisabeth Förster-Nietzsche, who saw herself as fighting for the cause of women, while insisting on traditional womanly virtues. Early feminists of the more progressive kind were skeptical of Nietzsche's exaggerated individualism, but many also appreciated the connection to life in Nietzsche's descriptions of pregnancy and birth.[26] It is therefore understandable that the interpreters of Nietzsche's philosophy of birth discussed in this interpretation of it think it through further in terms of the maternal, sexuality, and relationality. These interpreters reappropriate Nietzsche's philosophy of birth in a gesture against his appropriation of the feminine. Arendt's philosophy of natality also opposes the apolitical tendency of Nietzsche's solipsistic view of the creative individual, and extends the idea of birth as transfiguration to the sphere of the political.

The conception of birth has been interpreted as a transfiguring encounter with otherness that is a precondition for seeing oneself and the other in a new and different light. In bringing Nietzsche's thoughts on birth together with the ideas of these thinkers, a richer notion of birth evolves. Not only is Nietzsche's conception of birth transfigured through the encounter with these thinkers. Nietzsche's thought on the issue literally calls for a transfiguring encounter by its very insistence on openness to plurality.

NOTES

1. "Du bist immer ein Anderer," but in the English translation of *The Gay Science* (1974: 246 [307]), it is "you are always a different person."

2. *KSA* stands for Nietzsche, *Sämtliche Werke: Kritische Studienausgabe. KSA* is referred to for quotations from unpublished notes of Nietzsche.

3. See Nietzsche 1995: 169–225.

4. "'Die Menschen sind *nicht gleich!*'—So spricht—die Gerechtigkeit."

5. The emphasis on destruction as the origin of becoming relates to Freud's work on the death drive, but there are differences between Spielrein and Freud on this point that cannot be elaborated here.

6. See for example *KSA* 10, 29.

7. For further discussion see Köhler 2000: 36.

8. Kristeva 2002: 207.

9. Villa 1992: 275.

10. It has to be kept in mind that Arendt was a student of Martin Heidegger and Karl Jaspers, who with their books on Nietzsche laid ground for the reception of Nietzsche's philosophy in Germany after the Second World War.

11. Arendt's notions of promise and forgiveness as forms of our view of the past and dispositions toward the future in the public realm are also worked out with reference to Nietzsche's philosophy of forgetting, memory, and promise. See Lemm 2006.

12. For a helpful distinction between the value Nietzsche bestows on political thinking and his own (anti-democratic) political views see Brown 2000: 205–23.

13. See Stegmaier 2000: 67–91.

14. See Hannah Arendt, "'A Daughter of Our People': A Response to Gershom Scholem," in Arendt 2000: 392.

15. Oliver, who elaborates her idea of an ethics of intersubjectivity inspired by earlier versions of Kristeva's model of the mother-child relation, emphasizes the corpo-reality of this relation by locating it in the relation of the mother and the fetus (Oliver 1995: 195).

16. See Alan D. Schrift's introduction to *The Logic of the Gift: Toward an Ethic of Generosity* (Schrift 1997: 1–24).

17. "Ein Kind soll mir den Spiegel halten, auf dem die Welt geschrieben steht." *KSA* 10, 415. See also the chapter on the child and the mirror in *Thus Spoke Zarathustra.*

18. "Und wer die Menschen am meisten verachtete—war er nicht dadurch immer ihr grösster Wohltäter? Nehmt das Kind weg—sein Blick tötet." *KSA* 10, 559.

19. Hannah Arendt, "The Crisis in Education" (Arendt 1993: 173–96).

20. Hannah Arendt, "The Two-In-One" (Arendt 2000: 408).

21. For an analysis of the different meanings of plurality in Arendt's political thought, see Klockars 2008: 62–71.

22. "Jede Geburt ist der Tod unzähliger Wesen."

23. For Nietzsche, the problem is not the violence of the animal, for he considers the animal to be inherently innocent; rather does the problem lie with the violence that humans direct against their own animality. See Lemm 2006.

24. See Birmingham 2003: 53–74.

25. On the early reception of Nietzsche by feminists, see, for example, Diethe 1996.

26. Bäumer 1900: 385–95.

BIBLIOGRAPHY

Arendt, Hannah. 1958. *The Human Condition.* Chicago: University of Chicago Press.

———. 1978a. *The Jew as Pariah: Jewish Identity and Politics in the Modern Age.* New York: Random House.

———. 1978b. *The Life of the Mind.* New York: Harcourt Brace Jovanovich.

———. 1990. "Philosophy and Politics." *Social Research* 57: 1.

———. 1993. *Between Past and Future.* New York: Penguin.

———. 2000. *The Portable Hannah Arendt.* Ed. Peter Baehr. New York: Penguin.

———. 2002. *Denktagebuch.* 2 vols. Munich: Pieper Verlag.

Bäumer, Gertrud. 1900. "Die psychischen Probleme der Gegenwart und die Frauenbewegung." *Frau* 7: 385–95.

Betz Hull, Margaret. 2002. *The Hidden Philosophy of Hannah Arendt.* London: Routledge.

Birmingham, Peg. 2003. "The Pleasure of Your Company: Arendt, Kristeva and an Ethics of Public Happiness." *Research in Phenomenology* 33, no. 1: 53–74.

Brown, Wendy. 2000. In Schrift 2000: 205–23.

Diethe, Carol. 1996. *Nietzsche's Women: Beyond the Whip.* Berlin: de Gruyter.

Foucault, Michel. 1990. *The History of Sexuality.* New York: Vintage Books.

Honig, Bonnie. 1993. "The Politics of Agonism: A Critical Response to 'Beyond Good and Evil: Arendt, Nietzsche, and the Aestheticization of Political Action' by Dana R. Villa." *Political Theory* 21, no. 3: 528–33.

———. 1995. "Introduction: The Arendt Question in Feminism." In *Feminist Interpretations of Hannah Arendt,* ed. Bonnie Honig, 1–16. University Park: Pennsylvania State University Press.

Klockars, Kristian. 2008. "Plurality as a Value in Arendt's Political Thought." *Topos* 2, no. 19: 62–71.

Köhler, Joachim. 2000. *Who Was Friedrich Nietzsche?* Bonn: Internationes.

———. 2002. *Zarathustra's Secret.* New Haven, Conn.: Yale University Press.

Komprimidis, Nikolas. 2006. *Critique and Disclosure: Critical Theory between Past and Future.* Cambridge, Mass.: MIT Press.

Kristeva, Julia. 1986. "Stabat Mater." In *The Kristeva Reader,* ed. Toril Moi, 160–86. New York: Columbia University Press.

———. 2001. *Hannah Arendt.* New York: Columbia University Press.

———. 2002. *Colette.* Paris: Librairie Arthème Fayard.

Lemm, Vanessa. 2006. "Memory and Promise in Arendt and Nietzsche." *Revista de Ciencia Política* 26, no. 2: 161–73.

Nietzsche, Friedrich. 1966. *Beyond Good and Evil.* New York: Vintage Books.

———. 1974. *The Gay Science.* New York: Vintage Books.

———. 1976a. *Thus Spoke Zarathustra.* In *The Portable Nietzsche.* Ed. Walter Kaufmann. New York: Penguin.

———. 1976b. *Twilight of the Idols.* In *The Portable Nietzsche.* Ed. Walter Kaufmann. New York: Penguin.

———. 1980. *Sämtliche Werke: Kritische Studienausgabe (KSA).* 15 vols. Ed. Giorgio Colli and Mazzino Montinari. Berlin: de Gruyter.

———. 1992. *Ecce Homo.* London: Penguin.

———. 1995. *Schopenhauer as Educator: Unfashionable Observations.* Stanford, Calif.: Stanford University Press.

———. 1997. *Daybreak.* Cambridge: Cambridge University Press.

Oliver, Kelly. 1995. *Womanizing Nietzsche.* New York: Routledge.

Oppel, Francis Nesbitt. 2005. *Nietzsche on Gender. Beyond Man and Woman.* Charlottesville: University of Virginia Press.

Schrift, Alan, ed. 1997. *The Logic of the Gift: Toward an Ethic of Generosity.* New York: Routledge.

———, ed. 2000. *Why Nietzsche Still?* Berkeley and Los Angeles: University of California Press.

Spielrein, Sabina. 1912. "Die Destruktion als Ursache des Werdens." *Jahrbuch für psychoanalytische und psychopathologische Forschungen* 4, no. 1: 465–503.

Stegmaier, Werner. 2000. "Nietzsche, die Juden und Europa." In *Europa-Philosophie,* ed. Werner Stegmaier, 67–91 (Berlin: Walter de Gruyter).

Thorgeirsdottir, Sigridur. 2009. "Frauen im Leben Nietzsches / Women in the Life of Nietzsche." *Nietzsche Studien* 38: 410–19.

Vatter, Miguel. 2006. "Natality and Biopolitics in Hannah Arendt." *Revista de Ciencia Política* 26, no. 2: 137–59.

Villa, Dana R. 1992. "Beyond Good and Evil: Hannah Arendt, Nietzsche and the Aesthetization of Political Action." *Political Theory* 20, no. 2: 274–308.

Young-Bruehl, Elizabeth. 2006. *Why Arendt Matters.* New Haven, Conn.: Yale University Press.

Zerilli, Linda M. G. 1995. "The Arendtian Body." In *Feminist Interpretations of Hannah Arendt,* ed. Bonnie Honig, 167–94. University Park: Pennsylvania State University Press.

Zupancic, Alenka. 2003. *Nietzsche's Philosophy of the Two.* Cambridge, Mass.: MIT Press.

PART 4
An Ancient Tragedy

NINE

Antigone and the Deadly Desire for Sameness: Reflections on Origins and Death

VIGDIS SONGE-MØLLER

For my son Markus (1983–2003), who stayed with us too few years, each one a treasure forever.

Philosophy and Tragedy

Although the Greek philosophers from Heraclitus to Plato lived in the same period as the tragic dramatists, modern philosophers have made few attempts to analyze the relationships between Greek philosophy and the tragedies. Among the exceptions are Hegel and Nietzsche. Despite their considerable differences as philosophers, both Hegel and Nietzsche assess the philosophy and tragic drama of antiquity on the basis of the insights and the levels of reflection of which these two literary genres are capable. It is interesting that both writers, albeit to differing degrees, consider tragic drama more insightful than ancient philosophy. For Nietzsche, the insights found in the tragedies into the significance of death for human life tower above, for instance, Socrates' "optimistic" philosophy.[1] Hegel does not venerate the tragedies quite as highly as Nietzsche, but still he adduces them to illuminate the shortcomings of antique philosophy. Hegel believes, for example, that there is something self-contradictory in Socrates' attitude toward his own death. On the one hand, Socrates does not accept the decision of the jury in the lawsuit against him: when he is given "the liberty of suggesting a penalty different from the penalty which the accuser proposed" (i.e., penalty at death; Hegel 1995b: 440), he suggests free meals in the Prytaneum, since he is convinced that he has done nothing wrong. On the other hand, Socrates is not willing to flee from prison, as he easily could have done, but chooses to submit to the Athenian law. As a contrast to Socrates, Hegel refers to the heroine of Sophocles' *Antigone:* Antigone faces death in a simple, noncontradictory way. In his *Lectures on the History of Philosophy,* Hegel discusses Antigone and Socrates as analogous figures, that is, as tragic, heroic figures in literary/philosophical works.[2] In his youthful work, *Philosophy in the Tragic Age of the Greeks,* Nietzsche for his part regards the pre-Socratic philosophers

as a feature of the "Tragic Age," and hence as diverse types of tragic thinkers on the same level as Aeschylus and Sophocles.[3] Thus both Hegel and
Nietzsche disagree to some degree with the genre distinction that separates
tragic drama and philosophy. Or to put it another way, they seem to regard
this genre distinction as at least partially irrelevant to their interests.

For me as well, this genre classification seems unimportant. If, as a philosopher engaged in a philosophical project on sexuality, birth, and death,
I choose to study the relationship between the tragedies and ancient Greek
philosophy, it is because I suspect the tragedies may provide another type
of insight than that which dominated much of antique philosophy. In this
chapter I shall take Sophocles' *Antigone* as my point of departure and analyze how the question of origins, sexuality, and death are interrelated. I will
use fragments of Heraclitus, Parmenides, and Empedocles as a prism for my
analysis. I believe it can be fruitful to make a rough distinction between two
basic currents in Greek philosophy. The dominant current, not just in antiquity, but also in its influence on later philosophy, is what I call the Platonic
tradition. This I trace back to Hesiod, and I include within it, besides Plato
himself, Parmenides as one of its most important writers. These thinkers
represent a hierarchical approach to the world, advocating the ideals of
unity, stability, harmony, immutability, and immortality. It is tempting to
apply a literary characterization and call this type of thought "comic," in
contrast to "tragic" thought, where existence is characterized by irreducible,
nonhierarchical oppositions, which entail change, conflict, and transience.
Anaximander, Heraclitus, and Empedocles, along with the tragic dramatists,
can be seen as representatives of this latter current.

Knowledge, experience, and action play different roles in the tragedies
than they do in the Platonic tradition. Tragic insight does not lead to virtue,
harmony, and happiness, and even less to fundamental agreement, but rather
it shows us life's impermanence and inherent conflicts. In *King Oedipus,* as
in other tragedies, knowledge is fatal; Oedipus's discovery that he has killed
his father and married and had children with his mother means his life is at
an end. The experience of personal error produces insight, not of the type
that sweeps away guilt or unhappiness, but rather of a type that confirms
guilt and unhappiness as inescapable components of life.[4] In contrast to the
knowledge of the philosopher, that of the tragic hero generally results from
chance events of the kind that life, in contrast to methodic reflection, tends
to offer. Oedipus could not have foreseen that it was his father whom he
encountered and killed at the fateful crossroads. The tragedies show us the
fragility and unpredictability of life; *suddenly* harmony turns to a dream,

and conflict and unhappiness become real. Whereas philosophic insight is attained through contemplation and argumentation, tragic insight is gained through action and participation in unfolding conflicts.

The optimistic character of Platonic philosophy is associated with the minimizing of the body; the life that the philosopher dreams of is beyond death, a life incorporeal. In the tragedies, people have bodies that are individual, sexualized, and mortal. The sexualized meaning of the body becomes clear especially in death, which differs for men and women. They are killed or take their own lives in ways that emphasize their bodies as either feminine or masculine (Loraux 1991). In the tragedies, the presence of death—and hence of the body—is inseparable from what underlies the traditionally sharp genre distinction between tragic drama and philosophy: in the tragedies individuals are given voices in a way that is quite distinct from philosophy. The question of human existence is not one of abstract entities—the *idea* or *eidos*—as it is in the texts of Plato and Aristotle, where the ideal human is treated as equivalent to the ideal citizen, and women (and slaves) are regarded as a separate human category.[5] The figures in the tragedies have their own individual histories. Women and men are not merely representatives of their respective sexes; they act to some degree counter to and to some degree in accordance with their positions as men and women in the *polis*. Clytemnestra, in Aeschylus's *Agamemnon,* and Antigone, in Sophocles' *Antigone,* talk and behave as if they were men, in ways that collide with the behavioral norms of women at the time, yet they also come across as women in the traditional sense (as housewife, mother, daughter, sister). One could say that the clear distinction between women and men in the tragedies is simultaneously erased and emphasized, a situation that confronts the interpreter with different challenges from those involved in the interpretation of philosophical texts.

Philosophy and the *Polis*

Jean Pierre Vernant has shown that, in its origins, Greek philosophy cannot be dissociated from the city-state and the rise of democracy.[6] The fragments of the earliest philosophers—Thales, Anaximander, and Anaximenes—are permeated with political and juridical terms and expressions, and can in Vernant's opinion be read as commentaries on the governmental form of the city-state. Whereas Vernant claims that philosophy dissociates itself from the political discourse and develops its own terminology beginning with Parmenides,[7] I for my part consider I have shown that even the work of Parmenides reflects fundamental problems associated with the ideology of the democratic city-state.[8] I argue that this ideology is based on certain problematic ideals: the ideal of the state's unity and homogeneity, based on the idea of politically interchangeable citizens, the ideal of the state's stability and self-sufficiency, and—above all—the ideal of the state's ability to reproduce and perpetuate itself. Since the democratic city-state consisted only of men, or male citizens, this ideal of the state's self-reproduction entails a concept of the male citizen as a self-reproducing and self-sufficient being, or alternatively: the ideal of the self-reproduction of the city-state entails the view of the woman as (ideally speaking) superfluous.

The expression "the ideology of the democratic city-state" is borrowed from the historian and mythologist Nicole Loraux. For her it refers to how the Athenians viewed themselves, as belonging to a harmonious, indivisible, enduring, and self-sufficient community of equal—or rather politically identical—citizens,[9] as this is expressed in, for example, the autochthonic myth describing the origin of the Athenians[10] and in the city-state's official funeral oration for citizens killed in war.[11] The Athenians traced their origins back to the earthborn Erichthonius. According to this myth, the maternal source of all Athenian citizens is the earth, or more precisely, the earth of Attica. As Plato puts it in his dialogue *Menexenus* (238e–239a), the Athenians look upon themselves as "brothers, the children of one and the same mother." This family resemblance provides in turn the basis for their political equality (*isonomia*). Compared to other democratic institutions in ancient Greece, that of Athens was distinguished by its radical idea of equality. In Athens there was no hierarchy whatsoever among citizens; none was more of a citizen than any other, and hence political equality was absolute.[12] The founding of these radical ideas about sameness on the autochthonic myth brings together both democratic and aristocratic elements: sameness is based on shared family origins; in other words, what counts is being of the right, or of "good," birth (*eugeneia*) (Loraux 2000: 21–22). When, in the *Republic,* Plato describes the ideal state as a single unified family, which is in fact so close-knit as to resemble an individual,[13] he may be said to follow the city-state's official ideology.

It may seem paradoxical to regard Plato's philosophy as a kind a reflection on, or even as a justification of, the foundations of the democratic city-state, but personally I believe there is much to be said for this interpretation. Of course, Plato's aim was not a defense of democracy. Quite the contrary. But although he builds his political philosophy on the idea of fundamental differences between human beings and advocates a society divided into hierarchical classes with an authoritarian government, his goal is the same as that of democratic Athens: a unitary, indivisible, harmonic, and self-perpetuating state. In the *Republic* his aim is precisely to describe the preconditions for such a state.[14]

It is striking that the only explicit defense, or theory, of democracy in Greek philosophy is made by Protagoras as depicted by Plato in the dialogue that he named after that sophist. Plato has Protagoras describe the basis for democracy in the form of a myth (*Protagoras* 322a–323a); all humans have been granted the faculty of *techne politike*, which enables them to discuss political questions with one another. This specifically human capacity is not restricted exclusively to the male citizens, nor even to men in general. Plato's Protagoras claims that it is madness not to pretend to partake of political virtue (*politike arete*), or more specifically justice, "since one must have some trace of it or not be human" (*Protagoras* 323c). Admittedly, Protagoras describes this quality as a "manly virtue" (*andros arete, Protagoras* 325a), but he adds that for a state to be able to function, this virtue should be cultivated among every "man, woman and child" (*Protagoras* 325a). In other words, the line is drawn not between men and women, or between the free and those who are slaves, but between the civilized on the one hand and the "wild" (*agrioi*) on the other (*Protagoras* 327d). In this way Protagoras explicitly oversteps the bounds of Athenian democracy, which encompassed only male citizens. This means that Protagoras is, in fact, proposing universal democracy. Ironically, it is the anti-democratic Plato, and not Protagoras, who could be said to provide a theoretical basis for the ideology of the Athenian democratic city-state.

As already mentioned, not only Plato but also his predecessor Parmenides can be interpreted as reflecting on the ideological foundation of the democratic *polis*. Parmenides' philosophy has come down to us in the form of a poem he composed in the first half of the fifth century BCE. In his poem, Parmenides sketches a picture of the world, or of Being, as a homogeneous, self-identical and self-sufficient, unchanging, and eternal sphere. This sphere encompasses all that exists—which is the "like" (*homoion*) and the "identical" (*tauton*)—and excludes all that does not exist—the "non-identical" (*me tauton*).[15] This image of the sphere of Being is structurally analogous to the democratic city-state, which is constituted by the exclusion of the "non-identical," primarily women and slaves. Strictly speaking, women and slaves are not part of the city-state; they function as nonexistent entities of some kind in relation to what was in political terms the homogeneous city-state. Viewed in this way, Parmenides' poem can be said to provide a philosophical foundation for the city-state ideology.[16]

Tragedy and the *Polis*

We have seen above that ancient philosophy includes both implicit and explicit reflections on the nature of the democratic *polis*. To what extent can the tragedies be viewed as an alternative political discourse? In what sense can also the tragedies be said to illuminate problematic aspects of the city-state ideology? It is not entirely easy to determine the relation between the tragedies and Athenian democracy. Of course, there would be nothing controversial in claiming a close connection between Athenian democracy and the tragedies as an institution.[17] But when it comes to the subject matter of the tragedies, which is my main interest in the current context, the relation is more complex. Only a few of the tragedies deal either directly or indirectly with contemporary political circumstances. One that did was a work, now lost, by Phrynichus, a predecessor of Aeschylus, which dealt with the Persian conquest of Miletus in 494 BCE, a dramatic political event that ended in the Greek citizens of Miletus being reduced to slaves. When *The Conquest of Miletus* was performed, "the whole theater burst into tears; and the people sentenced him [Phrynichus] to pay a fine of a thousand drachms for recalling to them their own misfortunes. They likewise made a law that no one should ever again exhibit that piece" (Herodotus, Book VI, 20). This ban evinces a principle that seems to have been respected by later tragic dramatists, at least with regard to misfortunes that had befallen the Greeks themselves: "the principle of placing at a distance" (*le principe de la mise en distance*), as Pierre Vidal-Naquet has called it (Vidal-Naquet 2001: 11). Among the surviving tragedies there is only one that deals with a historic political event, namely Aeschylus's *The Persians* (performed in 472 BCE), which dramatizes the Athenians' victory over the Persians in 480 BCE.

The action of all the other surviving tragedies takes place in a mythical world. Even so, these works contain numerous allusions to the political circumstances and institutions of the day. The most obvious example is the close of Aeschylus's *Oresteian* trilogy, where Orestes is brought before a court that can be seen as a reference to the council that met on the Areopagus. However, neither here nor elsewhere is it a matter of direct reflection of, or clear standpoints on, the democratic institutions. The relation between the themes of the tragedies and political realities is of a far more indirect nature. "Tragedy is not a direct mirror of social and political circumstances, it is a shattered mirror," Vidal-Naquet writes (Vidal-Naquet 2000: 172). I consider this a good image: in the tragedies we find fragments and splinters that give us partially distorted, inverted, or disjointed pictures of reality. When one reads a Greek tragedy, it is relatively obvious that it is telling us something or other about the social and political circumstances of the time—if it did not do so, it would hardly have been so popular in its own day—but what it tells us is not so immediately obvious. With the image of the "shattered mirror," Vidal-Naquet also suggests that the tragedies could be a brutal mirror for the Athenians; they could produce cracks in certain illusions on which the Greek state was in various ways dependent. Nicole Loraux also offers a striking description of the relation between tragedy and the city-state ideology: she refers to tragedy as "antipolitical." Here she is playing on two senses of the Greek word *anti*: "in the place of"/"instead of" and "opposed to." Tragedy goes beyond the political and reminds us first and foremost of our mortality; thus it is something other than politics. But this very point—human mortality—was something that was suppressed in the ideology of the democratic city-state, a circumstance that the tragedies convey by taking issue with that ideology. In other words, the tragedies offer an alternative voice to that of the political discourse while at the same time opposing it. For Loraux, tragedy is "antipolitical" in the sense that it "diverts, rejects, or threatens, consciously or not, the obligations and prohibitions constituting the ideology of the city-state" (Loraux 2002b: 26).

In her book *The Divided City: On Memory and Forgetting in Ancient Athens,* Loraux discusses a decree set forth in Athens in 403 BCE on the reintroduction of democracy following the government of the Thirty Tyrants. The decree proclaimed, "it is forbidden to recall the misfortunes" (*me mnesikakein*). It was also formulated as an oath: "I shall not recall the misfortunes" (*ou mnesikakeso*).[18] Here the "I" was that of each individual Athenian, or of the Athenians collectively. The prohibition is paradoxically formulated: what is meant to be forgotten is named and hence recollected. The ban against performing a tragedy that reminds the Athenians of their misfortunes can be seen as another strategy aimed at collective forgetting. A similar strategy is to be found in Pericles' funeral oration for fallen soldiers, as recounted by Thucydides. Rather than talk about the dead soldiers, Pericles gave a speech about the splendors of democratic Athens: "I have sung the praises of our city; but it was the courage and gallantry of these men, and of people like them, which made her splendid" (Thucydides, Book II, 42). The life of the individual soldier served to perpetuate the "splendid *polis*," and the parents who had lost sons were simply called upon to produce more sons: "[T]hose of you who are of the right age must bear up and take comfort in the thought of having more children. In your own homes these new children will prevent you from brooding over those who are no more, and they will be a help to the city, too, both in filling the empty places, and in assuring her security" (Thucydides, Book II, 44). One son replaces another, just as one citizen replaces another. In keeping with this kind of relativization of the individual's life and death, Thucydides describes the time of the city-state as a kind of eternity, in which the city-state remains forever the same: "In this land of ours there have always [*aei*] been the same people living from generation to generation up till now, and they . . . have handed it on to us, a free country" (Thucydides, Book II, 36). This considerable emphasis in the city-state's funeral oration on the everlasting existence of the *polis* can be viewed as a strategy that serves, among other things, to suppress grief, or at least to keep it rigorously in check, in favor of praising the city-state's continued existence. The death of the individual must be forgotten, while the life of the city-state is celebrated.

In contrast, the tragedies serve precisely as reminders of death, suffering, and mortality. They find expression for grief and a determination *not* to forget. Elektra refuses to forget the murder of her father, just as Antigone refuses to forget her dead brother. In this regard the tragedies can be read as works of protest, or as voices opposed to the city-state's official policy of forgetting; they insist on the significance of death and of life's transience, and they insist on the reality of grief for those who remain. In Sophocles' *Antigone*, this insistence results in the downfall of an entire dynasty. And in the process, a number of the city-state's forgotten and excluded elements are rendered conspicuous: among other things, the inextinguishable presence of grief and the ephemerality not just of the individual, but also of the family and of society.

Antigone does not simply insist on death, she seems to yearn for it.[19] For Antigone, death is not something alien, but rather a place where she will be reunited with those who are "her own"—her immediate blood relatives; death for her is not first and foremost the end of life so much as the beginning of eternal coexistence with her immediate family. This yearning for death is a form of homesickness. Antigone's death wish can be understood, on the one hand, as an affirmation of what one might call the city-state's yearning for the continued self-reproduction of the unitary and homogeneous *polis*, and on the other as a rejection of this notion. It is an affirmation insofar as it is clearly of an incestuous nature and can therefore be read as a yearning for the reproduction of the closed, self-identical family, in other words, the reproduction of Sameness. But Antigone's death wish can also be read as a rejection of the same ideology: as a woman, Antigone does not want to be an accomplice in achieving the masculine fantasy of the *polis*, which, despite its exclusion of women, still depends on them. This contradiction is in many ways a feature of the tragedy as such, insofar as it challenges both the distinction between life and death and the distinction between man and woman. In other words, what is to be forgotten and what is excluded from the *polis* are both dramatized in the tragedy and brought into close contact with their contraries. Seen in this way, the tragedy can be said to highlight and reflect upon the city-state's policies of forgetting and exclusion. But the same thing is also achieved on another level: it is Antigone's radical rejection of any kind of Other, or of everything that is Alien, that sends her to the grave. Similar to the incestuous family, the Athenian *polis* was also founded on a radical exclusion of "the other," which included slaves, women, and all kinds of non-Athenians.[20]

There are several structural parallels between the incestuous family and the ideology of the democratic Athenian city-state, for instance in their concept of time. The concept of time that finds expression in Pericles' funeral oration, where the emphasis is on the city-state's durability, in the form of constant renewal, repetition, and the assertion of democracy's fundamental principles across the changing generations, is also present in the autochthonic myth. For the Athenians, their origin was not a stage in the past, but quite the opposite; it was associated with an unalterable *place*, the earth of Attica, which unifies the past, the present, and the future. Each birth can be understood as a repetition of the Athenians' mythical beginning. Continuity between the present and those origins is preserved, the death of the individual is relativized, or neutralized, and subsumed into the "eternal" life of the community. Antigone expresses a similar concept of time, linking it to her yearning to be reunited with her dead, incestuous family: "for I must please those down below a longer time than those up here, since I shall lie there always [*aiei*]" (74–76). Antigone is looking for an eternity where nothing will happen, rather than endure the shifting phases of human life. Oedipus solved the riddle of the Sphinx concerning the three stages of human life—childhood, adulthood, and old age—but went on to invalidate the distinctions between them by taking his father's place and being both husband and son to the same woman. Antigone follows in her father's footsteps by tragically enacting a fantasy of eternity rather than participate in a linear and finite human time. In other words, the tragedies can be read as a glaring critique of the city-state's emphasis on the community's eternal temporality and the suppression of the individual's, the family's, and society's impermanence.

In the following analysis of *Antigone*, I shall take a closer look at the parallels between the autochthony myth and incest, between the democratic city-state and the incestuous family. We might say that in the tragedies that deal with Oedipus and his family, the constitutive principles of the city-state ideology—unity, sameness or self-identity, and self-reproduction, and hence a kind of exclusion of the rest of the world—are transferred onto the family. It is as if, in his plays *King Oedipus, Oedipus at Colonus*, and *Antigone*, Sophocles were doing the opposite of what Plato would do some years later in his *Republic*. Whereas Plato wanted to clarify the concept of justice by writing in capital letters, that is, by proceeding from an analysis of the individual to an analysis of the state, we can say that Sophocles sought to clarify what was problematic about the city-state's ideology by superimposing this ideology on the family unit. This amounts to a transformation of the notion of community: in the family, in contrast to the city-state, the woman is included. This casts a very different light on the problematic aspects of a radical philosophy of unity and self-identity.

By means of my analysis of *Antigone*, I wish to investigate how the various themes already mentioned are interrelated: the rejection in the tragedies of the state policy of forgetting and its suppression of conflict, polarities, transience, and death; Antigone's yearning for absolute unity, her rejection of the Other, and her transgression of and challenge toward the city-state's unambiguous distinction between man and woman. The analysis of fragments by Empedocles, Parmenides, and Heraclitus will be used to illuminate *Antigone* and its eponymous heroine. Whereas I view Empedocles and Heraclitus as tragic thinkers on a level with Sophocles, the thoughts of Parmenides can be interpreted as a philosophical counterpart to Antigone's words and actions.

Antigone and the Problem of Origins

Hegel's analysis of *Antigone* has, more or less explicitly, been taken as the background for later interpretations of this tragedy, and even today it is difficult to write about this play without mentioning Hegel. Even where contemporaries are critical of Hegel's interpretation of *Antigone*, most of them focus, as did Hegel, on the opposition between Antigone and her uncle Creon. This opposition is, however, so obvious that one hardly has to be a Hegel to notice it and take it as the basis for one's analysis. One only has to recount the plot of *Antigone* for it to be clear: Creon is king of Thebes following the death of Oedipus's son, Eteocles, at the hands of his own brother, Polynices, who has laid siege to Thebes with a hostile army.

Polynices also dies as a result of his single combat with his brother. Creon declares Polynices a traitor, refuses him burial, and threatens the death penalty for anyone who defies his regal command. For Antigone, however, the dead Polynices is not a traitor, but a brother deserving of a decent burial. Thus the conflict is assured. Antigone defies Creon's prohibition and buries her brother. Creon imposes the death penalty, incarcerating Antigone in a cave, where she hangs herself. Antigone's death leads to the downfall also of Creon's family, for Haemon, Creon's son, who was betrothed to Antigone, takes his own life, whereupon Creon's wife, Eurydice, takes hers. Creon survives alone, recognizing the error of his ways.

According to Hegel's interpretation of the play in *The Lectures on the Philosophy of Religion*, Antigone and Creon represent two necessary moral aspects of the state's dialectic toward justice: on the one hand, "the love of the family, the holy, the inner, what is also called the law of the lower deities because it belongs to sentiments," on the other, "the law of the state, the authority of the government," as Hegel expresses it (Hegel 1995a: 665). This opposition is at the same time an opposition between the sexes: the timeless world of the woman with the family and the blood bond on the one hand, and the historic, moral world of the man, expressed through the laws of state, on the other. Although Hegel elevates Antigone to a divine level ("the heavenly Antigone, the noblest of figures that ever appeared on earth" [Hegel 1995b: 441]), it is Creon's values that stand highest; the conflict between the two scales of value is resolved in favor of masculine morality.

The conflict between Creon and Antigone is without a doubt the focus of the tragedy, yet it is by no means as clear and straightforward as Hegel seems to suppose. As the offspring of an incestuous union, Antigone can be viewed as someone who stands outside every kind of traditional family structure, and who therefore is also on the outside of any accepted form of community.[21] Accordingly, Antigone also explicitly distances herself from the traditional family by renouncing the prospect of husband and children and choosing instead to dedicate herself to her dead brother, or, more generally, by preferring death to life. For his part, Creon can be regarded as a spokesman for the traditional family. Seen in this way, the conflict between Antigone and Creon assumes a form quite different from Hegel's analysis. In a number of places Sophocles also plays on the lack of clarity in Antigone's and Creon's gender identities: whereas Antigone sometimes behaves and speaks like a man, Creon is given correspondingly feminine traits. This makes it difficult to view Antigone and Creon as clear-cut representatives of their respective genders. The gender struggle in the tragedy is played out in ways that are more subtle and ambiguous. Sophocles points up not just the issue of gender difference, but also other differences relating to both family and society: the difference between those who are inside and those who are outside the community of the family and the state, that is, the difference between "us" and "the other," between "friends" and "enemies," and not least the difference between parents and children. The negation of the latter difference has fatal consequences not just for Antigone herself, but also for Creon and hence for the royal house of Thebes.

The possibility that *Antigone* is first and foremost an investigation into and a meditation on the problem of origins and the significance thereof for the community is suggested in the tragedy's opening words, Antigone's greeting to her sister, Ismene: *koinon autadelphon* ("My own sister of common blood"). *Koinon* means "common," or "that which one has in common," which was a focal word in the political debates of the time and which also denoted a public, political community,[22] while *autadelphon* emphasizes the sisters' shared, or identical (*autos*), origin. The opening lines of *Antigone* are as follows:

> *Ismene, my own sister, sharing the self-same blood,*[23]
> *of all the evils that descend from Oedipus*
> *do you know one that Zeus does not fulfil for us,*
> *the two still living? There is nothing—no!—no grief,*
> *no doom, dishonour or disgrace that I've not seen*
> *counted among the evils that are yours and mine.*[24]

Antigone is appealing here to her sister's solidarity by referring to what the two of them have in common, both with each other and with their dead brother. That common bond is not romanticized; indeed, if anything, Antigone stresses its incestuous aspect. The incestuous community is defined by the common origin of the family's members, which means in effect that all of them—Antigone herself, her brothers, her sister, and her father—were conceived in the same womb; they are all children of Iocasta. This hermetically sealed unit, which includes so few and excludes so many, constitutes Antigone's world, both in space and in time. Antigone works with a sharp distinction between what is inside and what is outside, that is, between friends (*filos*, which also signifies that which is one's "own," that which belongs to one) and enemies (*echthros*). Antigone wants nothing but to be together with those to whom she belongs, with those whom she resembles. All her actions are directed "inward"—or "backward"—toward the common, unified origin of her small, closed community. In consciously choosing death rather than life, her brother and her father rather than her betrothed, her own origin rather than herself bearing children, fusion with the original unity rather than development and diversity, immobility rather than movement and change, she is seeking nothing more than the fulfillment of what is already contained as a seed not just in Oedipus's incestuous family, but also in Thebes as a whole.[25]

According to Thebes's own autochthonic myth, the city's first citizens sprang from the earth as fully grown warriors, where Cadmus, the founder of Thebes, had sown the teeth of a dragon. The family of Oedipus were descendants of these earth-born men. This autochthonic myth involves a clearly incestuous element: in Greek mythology, the earth was the Mother Earth of all gods, all humans, and everything that lives,[26] and Cadmus can therefore be said to have sown the dragon's "seed" in their common mother. Just as Oedipus has a double role as both husband and son in relation to Iocasta, in Thebes's autochthonic myth the distinction is unclear between the begetter (the dragon's teeth) and the begotten (what germinates from the dragon's teeth). The autochthonic myth can be said to involve incest on the level of society, insofar as it attributes all citizens to a single, common mother, namely the earth of the city-state.[27] In the same way as incestuous relationships cancel out differences of generation, so too did the Thebans; they failed to solve the Sphinx's riddle about the three stages of human life. In an incestuous way, the autochthonous Thebans did not accept the vicissitudes of time. One could say that when Antigone goes to her grave, the Theban royal house returns to its autochthonic origins.

Insofar as the tragic outcome of *Antigone* can be interpreted as a fulfillment of the Theban "destiny," it should also be possible to read it as a commentary on the autochthonic myth of the Athenians themselves;[28] this myth encapsulates a dream of a unitary and indivisible community, a dream that Antigone realized in tragic terms. When Antigone is incarcerated in her tomb, the end becomes one with the beginning; life comes to a close with the closing of the circle. For Antigone and her small, close-knit family, life ends in a very concrete sense. Everyone is dead, admittedly with the exception of Ismene, who could be viewed as a tiny glow of hope for continued life.[29] Creon also survives, but only as a "nothing" (1325), a "living corpse" (1167). Throughout the tragedy, Creon has identified himself with the state, and we can view his reduction to "nothing" as the obliteration of the bedrock on which Thebes stood. The incestuous fulfillment of Thebes's autochthonic origin has shaken the state to its foundations.

Parmenides and Antigone:
The Denial of Change and Difference

Antigone's inclination toward absolute unity and inertness can be seen as a parallel to the philosophy of Parmenides. "It is the same where I begin; for I shall come back there again," writes Parmenides in fragment B 5. Parmenides' entire poem is concerned with sameness, with unity and the self-identical, which he visualized in the form of the sphere of Being. Being is, according to Parmenides, "whole, alone of its kind,[30] immovable and complete. It was not once nor will it be, since it is now altogether, one, continuous" (B 8.4–6), and "it remains the same in the same, it lies by itself and abides firmly where it is" (B 8.29–30). These characterizations of Parmenidean Being would be an appropriate description of the family community of which Antigone dreams.

Parmenides constructs his homogeneous, self-identical Being so as to exclude all and every form of difference and contradiction, which, according to Parmenidean logic, would entail annihilation and death. If we look closer at Parmenides' poem, we will see that it establishes a close, and necessary, connection between birth/becoming and death: whatever has come into being will perish, whatever is born will die.[31] His aim in constructing Being in this way seems to be everlasting existence, beyond destruction and death. In his search for an eternal being, Parmenides consequently postulates a being that does not involve origin or birth. The eternity that Parmenides is looking for is an eternal present (*nun estin*, B 8.5) close to the eternal time that Antigone seeks in death. Whereas the ordinary condition of human life has an end, the company of the dead will endure forever, and thus Antigone prefers death to life: "for I must please those down below a longer time than those up here, since I shall lie there always [*aiei*]" (74–76).[32] Or to put it another way, Antigone seeks eternal life in death, admittedly a life where nothing happens, or at the most an eternal repetition of the same. Parmenides' eternity entails a similar conception of eternal life, in the form of an unending repetition of the same. This I shall examine in greater detail.

Parmenides' poem introduces three named and clearly personified goddesses—Dike, Ananke, and Moira—who strive to keep secure the bonds that hold Being, an endeavor suggesting that force is needed to hold Being intact and in place.[33] One of the words in the poem commonly translated as "bonds" is *pedai* (28 B 8.14), meaning "fetter," a kind of shackle originally used to prevent prisoners from escaping. The role played by the goddess of fate, Moira, in Parmenides' poem further emphasizes that Being is constrained. Whereas in mythology, Moira is the one who determines the individual's moment of death by cutting the thread of life, in Parmenides' poem she prevents the bonds that secure Being from being broken. In the poem, the fine thread of life has been transformed into unbreakable bonds, which protect Being from coming into contact with Not-Being. Parmenides seems to be saying that the bonds around Being are a means for forcefully keeping death and decay away from Being. In describing these bonds as fetters, he suggests that Being is in danger of breaking free, which, if it did so, would have catastrophic consequences: annihilation, or death, would ensue. Like a prisoner, Being also struggles for liberation, yet liberty would result in death.

This implies that Parmenidean Being is not a purely static phenomenon, a kind of lifeless reality. What Parmenides calls "Being" seems if anything to be something active; it is something that happens—in other words, it is to be understood in a verbal rather than a substantive aspect. Such an interpretation of the Parmenidean concept of Being differs from the predominant view, which has taken Parmenides' "pure Being" as entailing absolute immobility.[34] The principal argument for this view comes from Parmenides himself, who describes Being as motionless (*akineton*): "motionless, in the limits of mighty bonds, it is without beginning and never-ceasing" (B 8.26–27). However, the fact that Being is described as "motionless" does not preclude a state of activity. "Motionless" is in fact an unfortunate translation for *akineton*, since it immediately suggests a state of quiescence. "Unshakable" comes closer to Parmenides' meaning. According to Loraux, the fundamental sense of *kinesis* is "shaking" (Loraux 1987: 108). In the Greek city-state there was a constant fear of *kinesis*, in the form of *stasis*, or civil war. *Stasis* was a condition of deadlock in political conflicts. The danger in such cases was that they might undermine the unity of the *polis* and even lead to its breakdown. The fear of civil war found what is probably its best expression in Thucydides (Book II, 20), who was particularly afraid of the possible total breakdown of order that might result from such conflict. Thucydides tells us that when the unity of a state breaks down, not even words retain their meaning—even language is lost. Parmenides' emphasis on the "motionlessness" of Being should be viewed against this background. The implication is not that Being is totally inert, but rather that it is so well secured that it cannot be shaken. If it were not for the bonds, the unity of Being, and hence Being as such, would be at risk of disintegration.

We should also note that, in the sentence just quoted (B 1.26–27), Being is described as "without beginning" (*anarchon*) and "never-ceasing" (*apauston*); that is, it has no *arche*, and will never cease (*pauesthai*) to be. If we examine how these two words—*arche* and *pauesthai*—are used in Greek texts, we find that they are always associated with activities or events. An *arche* is what initiates an action or event, and it is always an action or event that is said to cease (*pauesthai*). It is therefore possible to interpret Parmenides as claiming that Being is itself a kind of action or event that has neither beginning (origin) nor end (ceasing, annihilation).

> But since there is a furthest limit, it is everywhere accomplished;
> like the body of a well-rounded sphere,
> from the middle in every direction of equal strength. (B 8.42–44)

In this famous image of Being as a sphere, it is described as "complete," or "accomplished." In other words, the event that Being constitutes lacks nothing. It is complete in itself and is in this sense not on the way to becoming something (else), but is rather already and always at its goal. Being accomplishes—or reaches—its goal unceasingly.

This interpretation of Parmenidean Being as an accomplished action, or a consummated life, tends at the same time to view his philosophy as a fantasy about a life without birth and death. This fantasy seems closely related to that of Antigone concerning an eternal life in the grave together with her "own." What I have interpreted as "life," however, is construed by Nietzsche as death. For him, Parmenidean Being is "the rigor mortis [*starre Todesruhe*] of the coldest, emptiest concept of all, the concept of being" (Nietzsche 1998: 80). To describe Parmenides' concept of Being as "petrified immobility" (*starre Ruhe*) is in my view misleading, although I consider there is some justification in characterizing it as a kind of death. Both Parmenides and Antigone seem to have erased the difference between life and death. Antigone strives for a life in death, while Parmenides fantasizes about a life beyond birth and death. Antigone chooses the dead as her future family, and, in a paradoxical way, she looks toward the future; when united with "her own," she will be able to remain "a longer time" than a human life would allow (74). The future she is looking for is not a human future so much as an everlasting Parmenidean Now, where past and present are transcended—without birth and death, without growth and change, beyond the vicissitudes of time.[35] Whereas the Parmenidean eternity is Being, or existence, in itself, the eternity that Antigone dreams of is a sheer nothingness. In *Antigone*, Sophocles holds up a mirror to Parmenides' "comic" dream of eternity, portraying it as a tragic illusion.

It would hardly be an overinterpretation to see the grave as analogous to Iocasta's womb. Antigone's death wish unites the tomb and the womb, the end and the beginning of life. Henceforth, this unity is to be her home, her family (cf. *oikesis*, 892). In Greek, *oikos* denotes at one and the same time "family," "home," and "house." It is a term that describes both the continuity of the family across its various branches and the family's linkage to a *place*, in other words to the house and earth where the family resides. Antigone, who regards herself as homeless among the living,[36] wants to establish a "home" that is impervious to temporal change and not associated with place. In the conceptual world of the Greeks, this could hardly be anything other than nothingness. It is interesting to note that the word that Parmenides uses to link the beginning and the end in the above-quoted fragment 5 ("It is the same where I begin; for I shall come back there again") is *ksynon*, an equivalent to *koinon*, which is also the very first word in *Antigone* and can be seen as decisive for Antigone's entire fate; the community that Antigone seeks and that she finally finds in death is closer than any that a human community could endure. In other words, the type of unity that, according to Parmenides, keeps Not-Being and death—and hence also birth and becoming—at bay, is portrayed in Sophocles' tragedy as an unlivable unity.

One place where Antigone's yearning for the One and for Sameness is made brutally clear is in a verse that many interpreters have been inclined to view as inauthentic: she would not have defied Creon's ruling if it had been a husband or her own child who had been denied burial.[37] Neither a child nor a husband is unique and irreplaceable; one can find a new husband, and one can have a new child, but a brother is something else: "I would never have defied the citizens to do this labor if the oozing corpse were that of my own child, or if my husband lay there dead. . . . My husband dead, I could have had another, and a child from someone else, if I had lost the first; but with my mother and my father both concealed in Hades, no more brothers ever could be born" (905–12). Provided husband and child have no incestuous linkage, they point outward, toward the world beyond the hermetically sealed family, and since they involve the world outside, they can also be multiplied. In contrast, Polynices draws her in toward the unitary, self-identical source, where reproduction involves repetition of the same. Antigone, her brother, father, and mother constitute a unique unit with clear boundaries toward the world beyond. It is this original, homogeneous unit that Antigone wants to preserve, and that Sophocles shows us the impossibility of preserving. Antigone's brutal rejection of Ismene,[38] who is also of the same blood as Antigone, clearly demonstrates that her principal concern is not the honoring of the blood bond. It is only by being reunited with Polynices and Oedipus in their somber bridal chamber[39] that Antigone can dream of continuing the reproduction of Oedipus's family, in the form of identical replicas of the source.

Antigone's relativization of husband and child is, however, ambiguous, since in many ways it accords with the official attitude of the city-state toward the family. Creon attempts a similar relativization in his brusque dismissal of Ismene's question about whether he would kill the bride of his own son: "[T]here are other plots of land to plow" (569), he says. One of the peculiarities of Athenian democracy was that, from a political point of view, all citizens were *equal* (*homoioi*), in the sense that they are interchangeable within the various political institutions. As already mentioned, in his funeral oration Pericles comforted the parents of soldiers who had died in battle with the hope of new sons. Although it might sound anachronistic, this is a cynical comfort that reflects the wishes of the state rather than the parents. While the parents grieve for their dead sons, the *polis* is in need of new citizens to replace the fallen. It might appear that Sophocles, in having Antigone argue that her brothers—in contrast to a husband or a child—are irreplaceable, is deliberately using the ideology of the city-state to undermine its own foundation. To put it another way: Antigone's argument here is, as in so many cases, a brutal radicalization of the city-state ideology.

Antigone's incestuous yearning for her brother and her father has also been noted and analyzed by others. Hegel, too, places considerable emphasis on Antigone's love for Polynices, but rather than interpret this from the incestuous angle, he sees the love between brother and sister as one of the highest forms of love; it is love toward someone of the same blood, yet not of a sexual nature, and it is voluntary and not self-serving. And it is in this kind of love that the feminine achieves its highest expression: "Consequently, the feminine, in the form of the sister, has the highest *intuitive* awareness of what is ethical."[40] This romantic reading of Antigone's yearning for her brother not only disregards all the sexual imagery and connotations that occur in the text, it also disregards the unusual relationships that hold between the various members of Oedipus's family. It would have been difficult to accommodate this almost monstrous community within Hegel's notion of "ethical life." It is hardly a model family that could be integrated into the State. Quite the opposite: it threatens the community's very existence.

The sexual aspect of Antigone's longing for her brother is hinted at as early as in the opening dialogue between Antigone and Ismene: "I'll lie there, dear to him, with my dear friend" (73–74). Both "dear" and "friend" are translations of the Greek word *filos*. Admittedly, *filos* has no directly sexual connotations, but characterizes rather a familial relationship, or what "belongs" or is "dear" to the subject. If the reader, or the audience, fails at this point to interpret Antigone's words in a sexual sense, they are given this kind of meaning—and quite unambiguously so—later in the tragedy, as when, for example, Creon says to Haemon, who longs to win Antigone as his bride: "So spit that girl away just like an enemy and let her marry someone else, in Hades' house" (653–54), or when Antigone herself exclaims: "Oh grave! Oh marriage chamber! Oh you caverned dwelling-place, eternal [*aiei*] prison where I go to join my own" (891–93). Although there is nothing unusual about the comparison of the grave of an unmarried woman with her marriage chamber, it nevertheless reinforces the impression of Antigone's erotic yearning, primarily toward Polynices, but also toward Eteocles and Oedipus.[41] Her "homesickness" is not clearly distinguished from her desire to meet her brother in their shared "marriage chamber." Here Antigone turns the traditional relationship between home and marriage on its head: when a young woman in the city-state married, she had to leave her family, that is, the home of her father, in order to become part of her husband's household, which would never be "home" to the woman in the fullest sense. To some degree she remained a perpetual alien, a kind of guest on a long-term visit in her husband's home.[42] This tenuous status meant that a woman kept a bond to her original family throughout her marriage. For instance, her dowry was to be maintained intact for as long as she was married so that it could be returned to her father in the case of divorce. Antigone evidently did not want any change of family: her original home should remain such for all eternity. It is also worth noting that Sophocles has Antigone die in a way that was otherwise reserved in the tragedies for married women; among the tragic heroines, Antigone is the only unmarried girl to take her own life,[43] a fact that helps to blur the distinction between her status as Polynices' sister and his wife.

In *Antigone* the city wall symbolizes the limits of human community. The banishment of the dead Polynices and the still living Antigone beyond the city wall, out into the wild and open landscape, amounts to a clear exclusion from the living human community. This is clearly indicated in the way Antigone buries Polynices: the sand she scatters on her brother's corpse will have no lasting effect. It will blow away, exposing the corpse as food for scavengers (1016–18). However, in denying Antigone and Polynices a place within the *polis*, Creon demonstrates contempt for divine law; he thereby recognizes the laws of the state alone, in other words, his own laws. Haemon tells his father that the citizens of Thebes do not agree with Creon's brutal judgment of Antigone for having acted in accordance with acknowledged divine laws, and he insinuates that the state over which Creon rules embraces no one other than himself: "There's no true city that belongs to just one man" (737), and "You'd do well ruling in a desert by yourself" (739). Creon identifies with the state to the extent that he seems to confuse the citizens of Thebes with himself, thus disregarding the diversity that a city must of necessity encompass. It would appear that Aristotle's criticism of Plato's ideal state could also be applied to Creon's Thebes: the state tends to resemble an individual, and its ideal is unity at the expense of diversity.[44] The city walls of Thebes, the city's overshadowing architectural feature, can be compared to the bonds that run around Parmenidean Being; they encompass sameness and exclude diversity. The aim is to preserve the self-identical community and its life and to shut out death and Non-Being. Creon does not succeed in his undertaking. After Antigone has hanged herself inside her cave, and both his son Haemon and his wife Eurydice have taken their own lives, Creon remains, empty-handed, and exclaims: "I who exist no more than nothing" (1325). Non-Being has caught up with Creon, and hence also with the *polis* with which he identifies.

Sophocles and Parmenides show two contradictory images of reality. While Parmenides presents unity and sameness as true Being, Sophocles wishes to demonstrate that it is an absolute Nothing, or perhaps more correctly, that the yearning for such absolute unity and sameness results in death and total infertility. Both Creon and Antigone operate, as does Parmenides, with clear boundaries between what is "inside" and what is "outside." For Sophocles this clear demarcation is the primary cause of the tragic outcome; for Parmenides it is constitutive of existence. Whereas Parmenides' poem presents an unreserved praise of unity, sameness, and immutability, the tragic dramatist can be said to provide a revealing inversion of these ideals.

Empedocles and *Antigone:* When "All Becomes One"

"My nature joins in friendship, not in enmity," Antigone says (523). But the love that she sees as the goal of her life is a sterile form of love, since it clearly has no aim but death. Empedocles also provides a description of this kind of love.

The words *filos* (friend) and *echthros* (enemy, foe) are used in *Antigone* in a variety of ways. When used by Antigone herself, *filos* refers to a family member, although the term does not include all members of the family. No sooner has Ismene declined to help her sister in burying their brother ("I am overpowered by force; I shall obey those who are in authority," 66–67) than Antigone excludes her from this narrow circle of "friends": "If you speak so, you'll be a hateful enemy to me, and justly hated by the dead man, too" (93–94). Antigone wants nothing whatsoever to do with those who are not her friends, and this clear distinction between the categories of friend and foe also turns out to be physical in nature; Antigone enters her tomb in order to be reunited with her family and separated from all others. Creon uses *filos* in quite another way, albeit one that is equally unambiguous. In his conceptual world, *filos* and *echthros* carry political connotations; friends are those who defend and show solidarity with the *polis*, in other words, with himself,[45] while enemies are those who in his view threaten the *polis*. For Creon as well, friends and enemies are not stable entities, but rather values that arise within the political space and over which one exerts control: "nor would I ever count a man as my own friend who is an enemy of this land" (187–88).[46]

Although Antigone and Creon apply the terms "friend" and "enemy" to different groups of persons, structurally they use the words in the same way: "friend" denotes a person whom one integrates into one's own community, while "enemy" denotes a person one excludes from that community, regardless of whom that community encompasses. This pair of terms is at first glance reminiscent of Empedocles' use of the terms "love" (*filotes*) and "hate," or "strife" (*neikos*). For Empedocles, love and hate are the fundamental forces of being, the two forces that, collectively, give rise to life, growth, change, and death. Love unites distinct elements, while hate separates them. Whereas both Antigone and Creon seek to cultivate friendship and to expel, or suppress, every possible enemy from their respective communities, Empedocles stresses the need for both of these forces to exist in tandem.

One of the most idiosyncratic elements of Empedocles' philosophy is his theory that the universe undergoes a cyclical development in which the harmony of love and the conflict of hate alternate in supremacy:

> A twofold tale I shall tell: at one time they [i.e., the element / the roots] grew to be one alone out of many, at another again they grew apart to be many out of one. Double is the birth of mortal things and double their death. For the coming together of all things brings forth and destroys the one, the other is nurtured and flies apart as they grow apart again. And these things never cease their continual interchange, at one time coming together through Love, whereby all becomes one, now again each carried apart by the hatred of Strife. (Empedocles B 17.1–8)[47]

These verses are far from unambiguous, and I shall merely point out one possible interpretation. Empedocles seems here to be saying that all things in the organic world come into being and find their end in two different ways, depending on where in the cycle those things happen to occur. During one phase love has total supremacy, at which point the four elements, or "roots," as they are also called, are attracted toward one another and united to the extent that "all becomes one" (Empedocles B 17.7). During this stage the elements become so completely interfused that they are no longer capable of productive connections. In other words, during this phase there is absolutely no possibility of becoming or of change. In the opposite phase, strife and hate have supremacy, with the consequence that no kind of binding force is effective. On the contrary, the elements strive to separate from one another. Also this phase is sterile in the sense that productive associations cannot occur. Empedocles must have pictured the intervening phases as governed by a combination of love and hate, of productivity, birth, and death.

During the phase when love has total supremacy, the universe, or everything that exists, assumes the form of a sphere, which is partially described in words similar to those used by Parmenides to describe his own sphere: it is "everywhere equal to itself" (Empedocles B 28). This must mean that the four elements are so intermingled and permeated with one another that any one part of the sphere is indistinguishable from any other. This phase is characterized by total calm and immobility. Here the force of love has cancelled out the existence of all that formerly existed, merging everything into a single total unity. The force of love, or the "coming together," as the quoted fragment puts it (B 17.4), leads to the cessation of becoming. By completely banishing its own contrary—the conflict that keeps extant entities distinct from one another—love has annulled its own associative and productive function. Love has become sterile.

In other words, love is not just a precondition for birth; when it reigns supreme, it also destroys the possibility of birth. This enables us to understand the fragment B 17.4: "For the coming together of all things [i.e., Love] brings forth and destroys the one [i.e., birth]." In effect, Love is a two-sided force, in that it both creates and destroys. In the phase of Love's supremacy, strife, enmity, and hate are forced toward the sphere's periphery. These phenomena exist, but have no active function during this phase.

Empedocles' theory of love as attraction between what is dissimilar, and of conflict as repulsion between dissimilar elements, implies that conflict also entails attraction, namely between what is similar. When conflict intrudes and makes its presence felt, the different elements begin to distance themselves from one another: water is repulsed from air, air from fire, fire from earth, and so on. At the same time, elements seek out their like: water converges with water, earth with earth, fire with fire, and air with air. In other words, in this second phase, the elements clearly emerge as what they are. It is no longer so that everything is interfused with everything else. When the individual elements become visible, opportunities arise for the force of love to function as it should—as a force that unites dissimilars, and one that is therefore productive. But the presence of conflict is always a precondition for love to be able to function as a productive force. Life and fertility depend on hate creating distance between distinct elements, a distance that love can strive to overcome.

The cosmic condition of total love, in which everything has become one, can be viewed as a parallel to Antigone's dream of the family's total unity, as something that can be achieved only in death and that implies the total collapse of Oedipus's line. Love, which was originally the basis for both fertility and growth, has become too close and, as a consequence, a merely annihilating force. One could also invert the picture and say that for both Antigone and Creon it is not love, as Empedocles uses the word, but hate that governs; both tend to isolate what is "the same"—Antigone her own self-identical family, Creon the citizens, his sole concern being the unity of the state—and exclude what is "dissimilar." Each is left standing on her/his respective side of the dividing line with no hope of meeting the other. Total love, which is utterly fixated on one's "own," seems to entail total hate for "the other." Neither the incestuous family nor the state that excludes all diversity amounts to a viable human community; instead, both constitute forms of chaos, that is, communities lacking in difference and hence without structure and destined to disintegrate.

Heraclitus and *Antigone:*
The Fragile Difference between Life and Death

Heraclitus can also be read as a commentary on *Antigone*, or as a commentary on the kind of community with which the play takes issue. Like Empedocles, Heraclitus views disagreement and strife as constitutive of a community. The strongest community is the one that is built on inner conflicts: "That which is in opposition is in concert, and from things that differ comes the most beautiful harmony" (Heraclitus B 8).[48] Whereas Empedocles' poem concentrates primarily on the necessary interplay of love and hate in the organic world, the aphorisms of Heraclitus, while also concerned with organic creation and disintegration, are more directly associated with a political discourse. A little anecdote may shed some light on this. Plutarch relates that the citizens of Ephesus once asked Heraclitus for his opinion on the political agreement that reigned in the city-state. Heraclitus said nothing in reply, but "took a cup of cold water, sprinkled it with barley-meal, stirred it with penny-royal, drank it up, and departed," all in complete silence.[49] What is being described here is the drink *kykeon*, which Heraclitus comments on in fragment B 125: "Also *kykeon* disintegrates (*diistatai*) if it is not stirred (*kinoumenos*)." The vocabulary here is political and plays on *stasis* (civil war): when *stasis* dominates, the city disintegrates. But Heraclitus expresses himself in a manner that is ambiguous, if not indeed paradoxical; not only does *diistatai* refer to *stasis*, so too does *kinoumenos*, which is formed from *kinesis* (movement, shaking), which can be used as a synonym for *stasis*, but which Heraclitus prescribes as a remedy against that very condition.[50] If we consider the fragment in the context of Plutarch's anecdote, what we read out of it is that Heraclitus is warning his fellow citizens against striving for unity and passive harmony at any price. Diverse elements have to be confronted with one another and "integrated"; if this does not happen, unity will break down, or be divided in two. This is a different kind of unity than the one that the Thebans and the Athenians fantasize about in their myths of origin and that Creon and Antigone seek to achieve within their spheres, respectively, of the family and the state. It is also a very different concept of harmony than the one we find in Plato, who for his part inherited it from the Pythagoreans. For the Pythagoreans, harmony was a unifying force between the dichotomous elements of existence: between light and darkness, male and female, good and evil.[51] The contraries here are obviously of a hierarchical nature, and harmony ensures that the "best" element stands above, or governs, the "worst" element. Similarly, the harmony that Plato constructs in the *Republic* is a static hierarchy among the various groups within the state, not, as in Heraclitus, a harmony of tensions between conflicting but equal elements.

Not only a political community, but existence as such consists, according to Heraclitus, of opposing elements, or forces, which relate to one another and keep one another apart in a harmonious tension: "They do not understand how what is diverging is converging with itself: a back-turning harmonia, like a bow and a lyre" (B 51).[52] In Heraclitus's view, the nature of existence is such that there *must* be tension between its various elements. If one of the participants in a relationship of tension gains complete dominance, then existence will disintegrate. One specific example of such an opposition, whose elements are mutually dependent on one another and which constitute "the most beautiful harmony" (B 8), is that between dryness and wetness in nature. If dryness wins out over wetness, the relation of opposition would cease, resulting in eternal drought and the end of all life. The order, or structure, of nature *is* the relationship of tension that exists between contraries. If this relationship ceases then so too does life, and the order (*logos*) of nature will collapse.

Thus, the opposites belong to a common unity, which is dependent upon difference and strife in order to exist: "One should know that war [*polemos*] is common, and strife [*eris*] is justice; and that everything comes about in accordance with strife and necessity" (B 80). It might be surprising that Heraclitus sees strife as the bond that holds individual beings and powers/qualities together in a common existence. Existence as such, as well as the existence of individual entities is, according to Heraclitus, dependent on an *active relation* between opposites. This active relation can be seen as life itself, or that which upholds life. Thus, Heraclitus's philosophy excludes all-embracing unity and sameness.

I believe *Antigone* can be read along the lines of Heraclitus; for a community to hold together, it must contain opposites, which, we should note, stand in relation to one another. There has to be something that keeps the opposites apart, not least in the sense that there are clear distinctions between the elements that make up the entirety. Antigone's striving for consummate unity is at the same time an attempt to annul distinctions. In Antigone's family it is primarily the distinctions between generations that have been annulled: the distinctions between mother and wife, mother and grandmother, father and brother, and so on. The tight community of the Oedipus family is not one that manages to keep distinctions separate; on the contrary, they collapse into one another. The identity of every family member is unclear, and this is also a recurrent theme in *Antigone*. The identity of Antigone herself is shifting in many ways; this is true not just of her relationships to other members of her family and of her gender, but also to the ambiguity of whether she belongs among the living or the dead.

For Heraclitus life and death are the outer extremes of existence, while at the same time standing in a close but fragile relationship with one another: "The name of the bow [*biós*] is life [*bíos*], its work is death" (B 48). This remark plays on words. The only thing that distinguishes the Greek word for a "bow" from the word for "life" is the accent; *biós* means "bow," while *bíos* means "life." The term for "bow" can therefore be construed as "life." But the effect of the bow (its "work") is to kill. Thus the pun exposes a double meaning, in the form of a contradiction, in the bow as such and in its broader connotations. The purpose of the bow is both life and death, and this is so on a number of levels. Both the warrior and the hunter use the bow to sustain life, but in both cases this involves taking the life of another. But Heraclitus points out that the "life" of the bow itself (its work) is also death. The activity of the bow involves not just the killing of an enemy or an animal; in a certain sense it also leads to its own death: the "life" of the bow ceases when all force is released from it and it slackens. The "life" of the bow consists in that one moment when the tension is released. The transition from "birth" to "death" is condensed here to a single moment; the bow's life is also its death. Interpreted in this way, this little fragment offers a picture of Heraclitus's conception of *physis*. *Physis* is existence in the moment of tension between birth and annihilation, between life and death.

It is precisely this highly charged opposition between life and death that has vanished from Antigone's world. Antigone does not accept the distinctions between generations and the vicissitudes of time; she does not accept that the death of her parents should be followed by new generations, but attempts instead to melt these things into one, into a life in death.

Antigone's Mourning

Creon's prohibition against burying Polynices also includes an injunction against mourning him: "none may shroud him in a tomb or wail for him; he must be left unwept, unburied" (27–28); "the city has received a proclamation, not to honour him or wail for him" (203–204). Burial accords the deceased a conspicuous place among the living, and mourning ensures him a place in the consciousness of the living. Burial and grief prevent the deceased from being forgotten and becoming nonexistent. Creon's prohibition against burial and lamentation is effectively a prohibition against remembering Polynices, against according him a place in Thebes's further existence. This is also what the chorus hopes for the future of Thebes: "Now war is past, bring on forgetfulness" (151). Antigone's refusal to obey Creon's prohibition must be viewed as a refusal to forget her brother.

In the opening scene between Antigone and Ismene, the latter promises to keep Antigone's actions secret. But this very promise prompts Antigone to rebuff her sister still more forcefully: "Speak out! You'll be more hateful still if you stay silent. No, proclaim my plan out loud to all!" (86–87). Creon's guard, who together with his companions conceals himself within view of the corpse in order to discover who has defied Creon's prohibition, relates that he "saw this girl here wailing bitterly aloud, in the piercing voice of a mother bird who sees her nest is empty and her bed bereft of baby chicks. Just so did she, on seeing that the corpse was bare, cry out in lamentation" (423–27). Antigone's weeping is not put on for the guards, since she is unaware that they are observing the scene, so much as an impassioned expression of grief. At the same time, the *sound* itself seems important. Grief is not merely an inner, solitary phenomenon; it is no less important that it is exclaimed out loud. Even if her loud lamentation takes place outside the city walls, in effect, outside civilization, in the wilds of nature, it must still be conceived as a form of cultural expression and an attempt to give grief a place in the world of the *polis.*

As already mentioned, Athens adopted a range of strategies for forgetting the deaths of individuals, collective misfortunes, and human mortality. In *Antigone*—as in other tragedies—such strategies are explicitly challenged. Antigone's intense grief and forceful insistence on remembering her dead brother are given legitimacy, while at the same time her own project involves the suppression of mortality. Sophocles also shows how Creon's refusal to allow scope for grief within the *polis* backfires on him. In the final scene, Creon grieves aloud and without inhibition, thus indulging in the very grief that he forbade Antigone. Insofar as the rituals of grief were traditionally a woman's domain, he feminizes himself in a way he can barely reconcile with his self-image; in his final speech he describes himself as "without substance" (cf. *mataion,* empty, worthless; 1339). His rejection of grief has resulted in the loss of his own existence. He continues to live, yet merely, as we have already seen, as a "nothing" (1325), as a "living corpse" (1167).

Sexual Difference: Transgression and Affirmation

In reply to Haemon's accusation that his father rules exclusively on the basis of principles and political categories, without a thought for the individual (737, 739), Creon remarks ironically that Haemon "is fighting as the woman's ally, so it seems" (740). Haemon craftily concurs with his father: "If you're a woman; you're the one I care about" (741). Creon's determination to preserve his manliness and authority in his confrontation with Antigone, who in her rebellious actions seems to have behaved like a man, makes little impression on Haemon. He feels concern for both his father and his betrothed and appears to want Creon to adopt a position in this affair that the latter regards as feminine. Haemon seems to have seen that a traditionally feminine virtue—such as that of feeling concern for one's nearest and dearest—is a human virtue no more linked to one gender than the other. But not only does he recognize the need to step beyond a traditionally masculine position, he also seems to approve of Antigone's transgression of the traditionally feminine position; he accepts her speaking out in the public arena as if she were a man. Haemon thus comes across as a radical critic of the city-state's clear distinction between the "feminine" and the "masculine," and this further implies that he is a radical critic of the city-state's explicit gender hierarchy. It would appear that he recognizes the need for the city-state to embrace both women and traditionally feminine roles.

Antigone's burial and lamentation of her brother is a provocation to Creon in a double sense. Firstly, her actions offend against his, and hence also the state's, law, and secondly, this threatens his masculinity. The former is bad enough; the latter is an outrage. When Ismene declines to help Antigone in burying their brother, it is not because this offends against Creon's ruling, but because she and Antigone are *women*: "We must remember, first, that we two are by nature women and not fit to fight with men" (61–62). In Ismene's view it is part of the natural order (*physis*) that women are subservient to men. Antigone's transgression of this order, on which society is also built, is not just unnatural; for Ismene it also indicates that her sister is "in love with the impossible" (90). By contrast, Antigone regards her actions as "fine" (*kalon*): "To me it's fine [*kalon*] to die performing such a deed" (72).[53] We could say that what is fine in Antigone's actions is precisely that they break with the "natural." Antigone is conceived as *autonomous*, which is to say, as someone who acts according to her own standards. The chorus puts the point thus: "You were not struck by a wasting sickness or given the wage that is paid by the sword; you alone among mortals will go down to Hades still living, a law to yourself [*autonomos*]" (819–21).[54]

In Athens, the expression "fine death" was used in the state's official funeral oration. It was a term of respect: through his death the citizen strengthened the foundation for the city-state's continued existence. In other words, the "fineness" of death carried clear political connotations, which on Antigone's lips tends to become subversive. Her death does not serve the community of the *polis*, but is one of loneliness. Antigone herself emphasizes what is ambivalent in the "fineness" of her death: "Let me and the ill counsel that derives from me, suffer this awful fate [*to deinon*]; what I shall suffer will be far less dire than dying an ignoble [*ou kalos*] death!" (95–97). The word translated here as "awful" (*deinon*) has been the subject of considerable debate, not primarily in the context of this quote, but in discussions of the chorus's so-called ode to man a little later in the tragedy (332–75). The word *deinon* suggests an immoderation that is likely to encourage hubris. In the respective choral ode the theme is the "greatness" of humankind; more than any other species man manages to defy the powers of nature, an ability that can bring both blessings and misery. Mankind is creative, but his creativity is of an ambiguous nature; it is both constructive and destructive. There is only one thing humans cannot do, and that is flee from death: "Only from Hades will he fail to find escape" (360–61). In speaking of the "wondrous," and hence "awful," aspect of Antigone's action, reference is made not just to her total autonomy, which involves among other things the transgression of both gender categories and the laws of the state, but also to the goal of her action: death. Rather than seek to flee from death, she runs in full awareness toward it. Antigone transforms Creon's death sentence, which took the form of entombing her alive in a cave, into a death of her own choosing (autonomous); she hangs herself in a noose she has made from her veil (1220–22).

Jacques Lacan is one of those who have shown a fascination for Antigone's "beautiful" death and its ethical character (Lacan 1986: 285–333). He points out, among other things, that her action is without object. It is a moral action in virtue not of its aim, but rather of its having no aim; Antigone does not hope to achieve anything by her death, not even recognition.[55] Here one might object that the aim of her action is to underline her brother's right to burial, but Antigone does not seem to distinguish between the rights of the deceased and her own yearning for death. Her yearning is directed at a silent corpse and therefore expects no response (Sjöholm 2004: 109–10). Antigone fulfills her own individual yearning; and herein lies both what is "beautiful" and what is "awful" about her death. I consider it important to point out, however, that Antigone's insistence on fulfilling her own autonomous yearning is ambiguous. Ultimately she annuls her own individuality and identity by uniting herself with her incestuous family. Both Creon and Antigone negate the individual in favor of a kind of community that fails to recognize individual differences. This too is what is "awful" about her action.

Several commentators have noted that, through his disregard for individual distinctions, Creon enacts the ideals of the city-state. The political equality of the citizens in the democratic *polis* entails that, in political contexts, any one citizen is interchangeable with any other. Creon radicalizes this ideal by transferring it onto the family. Ismene seeks in vain to appeal to Creon's sense of Antigone's significance as an individual, both as a sister and as his son's prospective bride:

Ismene: How can I live my life without her, all alone?
Creon: Her—do not speak of her as someone still alive.

> Ismene: But will you really kill your own child's bride-to-be?
> Creon: Yes; there are other plots of land for him to plow.
> Ismene: Not like the harmony that fitted him to her. (566–70)

This total blindness to individual differences and ultimately to family bonds becomes Creon's downfall. In the closing scene, when Creon lingers on alone, bereft of wife and son, the state has utterly vanished from his horizon. He is no longer a statesman but merely a husband and a father, and he sees himself exclusively in the sphere of *oikos*. Creon's greatest fear, namely of succumbing to the feminine, catches up with him in the tragedy's conclusion, where he ends like a weeping, grieving woman. His fear of being feminized, and more generally of the gender hierarchy being undermined, was one of his explicit justifications for Antigone's punishment: "It's clear enough that I'm no man, but she's the man, if she can get away with holding power like this" (484–85). He identifies his entire existence with what it is to be a man: "But while I live a woman shall not rule" (525). It is this self-image that collapses when Creon recognizes his error. He has erred not just as a statesman, but also as a husband and a father, and he is left behind utterly deprived of an identity: "I who exist no more than nothing" (1325). This collapse of Creon's masculine identity is further highlighted after his final words by his being led into the palace, the domain of the women.

In the tragedy's opening scene the situation is the reverse: Antigone stands outside the royal palace and calls Ismene out to her, into the public, masculine domain. In this opening scene, both Ismene and Antigone are "out of place,"[56] a position that Antigone retains throughout the drama. In Pericles' funeral oration on the "fine death" of the hero, feminine virtue is defined as absence from the public space: "the greatest glory of a woman is to be least talked about by men" (Thucydides, Book II, 45). The exclusion of women from the public, political sphere was constitutive of Athenian democracy. By bandying words (*logos*) in direct confrontation with the head of state, and by *acting* independently, in defiance of Creon's word, which is law, Antigone offends radically against the woman's sphere. This offense she compounds by refusing to take on the task that was woman's crucial contribution to the *polis*: bearing the citizen legitimate children.

Even if Antigone's transgression of gender identity is ultimately legitimized through Creon's admission of having acted wrongly in condemning her actions, it is still this transgression that amounts to Antigone's tragedy. If the tragic consists in realizing one's own fatal errors, then Antigone herself must be described as tragic: while awaiting death, she no longer views the grave exclusively as a bridal chamber or death as a longed-for reunion with her own family, but also as a sterile conclusion to life: "He [Hades] leads me off unbedded, unaccompanied by wedding song, without a share in marriage or the nurturing of children; thus deserted by my friends I go alive, ill-fated, to the caverns of the dead" (916–20). The term "friends" has now acquired a new significance. Whereas, earlier on, Antigone had identified only her dead family as her friends, now she finds them also among the living, whom she had hitherto viewed as her enemies. Whereas she had formerly regarded death as a deliverance (cf. 462–66), she now grieves for the life she will never achieve. It is only now that she sees that being a woman (also) can involve giving life and perpetuating her kind within a non-incestuous family. In her final speech she accords herself an ambiguous status, as someone "out of place" among both the living and the dead: "I have no home among mortals, no home as a corpse among corpses, with the living or with the dead" (850–52). She still longs to be reunited with "her own" (891–99), but this yearning is shot through with pain at her imminent death.

Antigone's ambiguity is present on a number of levels. On the one hand, she demonstrates the need to include women in the state, as someone who has a right both to speak and to act. She also demonstrates the need to accommodate the individual in the *polis,* where every citizen is regarded as politically identical with every other. And she shows the necessity of granting even an "enemy," or an alien, a place in society, in terms of, for example, burial and public shows of grief. In other words, she shows the necessity of breaking down the rigid distinctions between those who are inside and those who are outside, between "us" and "the others." On the other hand, her incestuous longing for reunion with her own source can be interpreted in precisely the opposite direction. She is someone who imposes rigid boundaries between "friends" and "enemies," as does the city-state. As Sophocles portrays it, Antigone's transgression of the traditionally feminine position assumes a fatal direction, namely toward a radical identification with the city-state's masculine ideal. She is, in other words, transferring the "incestuous" political ideals of the unity and purity of the state onto the family.

As has often been noted, Antigone's repudiation of her femininity is already embodied in her name: anti-gone, which can be understood both as *anti-gyne* (*gyne* = woman) and as *anti-gone* (*gone* = offspring). As already mentioned, the Greek word *anti* has a double meaning; it means both "contrary"/"opposite" and "in place of." It is precisely this double meaning that we find in the Antigone figure. By speaking out and acting "autonomously" in the public sphere, she demonstrates the possibility of an alternative understanding of the feminine, while in preferring her dead brother to a living husband, she undermines one of the roles that (at least some) women have to play in human society. By means of his Antigone figure, Sophocles can be said to lay bare the city-state's ideological foundations. Antigone's incestuous family ideals hold up a mirror to the city-state, while her refusal to give life exposes the city-state's radical exclusion of women for what it is: a phantasm, which, if taken to its logical conclusion, would lead the city-state straight to the grave. Ismene's words in the opening scene— "We must remember, first that we are by nature women" (61–62)—gradually assume a twofold meaning. The fact that Antigone consistently ignores her sister's reminder points up both the limits and the truth thereof.

The manner of Antigone's death also both confirms and oversteps her gender. Her death accords with the way women die elsewhere in the tragedies. Whereas men generally tend to be killed by others, most of the female protagonists take their own lives.[57] This is certainly true of the married woman, who takes her life following the death of her husband, and usually by hanging. This was a form of suicide that was also practiced by young women in the Athens of the day (Loraux 1991: 9–10). Just as Antigone hangs herself in a noose that she has made from her veil, it was common to use items of clothing associated either with the woman's virginity or with her sexuality, such as a veil, a belt, or a headband.[58] When a woman dies by strangulation, the constriction closes the opening that is regarded as analogous to her genital opening.[59] Strangulation silences her in a double sense: both her "upper mouth" and her "lower mouth"[60] are silenced. In other words, the woman's way of taking her own life can be seen as a way of evading sexuality. Antigone refuses to live as a woman, but goes to her death as a woman. Yet precisely this womanly death is an evasion, not just of life, but perhaps first and foremost of a woman's life in an extremely patriarchal state, which Antigone in all her ambiguity both challenges and confirms.

What is peculiar to and tragic about Antigone is that no external voice, no voice from outside, penetrates through to her. Grief for her lost brother has captured all her longing. Antigone is isolated and alone in an extreme sense. Only some Other could have halted her on her path toward death. The idea of such an Other may possibly be present in her final words, in which she reflects on death as a loss of a woman's life, but by that point she is already on the way to her grave. Antigone's tragedy is, on the one hand, that she draws such clear boundaries between friends and enemies, between her own and the outsider, and on the other, that she loses her identity as a result of erasing the distinctions between herself and her family and between life and death. The Heraclitean bow, which holds opposites from one another in an internal relation of tension, is absent in Antigone. The riddle of the Sphinx offers her no challenge; she refuses to see human existence as a cycle consisting of different stages and in which time is of a linear nature and death sets an unavoidable full stop. In his *Antigone*, Sophocles shows us that the autochthonic and incestuous dream of unity, harmony, and absence of the Other is quite unworkable. In *Antigone* this dream is achieved in a radical and tragic manner, while at the same time the tragedy allows us to understand that the interplay between one's "own" and the foreign, between us and the Other, between birth, life, and death, is fragile, not just for the individual, but in any human community.

Translated from Norwegian by Peter Cripps.

NOTES

1. Nietzsche 2000. One of the things Nietzsche says here is: "I want to speak only of the most illustrious opponents of the tragic world-view, and by that I mean science, which is optimistic in its deepest essence, with its ancestor Socrates to the forefront" (85). It is implied here that the "tragic world-view" is superior to Socratic optimism. See also Nietzsche 2000, chs. 14 and 15.

2. "The fate of Socrates is hence really tragic"; "in what is truly tragic there must be valid moral powers on both sides which come into collision; this was so with Socrates." Hegel 1995b: 446.

3. Nietzsche 1998. Nietzsche considers also Parmenides to be a representative of the "Tragic Age," but this applies primarily to his *doxai* doctrine, or what is often regarded as the second part of his didactic poem, and which Nietzsche places in the tradition of Anaximander. According to Nietzsche, this is the "young" Parmenides, who only later conceived his "bloodless" and "un-Greek" ontology. In his view this divides "the two centuries of the Tragic Age . . . [into] two periods" (ibid., 69). I regard this division, not just within early Greek thought as a whole, but also within Parmenides' own philosophy, as highly plausible (see Songe-Møller 1999: ch. 8, "Parmenides"). My reason for not characterizing Parmenides as a "tragic" thinker in the following has exclusively to do with his ontology. It is perhaps especially the role that death plays in Parmenides' ontology that persuaded Nietzsche to regard the "older" Parmenides as someone who is distinct from his predecessors and who does not at first sight seem to belong to the "Tragic Age." In Nietzsche's view, Parmenides does not treat death as part of human life, but as "the rigor mortis of the coldest, emptiest concept of all, the concept of being" (1998: 80). Nietzsche maintains that, in his ontology, Parmenides takes refuge from the diverse and threatening vicissitudes of existence, and finds reassurance in the "terrible energetic striving for *certainty*" (ibid., 81).

4. Cf. Nietzsche 2000: "Let us consider the consequences of the Socratic principles: 'Knowledge is virtue; sin is the result of ignorance; the virtuous man is the happy

man': in these three basic forms of optimism lies the death of tragedy. For now the virtuous hero must be a dialectician, now there must be a necessary link between virtue and knowledge" (78).

5. Here I should refine my point: in Plato's dialogues Socrates comes across as an ideal person, and Plato's more abstract theories about human life are in many ways founded on the figure of Socrates. For a discussion of the role of Socrates as an ideal type, see Blondell 2002. It could of course also be debated whether Plato regards women as a distinct category of humans, or whether instead he transcends the gender distinction. This I discuss in Songe-Møller 2002 (Part II, "Plato, Love and Sexual Difference") and will not pursue further here.

6. Vernant 1982. See also "Geometry and Spherical Astronomy in the First Greek Cosmology," "Geometrical Structure and Political Ideas in the Cosmology of Anaximander," and "Space and Political Organization in Ancient Greece," in Vernant 1983.

7. Vernant 1983: "With Parmenides philosophy becomes independent. Each type of discipline, at grips with its own problems, has to develop its own ways of thinking and its own terminology and elaborate its own logic" (223).

8. See my book *Philosophy without Women*, especially chapter 3: "The Logic of Exclusion and the Free Men's Democracy. An analysis of the notions of equality and balance in Anaximander and Parmenides."

9. Cf. Loraux 2002b: "By 'ideology of the city-state' I mean, essentially, the idea that the city-state must be—and so, by definition, is—*one and at peace* with itself" (26).

10. See Loraux 1993. Here she discusses in depth the significance of the autochthonic myth for the ideology of the democratic Athenian city-state.

11. See Loraux's thorough study of the Athenian funeral oration in *The Invention of Athens: The Funeral Oration in the Classical City* (1986).

12. The class of citizens was, however, restricted to a small elite: of some 320,000 inhabitants of Athens only 40,000 were citizens. Probably about half the inhabitants were slaves; the remaining noncitizens were foreigners without citizenship, women, and children. Citizenship was a question of gender and birth (and, of course, age): according to the Periclean law of around 450 BCE an Athenian citizen must be "born of two citizens." Interestingly, this implies that both mother and father must be citizens, even though there were no female citizens. The definition of the Athenian citizen is obviously self-contradictory. Cf. Loraux 1993: 119.

13. See e.g. *Republic*, Book V, 462c, where Socrates is discussing the guardians' common ownership of women and children. Socrates asks rhetorically: "Then, is the best-governed city the one in which most people say 'mine' and 'not mine' about the same things in the same way? [. . .] What about the city that is most like a single person?" See also *Statesman* 258e–259d, where the government of a state and of a household are equated. Aristotle criticizes Plato's comparison of the ideal state with a family and ultimately with an individual: "Yet it is clear that if the process of unification advances beyond a certain point, the city will not be a city at all; for a state essentially consists of a multitude of persons, and if its unification is carried beyond a certain point, city will be reduced to family and family to individual" (*Politics*, Book II, 1261a).

14. For a more detailed discussion of such an interpretation of Plato's political philosophy, see my *Philosophy without Women*, part 2, "Plato, Love and Sexual Difference."

15. For *homoion*, see Parmenides, DK 28 B 8.22; *tauton*, DK 28 B 8,29; *me tauton*, DK 28 B 8,58. References to fragments of pre-Socratic philosophers are given according to the numbering established by Diels and Kranz in *Die Fragmente der Vorsokratiker*. The translations are my own, or Leonardo Tarán's (1965), sometimes with small changes.

16. A relatively thorough discussion of this idea will be found in my *Philosophy without Women*, ch. 3, "The Logic of Exclusion and the Free Men's Democracy. An analysis of the notions of equality and balance in Anaximander and Parmenides." See also ch. 2: "Thought and Sexuality: A Troubled Relationship. An Analysis of Hesiod and Parmenides."

17. The tragedies were performed during the public religious festival called the Great Dionysia, which took place in Athens in the spring once a year. The participating and competing tragedians were chosen by the archon, the highest elected politician. The tragic choirs were financed by a wealthy citizen, and the winner of the competition was chosen by a jury composed of citizens chosen by lot. An illustration of the public importance of the dramatic performances is the so-called Theoric or Festival Fund, which was used to enable the poorest citizens to pay their theater entrance fees. According to Paul Cartledge, the Theoric Fund had "an enormous symbolic significance as a token of democratic ideology" ("'Deep plays': theatre as process in Greek civic life," Cartledge 1997: 9). In classical times, the Theoric Fund was called "the glue of democracy" (ibid.).

18. Loraux 2002a: 148–152. None of the translations I have consulted in which the word *mnesikakein* occurs give the literal meaning to which Loraux draws attention: "to remember the misfortunes." The prohibition "not to recall the misfortunes" is linked to the amnesty for Athenian citizens who had fought on the side of the Thirty Tyrants; one should not remember "the misfortunes" these citizens had committed against Athens and the Athenian democracy. See Aristotle, *Athenian Constitution,* 40,2. Aristotle relates the story of a man who was condemned to death because he "began to remember what was painful" about citizens who had fought on the side of the Thirty Tyrants, and who had regained their citizenship following the return to democracy. The sentence was effective, "for ever since his execution, no one has remembered what was painful." H. Rackham (Loeb Classical Library) translates this passage thus: "for never since he was put to death has anybody broken the amnesty." See also Lysias, *Against Nicomachos,* and Plato *7th Letter,* 336e–337a.

19. See, for instance, 69–77. This is a central point in Cecilia Sjöholm's reading of *Antigone* in *The Antigone Complex: Ethics and the Invention of Feminine Desire.* The chorus also insinuates that Antigone has a death wish when giving their reasons for not defying Creon's proclamation: "No one's so foolish as to be in love with death" (*Antigone,* 220).

20. According to P. Vidal-Naquet, the democratic Greek city-state can best be defined in terms of a double exclusion: "the exclusion of women, which made it a 'men's club,' and the exclusion of slaves, which made it a 'citizen's club'" (Vidal-Naquet 1986: 206).

21. This is one of Judith Butler's principal points in her book *Antigone's Claim: Kinship between Life and Death,* which is the work that really opened my eyes to the crucial significance of the incest theme in *Antigone*. My analysis, however, has few points of similarity with Butler's.

22. See, for instance, Herodotus, Book III, 80.

23. This opening sentence (*O koinon autadelphon Isménés kara*) has proved difficult to translate. Cf. David Franklin and John Harrison: "No translation can convey Antigone's unusual way of addressing her sister (literally 'very sister of common blood'), which stresses the closeness of the tie of kinship," Sophocles 2003: 2.

24. English translation by Mary Whitlock Blundell, in Sophocles 1998.

25. The incestuous origin can be seen as a "closure" and stands as such in opposition to the notion of origin as natality, i.e., as a beginning of something anew. Cf. Arendt 1958: 9. It is interesting to note that for Arendt, natality is one of the fundamental conditions of political life. For a discussion of this, see chapters 3 and 8 of this volume.

26. Hesiod, *Theogony*. Cf. also *Antigone* 339–40, where Earth is described as "the highest of gods" and "the tireless immortal Earth."

27. On the relation between autochthony and incest in general, and in the Oedipus myth in particular, see Edmunds 1981: 235–38. Edmunds refers among other things to a report in Herodotus, Book VI, 107, that links incest and autochthony. According to Herodotus, the tyrant Hippias dreamt that he lay with his own mother, "and conjectured the dream to mean that he would be restored to Athens, recover the power which he had lost, and afterwards live to a good old age in his native country." Following this dream, Hippias landed with his fleet at Marathon. Herodotus tells us that, having landed, Hippias "sneezed and at the same time coughed with more violence than was his wont," whereby he lost one of his teeth, which fell into the sand and was not to be found. "Hippias believed that in this way his dream was fulfilled." Hippias seems here to have equated his teeth with the phallus and the earth with his own mother.

28. Several authors have pointed out the peculiar relationship between Thebes and Athens in antique myths and literature, in which Thebes is portrayed as a kind of anti-Athens. See, among others, P. Vidal-Naquet, "Oedipus in Athens" and "Oedipus between Two Cities: An essay on *Oedipus at Colonus,*" in Vernant and Vidal-Naquet 1998; Zeitlin 1990; and Blundell 1993.

29. Already in the opening verses, Ismene reminds Antigone that they are now the only two survivors from their family and that they too will be destroyed if they defy Creon's prohibition (58–60). Ismene seems here to be expressing a certain hope that she and Antigone might continue their line.

30. "Alone of its kind" is a translation of *mounogenes,* which can also mean "the only member of a kin/family/birth." In Parmenides' poem the word is often translated as "unique."

31. Cf. Parmenides, B 8.3: "Since it is ungenerated, it is also imperishable."

32. It is interesting to note that Sophocles uses here the same word for "lie" (*keimai*) as Parmenides uses in the above-quoted sentence, "it lies by itself and abides firmly where it is" (B 8.29–30). *Keimai* can also mean "to lie in bed."

33. See B 1.15 and B 8.13 (Dike), B 8.16 and B 8.30 (Ananke), and B 8.37 (Moira).

34. See, e.g., Guthrie 1978: "The complete immobility of the real, the impossibility of *kinesis* in any sense of the word, is for Parmenides the climax of his message" (36).

35. Cf. Parmenides, B 8.3–7.

36. Antigone describes herself as *metoikos* (850, 868), which in the 5th century BCE was a term for a non-Athenian living in Athens without a citizen's rights. Creon con-

firms Antigone's self-assessment: "she shall be deprived of any home (*metoikias*) up here" (890).

37. *Antigone* 904–20. Goethe was already suspicious of these verses; they reflect "a motive which is quite unworthy [of Antigone], and which almost borders on the comic." Goethe feels the paragraph ruins "the tragic mood, coming from the lips of a heroine on her way to her death." To him the passage seems "thoroughly artificial and far too much like a dialectic calculation." He says he would "give a great deal for an apt philologist to prove that it is spurious and interpolated" (Eckermann n.d.: "Gespräch am 28. März 1827"). The verses were, however, already known to Aristotle, who seems not to doubt their authenticity, but uses them as an example of an "incredible" statement (*Rhetoric*, Book III, 1417 a 27). For a summary of various opinions on the authenticity of these verses, see Hester 1971: 11–59, esp. appendix D, 55–58. Matt Neuberg, in "How Like a Woman: Antigone's 'inconsistency,'" refers to further literature on this subject and argues forcefully for the view that the verses are consistent with the picture of Antigone conveyed elsewhere in the tragedy (Neuberg 1990: 54–76). Even so, his argument differs from my own.

38. Antigone rejects Ismene's plea to share responsibility for the burial of Polynices (536–560).

39. Concerning Antigone's identification of the grave with her bridal chamber, see below.

40. Hegel 1977: VI, A, a ("The ethical world. Human and Divine Law: Man and Woman"), 274. The original reads: "Das Weibliche hat daher als Schwester die höchste *Ahnung* des sittlichen Wesens" (Hegel 1976: 336). For a thorough discussion of Hegel's interpretation of *Antigone,* see Steiner 1984: ch. 1.

41. For a discussion of Antigone's Oedipal desires, see Johnson 1997: 392–95.

42. Cf. Aristotle *Oeconomica,* Book I, 1344a, where the housewife is compared with a "suppliant" seeking refuge at her husband's hearthstone (*hestia*).

43. Other unmarried women who die in the tragedies are either killed or sacrificed (e.g., Iphigenia and Cassandra in Aeschylus's *Agamemnon*).

44. Creon employs the same analogy that Plato uses in the *Statesman,* between the government of the state and of the family: "For he who is a good man in his household will be shown to be a just man in the city too" (*Antigone* 660–61). For Aristotle's criticism, see above, note 13. It is worth noting Aristotle's warning against any attempt to achieve "the ideal of the fullest possible unity of the entire state, which Socrates takes as his fundamental principle": "even if any lawgiver were able to unify the state, he must not do so, for he will destroy it in the process" (*Politics,* Book II, 1261a). This means that plurality, not unity, is the condition of a state. Here, Hannah Arendt follows Aristotle. For her, plurality is a human condition: "men, not Man, live on the earth and inhabit the world. While all aspects of the human condition are somehow related to politics, this plurality is specifically *the* condition . . . of all political life" (1958: 7).

45. See 182–83, 187–89, 209–10.

46. Creon's use of the words "friend" and "enemy" has been studied by a number of authors, including Saxonhouse 1995: 72; Nussbaum 2001: 57; and Winnington-Ingram 1980: 129–33.

47. English translation from Kirk, Raven, and Schofield 1983, with some changes.

48. English translation by Kathleen Freeman, *Ancilla to The Pre-Socratic Philosophers* (1962).

49. Plutarch, *Concerning Talkativeness, Moralia,* 511b (reference from Loraux 1987: 111).

50. Cf. Loraux 1987: 108–12.

51. Concerning the Pythagorean table of principles, see Aristotle *Metaphysics,* Book I, 986a 24–27. The ten pairs of principles are: Limit and the Unlimited, Odd and Even, Unity and Plurality, Right and Left, Male and Female, Rest and Motion, Straight and Crooked, Light and Darkness, Good and Evil, Square and Oblong.

52. The English translation is adapted from the translations by Jonathan Barnes, in *The Presocratic Philosophers* (1982), and by Robin Waterfield, in *The First Philosophers: The Presocratics and the Sophists* (2000).

53. See M. W. Blundell's comment on her translation of this line: "'Fine' translates *kalos,* a powerful evaluative term with moral, aesthetic, heroic and aristocratic overtones" (Sophocles 1998: 22).

54. See Loraux 1997. Here Loraux discusses, among other things, the many occurrences of word combinations with *auto-* in *Antigone.*

55. For a thorough and insightful discussion of Lacan's interpretation of *Antigone* as a kind of ethics, see Sjöholm 2004, especially ch. 5. Sjöholm summarizes Antigone's ethics thus: "Antigone allows us to formulate an ethics in which the subject is not only autonomous but also exposed, not only finite but also destructive, not only vulnerable but also monstrous. Her action is undertaken without concern for the good, where values are shown and proven through the experience of rewards such as happiness or pleasure, and it is Antigone's lack of concern for the good—or knowledge or possible experience of it—that makes her into a symbol of ethical action" (125).

56. The expression is taken from Sourvinou-Inwood 1989: 152.

57. Here there are exceptions: Ajax and Haemon take their own lives, while Clytemnestra is murdered.

58. See, e.g., Schmitt 1977: 1059–73.

59. Both *auchén* and *trachelos* can mean both "neck" and "womb cervix" (Hippocrates, *Maladies des femmes,* Book III, 230, and Book II, 169).

60. Cf. Hippocrates, *Maladies des femmes,* Book III, 230: *to stoma tón métreón,* "the mouth of the mothers," *os uteri.*

BIBLIOGRAPHY

Arendt, Hannah. 1958. *The Human Condition.* Chicago: University of Chicago Press.

Aristotle. 1926. *Art of Rhetoric.* Loeb Classical Library. Cambridge, Mass.: Harvard University Press.

———. 1935. *Oeconomica.* Loeb Classical Library. Cambridge, Mass.: Harvard University Press.

———. 1944. *Politics.* Loeb Classical Library. Cambridge, Mass.: Harvard University Press.

———. 1952. *Athenian Constitution.* Loeb Classical Library. Cambridge, Mass.: Harvard University Press.

Barnes, Jonathan. 1982. *The Presocratic Philosophers.* London: Routledge and Kegan Paul.

Benveniste, Émile. 1937. "Expression indo-européenne de l'éternité." *Bulletin de la Société de linguistique de Paris* 38: 103–12.

Blondell, Ruby. 2002. *The Play of Character in Plato's Dialogues*. Cambridge: Cambridge University Press.

Blundell, Mary Whitlock. 1993. "The Ideal of the *Polis* in *Oedipus at Colonos*." In *Tragedy, Comedy and the Polis,* ed. A. H. Sommerstein et al., 287–306. Bari, Italy: Levante editori.

Bollack, Jean. 1986. "Né damné." *Theatre/Public* 70/71: 17–22.

———. 1988. "Destin d'Oedipe, destin d'une famille." *Metis. Revue d'anthropologie du monde grec ancien* 3, no. 1–2: 1, 159–77.

Butler, Judith. 2000. *Antigone's Claim: Kinship between Life and Death*. New York: Columbia University Press.

Cartledge, Paul. 1997. "'Deep Plays': Theatre as Process in Greek Civic Life." In *The Greek Companion to Greek Tragedy,* ed. P. E. Easterling, 3–35. Cambridge: Cambridge University Press.

Diels, Hermann, and Walther Kranz. 1951. *Die Fragmente der Vorsokratiker*. Berlin: Weidmann.

Eckermann, Johann Peter. N.d. *Gespräche mit Goethe in den letzten Jahren seines Lebens*. Herausgegeben von Paul Stapf. Wiesbaden: Emil Vollmer Verlag.

Edmunds, Lowell. 1981. "The Cults and the Legend of Oedipus." *Harvard Studies in Classical Philology* 85: 221–38.

Freeman, Kathleen. 1962. *Ancilla to the Pre-Socratic Philosophers: A Complete Translation of the Fragments in Diels*. Fragmente der Vorsokratiker. Oxford: Basil Blackwell.

Guthrie, W. K. C. 1978. *A History of Greek Philosophy*. Vol. 2: *The Presocratic Tradition from Parmenides to Democritus*. Cambridge: Cambridge University Press.

Hegel, Georg Wilhelm Freidrich. 1976. *Die Phänomenologie des Geistes*. Frankfurt am Main: Suhrkamp.

———. 1977. *The Phenomenology of Spirit*. Trans. A. V. Miller. Oxford: Oxford University Press.

———. 1995a. *Hegel's Lectures on the Philosophy of Religion*. Vol. 2: *Determinate Religion*. Trans. R. F. Brown, P. C. Hodgson, and J. M. Stewart. Berkeley and Los Angeles: University of California Press.

———. 1995b. *Lectures on the History of Philosophy*. Vol. 1. Trans. E. S. Haldane. Lincoln: University of Nebraska Press.

Herodotus. 1952. *The History of Herodotus*. Chicago: Encyclopædia Britannica.

Hesiod. 1988. *Theogony. Works and Days*. Trans. with an introduction and notes by M. L. West. Oxford: Oxford University Press.

Hester, D. A. 1971. "Sophocles the Unphilosophical: A Study in the *Antigone*." *Mnemosyne* 24: 11–59.

Hippocrate. 1982. *Maladies des femmes*. In *Oeuvre Complètes*. Ed. É. Littré. Vol. 8. Amsterdam: Adolf M. Hakkert; reprint of 1853 edition.

Johnson, Patricia J. 1997. "Woman's Third Face: A Psycho/Social Reconstruction of Sophocles' *Antigone*. *Arethusa* 30, no. 3: 369–98.

Kirk, G. S., J. E. Raven, and M. Schofield. 1983. *The Presocratic Philosophers: A Classical History with a Selection of Texts*. Cambridge: Cambridge University Press.

Lacan, Jacques. 1986. *Le séminaire*. Livre 7: *L'éthique de la psychanalyse*. Paris: Éditions du Seuil.

Loraux, Nicole. 1984. "Le corps étranglé." In *Le chatiment dans la cite,* ed. Y. Thomas, 195–218. Rome: École Francaise de Rome.

———. 1986. *The Invention of Athens: The Funeral Oration in the Classical City.* Trans. Alan Sheridan. Cambridge, Mass.: Harvard University Press.

———. 1987. "Le lien de la division." *Le cahier du collège international de philosophie* 4: 101–24.

———. 1991. *Tragic Ways of Killing a Woman.* Trans. Anthony Forster. Cambridge, Mass.: Harvard University Press.

———. 1993. *The Children of Athena: Athenian Ideas about Citizenship and the Division between the Sexes.* Trans. Caroline Levine. Princeton, N.J.: Princeton University Press.

———. 1997. *La main d'Antigone.* Postscript to Sophocles, *Antigone.* Paris: Les Belles Lettres.

———. 2000. *Born of the Earth: Myth and Politics in Athens.* Trans. Selina Stewart. Ithaca, N.Y.: Cornell University Press.

———. 2002a. *The Divided City: On Memory and Forgetting in Ancient Athens.* Trans. Corinne Pache with Jeff Fort. New York: Zone Books.

———. 2002b. *The Mourning Voice: An Essay on Greek Tragedy.* Trans. Elizabeth Trapnell Rawlings. Ithaca, N.Y.: Cornell University Press.

Lysias. 1957. *Against Nikomachus.* Loeb Classical Library. Cambridge, Mass.: Harvard University Press.

Neuberg, Matt. 1990. "How Like a Woman: Antigone's 'Inconsistency.'" *Classical Quarterly* 40: 54–76.

Nietzsche, Friedrich. 1998. *Philosophy in the Tragic Age of the Greeks.* Trans. with an introduction by Marianne Cowan. Washington, D.C.: Regnery Publishing.

———. 2000. *The Birth of Tragedy.* Trans. with an introduction and notes by Douglas Smith. Oxford: Oxford University Press.

Nussbaum, Martha C. 2001. *The Fragility of Goodness: Luck and Ethics in Greek Tragedy and Philosophy.* Cambridge: Cambridge University Press.

Plato. 1900–1907. *Opera.* Ed. John Burnet. Oxford: Oxford Classical texts.

———. 1997. *Complete Works.* Ed. John M. Cooper. Indianapolis: Hackett.

Plutarch. 1957. *Concerning Talkativeness.* In *Plutarch's Moralia.* Loeb Classical Library, vol. 6. Cambridge, Mass.: Harvard University Press.

Sampson, Kristin. 2005. "Ontogony: Conceptions of Being and Metaphors of Birth in the *Timaeus* and the *Parmenides.*" Ph.D. thesis, University of Bergen.

Saxonhouse, Arlene W. 1995. *Fear of Diversity: The Birth of Political Science in Ancient Greek Thought.* Chicago: University of Chicago Press.

Schmitt, Pauline. 1977. "Athéna Apatouria et la ceinture: les aspects féminins des Apatouries à Athènes." *Annales. Économies Sociétés Civilisations:* 1059–73.

Sjöholm, Cecilia. 2004. *The Antigone Complex: Ethics and the Invention of Feminine Desire.* Stanford, Calif.: Stanford University Press.

Songe-Møller, Vigdis. 1999. *Tanker om opprinnelsen: Tidlig gresk filosofi fra Hesiod til Demokrit.* Oslo: Cappelen Akademisk Forlag.

———. 2002. *Philosophy without Women: The Birth of Sexism in Western Thought.* London: Continuum.

Sophocles. 1997. *Antigone.* Bilingue. Traduction de Paul Mazon. Introduction, notes, postface de Nicole Loraux. Paris: Les Belles Lettres.

———. 2003. *Antigone.* A new translation and commentary by David Franklin and John Harrison. Cambridge: Cambridge University Press.

————. 1998. *Sophocles' Antigone.* Introduction, translation, and essay by Mary Whitlock Blundell. Newburypost, Mass.: Focus Publishing.

Sourvinou-Inwood, Christiane. 1989. "The Fourth Stasimon of Sophocles' *Antigone.*" *Bulletin of the Institute of Classical Studies* (University of London) 36: 141–65.

Steiner, George. *Antigones.* 1984. New Haven, Conn.: Yale University Press.

Tarán, Leonardo. 1965. *Parmenides: A Text with Translation, Commentary, and Critical Essays.* Princeton, N.J.: Princeton University Press.

Thucydides. 1982. *History of the Peloponnesian War.* Trans. Rex Warner, with an introduction and notes by M. I. Finley. London: Penguin Books.

Vernant, Jean-Pierre. 1982. *The Origins of Greek Thought.* London: Methuen.

————. 1983. *Myth and Thought among the Greeks.* London: Routledge and Kegan Paul.

Vernant, Jean-Pierre, and Pierre Vidal-Naquet. 1988. *Myth and Tragedy in Ancient Greece.* Trans. Janet Lloyd. New York: Zone Books.

Vidal-Naquet, Pierre. 1986. *The Black Hunter.* Trans. Andrew Szegedy-Maszak. Baltimore, Md.: Johns Hopkins University Press.

————. 2000. *Les grecs, les historiens, la démocratie. Le grand écart.* Paris: Éditions La Découverte.

————. 2001. *Le miroir brisé. Tragédie athénienne et politique.* Paris: Les Belles Lettres.

Waterfield, Robin. 2000. *The First Philosophers: The Presocratics and the Sophists.* Oxford: Oxford University Press.

Winnington-Ingram, R. P. 1980. *Sophocles: An Interpretation.* Cambridge: Cambridge University Press.

Zeitlin, Froma. 1990. "Thebes: Theatre of Self and Society in Athenian Drama." In *Nothing to Do with Dionysos? Athenian Drama in Its Social Context,* ed. J. Winkler and F. Zeitlin, 130–67. Princeton, N.J.: Princeton.

NOTES ON CONTRIBUTORS

SARA HEINÄMAA is Professor of Theoretical Philosophy at Uppsala University and Senior Lecturer of Theoretical Philosophy at the University of Helsinki. She currently works as Academy Fellow at the Helsinki Collegium for Advanced Studies and leads a research group, *European Rationality in the Break from Modernity*, financed by the Academy of Finland. Heinämaa's expertise is in phenomenology and existential philosophy, and her work is focused on the problems of perception, embodiment, personhood, and inter-subjectivity. She is author of *Toward a Phenomenology of Sexual Difference* and two other volumes on the phenomenology of the body. She has published widely on Husserl, Merleau-Ponty, Beauvoir, and Irigaray, and is a co-editor of two volumes in history of the philosophy of mind, *Consciousness* and *Psychology and Philosophy*.

ROBIN MAY SCHOTT is Senior Researcher at the Danish Institute for International Studies, in the section for Holocaust and genocide studies, and Research Professor at the Danish School of Education (DPU), Aarhus University. She is author of *Discovering Feminist Philosophy: Knowledge, Ethics, Politics* and *Cognition and Eros: A Critique of the Kantian Paradigm*, and editor of several books, including *Feminist Philosophy and the Problem of Evil* (Indiana University Press, 2007). For some time she has focused her research on the concept of evil and issues of conflict, war, and gender—including the issue of mass war rape. More recently she also has been working on philosophical analyses of school bullying as part of the group research project "Exploring Bullying in Schools" at DPU.

VIGDIS SONGE-MØLLER is Professor of Philosophy and chairperson of the Department of Philosophy, University of Bergen. Her publications include *Philosophy without Women: The Birth of Sexism in Western Thought; Tanker om opprinnelsen: Tidlig gresk filosofi fra Hesiod til Demokrit* (Thoughts on Origins: Early Greek Philosophy from Hesiod to Democritus); and *Zwiefältige Wahrheit und zeitliches Sein: Eine Interpretation des parmenideischen Gedichts* (Two-Sided Truth and Temporal Being: An Interpretation of the Poem by Parmenides). Her focus of research is ancient Greek philosophy, especially the pre-Socratics and Plato, as well as contemporary feminist philosophy, which she uses to give feminist interpretations of classical texts—in particular by Hesiod, Anaximander, Parmenides, and Plato.

SIGRIDUR THORGEIRSDOTTIR is Professor of Philosophy at the University of Iceland. She studied philosophy in Boston and Berlin. She has published *Vis Creativa: Kunst und Wahrheit in der Philosophie Nietzsches* (Vis Creativa: Art and Truth in Nietzsche's Philosophy) and *Kvenna megin* (Women's Side), and has edited and co-edited books on the philosophy of Simone de Beauvoir, the philosophy of Hannah Arendt, and family and justice. Thorgeirsdottir is chairperson of the board of the EDDA Center of Excellence, and chairperson of the board of GET, a transnational gender equality training program for fellows from developing countries at the University of Iceland.

INDEX